FIG. 1. An Old New England Schoolhouse

AMONG

COUNTRY SCHOOLS

BY

O. J. KERN

SUPERINTENDENT OF SCHOOLS, WINNEBAGO COUNTY
ILLINOIS

GINN & COMPANY
BOSTON · NEW YORK · CHICAGO · LONDON

The Athenæum Press

GINN & COMPANY · PRO-
PRIETORS · BOSTON · U.S.A.

THIS BOOK IS DEDICATED TO ALL THOSE WHOSE
FEET HAVE WANDERED OR MAY WANDER
ALONG COUNTRY ROADS, OVER FIELDS,
THROUGH WOODLAND, TO THE
COUNTRY SCHOOL

PREFACE

This book is not a scientific treatise on education nor a manual of methods for the teacher. This may be the need for the country school. If so, some one better fitted must undertake the task of its preparation.

This little volume is not even a book on agriculture. It may be fairly questioned whether or not the country school-teacher needs something else before a text-book on the science and practice of farming.

In a personal letter to the author dated December 19, 1904, the Honorable James Wilson, United States Secretary of Agriculture, says:

> You have many delightful things in that write-up of yours, and it seems to me that you should not stop short in speaking to the public through your pen. We are needing, and needing very much, agricultural text-books. I have said this before to a great many people, and have asked if they could not write one directed to the farm child through farm topics. Something is being done along that line, but there is a great deal yet to be done.

The author hopes that this book will prove suggestive to the teacher and school officer who are striving for the spiritualization of country life through the medium of the country school. He believes that a careful reading of its pages will show a practical way of interesting the "farm child through farm topics."

What is thus offered is the result of seven years of very earnest thought and hard work in an endeavor to secure for the country child his rights so far as an educational opportunity is concerned. The country school should have that freedom which country life affords. This book has but little to say about the mechanics of school management.

In the training of children and the development of character no greater opportunity can be offered than that now belonging to the teacher in the country school. The author hopes these pages may prove helpful in the way of making the teacher a greater inspirational force in country life. Likewise no such opportunity was ever presented to a school officer as is now before the county superintendent of schools. It is his privilege to become a real leader in an educational way and to do original constructive work in the evolution of the country school to meet the new conditions of country life.

In the development of the country school discouragements will come and seemingly insurmountable obstacles will block the way. It is no time, then, to become despondent or cynical. Go out under the stars and breathe the resolve in prayer to be true to right ideals. The reward is to the one who remains steadfast to the end.

O. J. K.

HIGHLAND, ROCKFORD, ILLINOIS
July, 1906

CONTENTS

CHAPTER I

THE NEW COUNTRY LIFE

CHAPTER II

THE RIGHTS OF THE COUNTRY CHILD

CHAPTER III

OUTDOOR ART: BEAUTIFYING SCHOOL GROUNDS

CHAPTER IV

SCHOOL GARDENS

CHAPTER V

INDOOR ART AND DECORATION

CHAPTER VI

SCHOOL LIBRARIES

CHAPTER VII

A FARMER BOYS' EXPERIMENT CLUB

CHAPTER VIII

EDUCATIONAL EXCURSIONS TO THE COLLEGE OF
AGRICULTURE

CHAPTER IX

THE COUNTRY SCHOOL AND THE FARMERS' INSTITUTE

CHAPTER X

THE NEW AGRICULTURE AND THE COUNTRY SCHOOL

CHAPTER XI

THE FINANCIAL PHASE OF THE COUNTRY-SCHOOL PROBLEM

CHAPTER XII

CONSOLIDATION

CHAPTER XIII

THE TRAINING OF TEACHERS FOR COUNTRY SCHOOLS

CHAPTER XIV

MANUAL TRAINING IN THE COUNTRY SCHOOL

CHAPTER XV

A LAST WORD

LIST OF ILLUSTRATIONS

AMONG COUNTRY SCHOOLS

CHAPTER I

THE NEW COUNTRY LIFE

Truly this is a new age for country life. In a material way this truth seems to need no proof. The self-binder and the cream separator are tangible things, labor-saving and profitable. High-bred varieties of grains and fruits

FIG. 2. A Two-Row Corn Cultivator

are grown with marvelous results; while the facilities for quick communication in the use of the telephone, in the daily delivery of mail, and in the trolley line put the farm in close touch with the whole world.

The past quarter of a century has witnessed a great development in all things relating to the farm. The story seems too marvelous to believe. The Illinois country lad who, in the centennial year of 1876, plowed corn and bound grain by hand in the hot July sun little dreamed of the conquests to be made in the domain of agriculture. When, as a city man, in 1904 he helped to observe another centennial of the beginning of our national expansion, by attending the Louisiana Purchase Exposition, the Palace of Agriculture told him the new story. Invention has done much to lighten the burden of the farmer and to make his efforts more remunerative by furnishing the right kind of machinery. The exhibits told the story of labor-saving machinery. As a country boy, husking corn during the frosts of November, he thought not of selection and breeding of corn. As a man, standing before the exhibit of the Illinois Experiment Station in the Palace of Agriculture at St. Louis, he saw the results of seven years of patient, careful work in the development of high-bred corn. Science at last is working for and with the farmer.

As a boy, plowing the rich soil of central Illinois, little thought had he about soil fertility. To him, as a man, comes the soil-survey bulletin with county map showing types of soil in areas as small as ten-acre lots. Inoculation of soil with bacteria for certain fertility-restoring crops seems a fairy tale. And all this in the short space of twenty-five years.

No less significant are the new methods of communication in bringing a different spirit to country life. No longer is the farmer compelled to roam over half a township in his efforts to secure extra help for his threshing or harvesting. A few minutes at the telephone arrange all the

details for "swapping work." Or it may be that the binder
or mower has broken down right in the midst of a very
busy time. The old way was to leave the machine in the
field and let the hired help loaf around, while the farmer
hitched up and drove several miles for the needed repairs,
and then perhaps had to telegraph to the factory in a

FIG. 3. A New Country Road

distant city. The loss of a few hours meant the loss of
several hundred dollars' worth of golden grain if the
weather was bad. To-day the long-distance phone in
three minutes calls up supply house or factory; the
needed machinery is sent out by the night express, and
the early morning trolley car brings the needed relief to
the farmer's door ready for the beginning of a new day's
work. The average farmer is quick to take advantage of

all this because there is money in it. But how about the improvement of the country school? Has it kept pace with this material progress? Is there money in that also?

In 1876 the country lad, who dreamed not of telephones, self-binders, corn with a high percentage of protein, alfalfa bacteria, or the coreless apple, made his weekly journey Saturday afternoons to the country store for the mail. Perhaps there was a letter from the folks back in Indiana. Certainly there was a weekly paper or two; if only one, it was a party organ of the same political faith as that of the boy's

FIG. 4. A New Means of Communication for the Farm

father. From such sources the boy read the news a week old and incidentally found out that all the wisdom and patriotic virtue necessary for the preservation of free institutions was found in one party only. The weekly religious paper applied the same narrowing policy to its particular field.

To-day how different! For years the government at national expense had been delivering mail to the city people, but now the farmer has his daily mail at the expense of the same government. News a week old, with market quotations as ancient, does not satisfy the farmer to-day. He demands the great metropolitan daily, and the post-office department delivers it to him by ten o'clock in the morning. He wants to know what was doing last night at Port Arthur, yesterday's total receipts and top prices for live stock in Chicago, or the attitude of patriots in legislative halls towards election reforms or railway rate regulations. Strange to say, many farmers fought against all these innovations in the way of quick methods of communication,

FIG. 5. A Steam Roller and a Road Scraper

urging that the daily delivery of mail would increase taxes and that the mail boxes would be robbed by bad boys; that the trolley car going across the fields would shade the corn too much and that the yield per acre would thus be decreased. But they survived the change and prospered under it. They recognize the material benefits, and further changes will not be so difficult to accomplish.

But how about the children in the district school, without maps or necessary apparatus, and with text-books in history and geography copyrighted in 1883 and the same book which has been in almost constant use by various members of the family since 1893? Is the telephone, daily mail, or trolley line to touch only the financial or social interests of the farmer? Are these his only interests?

Things spiritual as well as material make us conscious of the new country life. The spiritualization of country life now going on requires closer study to catch its full significance than does a survey of farm machinery or growing crops. The farm home is no longer isolated. Newer and better comforts of life are coming to the country home. Music, magazines, high-grade literature, are creating better ideals of living. The improved material conditions of the American farmer make possible a richer life for the American country home. We have passed from the period of settling the country into that of settling down in the same country, and he who would attempt to create a new educational ideal with reference to the district school must, if possible, be imbued with the spirit of the new life that is unfolding. The significance of this change is thus expressed in a recent editorial in *The World's Work*.

In a sense we have settled the country; and now we are beginning to settle down. We are reaching a period of an equilibrium of opportunity.

This large fact explains many changes in the direction of our activities, and a corresponding change that is taking place in our national character; for what we do makes us what we are. It is a key to the larger tendencies in present American life.

The difference between a period of settling and a period of settling down is the difference between adventure and development. It is expressing itself in a hundred ways, — in intensive instead of extensive farming, in the concentration of industry instead of duplicating it, in building better homes instead of seeking other homes, in doing the jobs we have in hand better rather than seeking other jobs. All this means greater efficiency. It means sticking closer to business. It has much to do with the production of great wealth, which makes the last decade a period in our history which stands out by itself. It has much to do with the great movements to consolidate industry. It brings us back to all kinds of home problems, — to the proper building and government of our cities and to the almost universal tendency to improve country life.

Now this improvement in country life is manifested in better homes and barns, better roads, and the substitution of the carriage for the old lumber wagon for church and

FIG. 6. A Farm Scene

social visits. The increasing use of flowers, trees, and shrubbery around the country home tells of the growth of a love for the beautiful in country life. The great farmers' institute movement is contributing to the intellectual growth in country life. Has the improvement of the country school kept pace with other things? If so, why are so many people leaving the farm and moving to the cities to educate their children? Would good schools out in the fields help the movement back to the country? Is it desirable that people continue to drift to the great centers of population?

Why are the country schools so small, and where are the people?

According to the United States census reports the population of Winnebago County, Illinois, including the city of Rockford, increased 19.7 per cent in ten years, the population in 1890 being only 39,938, while in 1900 it reached 47,845.

The following table gives the population of each civil unit in the county. The civil units outside of the city of Rockford are properly called "towns," though many call them "townships." The report shows how in ten years the city of Rockford has increased in population, while the country communities have decreased.

	CENSUS	
	1900	1890
Burritt	658	733
Cherry Valley (with village)	1,014	1,105
Durand (with village)	1,256	1,223
Guilford	1,042	969
Harlem	837	695
Harrison	550	577
Laona	577	664
New Milford	761	865
Owen	667	762
Pecatonica (with village)	1,677	1,796
Rockton (with village)	1,561	1,492
Roscoe (with village)	811	894
Seward	1,022	960
Shirland	520	491
Winnebago (with village)	1,216	1,422
Rockford	2,767	1,618
City of Rockford	31,051	23,584

An analysis of the above table shows that ten county towns had decreased in population, while the city of Rockford had increased 7467, or 31.6 per cent. The town of Rockford shows an increase of 1149, but that increase is suburban to Rockford, and a greater portion has been annexed to the city since the federal census.

The growth of the city of Rockford and the country communities outside since the organization of the city and county is shown in the following table.

Year	Winnebago County	City of Rockford	Year	Winnebago County	City of Rockford
1840	4,609		1880	17,376	13,129
1850	9,680	2,093	1890	16,354	23,584
1860	17,512	6,979	1900	16,794	31,051
1870	18,252	11,049			

The increase in population for 1900 in Winnebago County is because of suburban population, as the city of Rockford is included in the town of Rockford. In truth, there has been a steady decrease in country population since 1870.

I do not offer a few statistics from one county as proof positive that similar conditions obtain in every county in the United States; but if small country schools indicate a decrease in population, then the reports of nearly every state superintendent in the great Middle West and in some eastern states verify the fact. At any rate, if any teacher is interested in finding out all she can about her own county, she can ask the county clerk for the United States census reports on file in his office. A few figures there of local reference might have as great an educational value in the schoolroom to country children as the study of the population of the fifteen largest cities in the world.

It is not expected that every one born in the country should remain in the country. That would be a serious mistake for several reasons. But is there not a tendency to disparage country life and interests?

The Right Honorable James Bryce of England, author of *The American Commonwealth*, visited America in 1870, in 1883, and again in 1904. In the *Outlook* for March 25,

1905, appeared the first of Mr. Bryce's two articles on "America Revisited." Both articles are worthy of serious study by every country school-teacher. He bears testimony that this is a new age for country life in the

Fig. 7. A Country Road

United States. In speaking of the changes of a quarter of a century, with special reference to the growth of manufactures, Mr. Bryce writes as follows :

The growth of manufactures might have been predicted half a century ago, for even then it was known that there were vast deposits of coal and iron, that the American people were highly inventive, and that the increase of population would create a prodigious demand for goods. One result, however, of the extension of manufactures may not have been so fully foreseen. I mean the change in the character

of the occupations and dwelling places of the people. They are ceas-
ing to be a folk of country dwellers. It is not only that the great
cities extend themselves with amazing speed, and that many of the
mineral areas are becoming so covered with villages as to differ little
from cities. There is a general disposition to migrate from rural districts to centers of population, where a brisker life and more amusements can be enjoyed. The change is all the more remarkable because
agriculture continues to be prosperous. It has been accelerated by
those applications of machinery to agricultural work which enable

FIG. 8. A Country Schoolhouse

a farm to be worked by a smaller staff than was formerly needed.
Wherever one travels in the eastern and northern states one sees
new towns rising along the lines of railroad and the older towns spread-
ing out. The eye as well as the census table tells one that the people
are becoming a people subject to city influences. Already, though the
population which lives outside towns with less than eight thousand
inhabitants is numerically larger (almost two thirds), still it is urban
ways and habits, urban opinion, urban tendencies, that are beginning
to prevail in the United States. This process goes on steadily. It
will go on all the faster because the good land of the Northwest has
now — so one is told — been practically all taken up, while even the
irrigation of the dry lands of the South-Central West cannot redress
the balance by providing a new rural population to set against the
increase of the cities. This is one of the new facts which strikes a

visitor, and especially an Englishman. Thirty-five years ago England was already a country of city dwellers, and the United States seemed by contrast a country of agriculturalists. Before long the United States will be like England, and, one may almost add, like Germany also, a land in which the urban type of mind and life will preponderate. The change may be regrettable. Jefferson would have regretted it. But it is unavoidable. It will tend to increase that nervous strain, that sense of tension, which Americans are already deemed to show as compared with the more sluggish races of Europe. There will be less repose than ever in life. Health may not suffer, nor the death rate increase, for cities can now be made to show as low a mortality as most country places. In London we have brought down the rate since 1870 from twenty-three to seventeen per thousand. Yet the physical strength of the average man may not be quite the same; and his mental constitution will almost certainly be different. It may not be inferior,— indeed, it may be more alert and versatile; but it will be different.

Is the continued migration from the country to the city unavoidable? It is true that about all of the best land is taken. Irrigation will increase the acreage available for farming. But it seems to me that scientific methods of farming — intensive farming — will make possible the support of a yet larger population not urban in "type of mind and life." The trouble has been that too often the country child in his education has been led to believe that agriculture does not furnish sufficient intellectual development and financial success to warrant a longer stay on the farm. Hence the pilgrimage to the city, where "a brisker life and more amusements can be enjoyed." The influence of these has not always been of the most wholesome character. Many a boy has quit the farm, not because of the hard work only, but because day after day, month after month, he experienced only hard work.

The training in the country school of the future should aim to conserve all that is best and richest in a "type of mind and life" distinctly *country*. The possibilities of intellectual growth, literary culture, and social enjoyment are as great — or will be so — among the clover blossoms in the field as among the flowers blooming in the city park; in raising high-bred corn as in practicing law or selling ribbon over a counter in a large department store.

FIG. 9. His First Day

I plead for the spiritualization of country life. Education must do this. A new educational ideal in the country school will lead the boys and girls to see more of the " divine joy of living" in the country. These boys and girls on the farms are the men and women of a great to-morrow in country life and in the life of the nation as well. The country school should be so organized as to meet the new conditions of life. It ought not to be continually necessary for country people to desert the farm for the city that their children may have art, music, libraries, lectures, and social intercourse. The proper organization and administration of the country schools will bring to the farm all these things.

These spiritualizing influences, unfettered in the freedom of simple country life, unobstructed by the dissipations of an artificial, complex life of a great metropolitan center, will produce the choicest flower of our civilization. A nobler dignity will be conferred upon agriculture. This educational product is the new type of the American farmer, a man strong in his personal virtues and mighty in his influence for civic righteousness. This is an ideal, but it is a practical ideal. Already *things done* encourage the hope of realization. It is true that not much can be done with many adults. Their ideals are of the past. The great promise, the great hope, is with country children.

CHAPTER II

THE RIGHTS OF THE COUNTRY CHILD

If I were to formulate an educational creed for the country school, it would contain but two articles, namely: (1) the country child is entitled to every whit as good an educational opportunity as that enjoyed by the most favored city child attending the American public school; (2) to secure this right for the country child the country people must expend more money on the country school and expend it in a better way.

I believe in consolidation, and my educational decalogue for school officers and teachers may be reduced to one simple commandment, namely, Thou shalt enrich and enlarge the life of the country child.

This is a simple creed. It does not claim that the country school shall be the same kind of a school as the city school. There is a difference of environment that must be considered. The country school for its specific work should be just as efficient as the best city school is for its specific work. There are certain fundamentals that are common to both systems, and it is the country child's right to have these fundamentals taught him without so much educational waste. The second article of the creed recognizes the fact that as a general rule one cannot get something for nothing, while on the educational commandment *in uno* hang all the law and the prophets, so far as patron and teacher are concerned in their training of the country child.

The last fifteen or twenty years have witnessed great advancement in the educational interests of the towns and cities. Large sums of money have been expended for material equipment in the way of better buildings, laboratories, libraries, manual training, etc. Superintendents and teachers in cities have become more efficient and are better

FIG. 10. Among the Oaks

paid. A strong effort has been made to adjust the course of study to practical conditions of life. Business courses have been introduced into high schools, and the general public seems to manifest a deeper interest in the entire educational machinery. The growth of towns and cities has been phenomenal, and the resources of the people have been taxed to the utmost at times to provide every child with the best educational advantages.

Many farmers, feeling that the country school did not furnish sufficient training for their children, have moved to the cities to be under the influence of better schools, or have sent their children to board in the nearest town. Some have complained that the city school has educated their children away from the farm. A moment's reflection is sufficient to show that the city school is for the city child, with a course of study more or less suited to conditions in which the city child must earn a living. It is not expected that a city high school will teach country children much about the farm and its interests. The city child, who after leaving school enters a profession or works in

FIG. 11. Among the Oaks

the counting-room, store, or factory, does not need to know about the care and composition of soil, rotation of crops, breeding and selection and care of animals and plants, feeding standards for stock, etc. But the country boy, who remains on the farm, must know about these things, if he is to be a successful farmer in this new age of scientific agriculture; and the country school should help him along these lines. The educational uplift, in its fullest sense, cannot come to the country child from "three R's" alone. These certainly need to be better taught; but to claim that these alone are sufficient is a refusal to see progress.

Fig. 12. An Old Schoolhouse in Winnebago County, Illinois

As well ask the farmer to make a success of life with the machinery and methods of thirty years ago.

Let us give the country school all credit for the great work it has done. What we desire for it is that it shall improve in at least the same ratio as the rest of rural institutions. It is to do a still greater work. What are the most efficient means to increase the usefulness of the country school? This is the question that should appeal most strongly to the American farmer. However much we may disagree as to the ways and means, any one who has given any serious study to the country school in all its relations must conclude that there is need of increasing its usefulness.

Yes, there is a wide gulf between the alley of a great city and a country lane; the children loitering along each have to be reached in different ways. At the meeting of the Department of Superintendence at Milwaukee, Wisconsin, February, 1905, Mr. Ben Blewett of St. Louis, Missouri, very forcibly contrasts the city system with the country system. Mr. Blewett was a member of the Jury of Awards, Group I, Elementary Education, at the Louisiana Purchase Exposition. In his paper at Milwaukee, on "Lessons from the United States Exhibit of Elementary Education," he speaks as follows, with reference to the

FIG. 13. A New Schoolhouse in Winnebago County, Illinois

problems of the city system of education, in an effort to secure the city child in his heaven-born rights.

The great mass of humanity compacts by centripetal force till life in its congested portions is distorted out of all semblance to natural health. A home becomes a few square feet of standing room in a caravansary, and the child is deprived even of the solace of a neighbor's cellar door for a sliding place; no refuge anywhere, — the sky, the far-off roof of an artificial canyon; the earth, a floor of granite; his neighbor, the fellow who crowds him.

This seems like tragedy to us who, when children, looked through clear air up to the sun and talked with fairies under sheltering trees.

How can you educate into decent citizenship a child pent up this way? Here is a question peculiar to the great city. And it should be the glory of our profession that there have been hearts that throbbed at the pathos of it all, and brains that joyed in contending with the difficulties.

In vivid contrast to the above, Mr. Blewett paints the country-school problem. He says:

The condition of the rural school is the problem that involves the welfare of more people than any other. The importance of this problem lies both in the number immediately affected and indirectly in the potency of these lives in giving character to the nation. However enticing it may be, the life of the great towns is artificial and misshapen by the pressure of the great throngs. In its atmosphere the human forces are devitalized and dwindle into abnormal weaknesses. This is so true that the great enterprises of the city are sustained only by the infusion of men who have held plow handles or wielded the ax.

The old story of the giant Antæus, like all great myths, is but the embodiment of a natural law. To get his strength and to hold his strength the child must touch his mother earth, must struggle with the cold and heat, must know how plants grow, must experience how the knot yields to the skillful wedge, must wrestle with labors that test his endurance, and must feel the joy of his own masterfulness. The demands of his life develop in the country boy a self-reliance and a faculty for adaptation which, though hidden under a cloak of awkwardness, give him a power not possessed by the child who has not had this natural training. It is from such people that the leaders of the world come.

The great centers of population act as maelstroms which gather into their swirling rush all that the outermost circles of their influence can reach. To counteract this tendency, to hold the youth on the farms, so to organize his life there that his natural longing for social intercourse will be satisfied, — to accomplish these ends some of the strongest efforts of our schoolmasters are being made.

This is what I am pleading for, — the enlargement and enrichment of the life of the country child.

It is true that many of the leaders in finance, statecraft, and great mercantile enterprises have come from the country. This is ofttimes offered as an argument that the country school that can produce such material needs no improvement. But the greatness of a Lincoln or a Garfield can hardly be attributed to the district school alone; and so with many others now holding responsible positions. They had an educational training in home duties on the farm, and possibly they could have made a success in life

FIG. 14. Crab Apple Blossoms beside a Country Brook

in spite of schools. We pick out the half-dozen boys in a county, perhaps, who have become famous. But how about the great number unheard of in after life? Did they play their part well in the struggle? Did they enjoy their rights as children in the country schools? Besides, the general level of intelligence has been raised since the boyhood of the man from the farm, now either a merchant prince or a learned jurist in a great city. The competition is keener; new conditions obtain; a new industrial age presents problems whose solution will test fully the stability of our free institutions. Hence the boy who leaves the country school for the city must be much better prepared than the boy of thirty years ago.

But perhaps we should not be overanxious about the five or ten per cent who doubtless will succeed in spite of any or all schools. Our chief concern in this new age should be to secure an equality of educational opportunity for the great mass of country children who get no other training for life's duties, so far as books are concerned, than that acquired in a miserable building with bleak, unkempt grounds, with no library or necessary educational equipment, with a short school year of four or five months, and all in charge of an untrained, underpaid teacher. This picture is not overdrawn, but I do not wish to dwell on its dark side. My belief has been that to help along an institution or an individual that needs help is to select the good qualities and to magnify them in order to show how the reform may be effected. While this is true, yet let us not be carried away with the soulful eloquence of the patriot who on stated occasions tells us that the public school is the safety of our republic, — or words to that effect, — and that the teacher is doing priceless service to the country. To be sure, this service is *almost* without price, reaching as low as $28 per month for four months of the year. The lowest salary paid a janitor by the city of Rockford is $320 per year for taking care of a four-room school building.

The country child has rights. He is entitled to a square deal in opportunities to enjoy the best that the civilization of the world thus far has produced. To him should come art, music, and literature. Millionaires are founding libraries and art galleries for city children, but who is doing a like service for the children living in the fields ? True, a poem, a picture, or a song, as an educational agent, is likely to be regarded as a fad by the man whose mind for the last thirty years has run chiefly to corn and hogs. Such a man thinks that there is no use in putting a five-thousand-dollar education on a fifty-cent boy. As a plain business proposition there is no use in wasting so much good money on such an insignificant thing. But this kind of man is more likely to give a fifty-cent education to a five-thousand-dollar boy, — a ten-thousand-dollar boy, perhaps, in possibilities. With charity for such a father, let us

FIG. 15. Where the Water Lilies Grow

do the best we can for his children as God gives us the ability to see the best.

More than all else, the country child has a right to that inspirational leadership which can come only from the genuine teacher. At the beginning of this chapter was given an educational creed of two articles, acceptable, I trust, to country patrons, school officers, and teachers. Following is a " Teacher's Creed " that is worth quoting.

A Teacher's Creed

I believe in boys and girls, the men and women of a great to-morrow; that whatsoever the boy soweth the man shall reap. I believe in the curse of ignorance, in the efficacy of schools, in the dignity of teaching, and in the joy of serving another. I believe in wisdom as revealed in human lives, as well as in the pages of a printed book; in lessons taught not so much by precept as by example; in ability to work with the hands as well as to think with the head; in everything that makes life large and lovely. I believe in beauty in the schoolroom, in the home, in daily life, and out of doors. I believe in laughter, in love, in all ideals and distant hopes that lure us on. I believe that every hour of every day we receive a just reward for all we are and all we do. I believe in the present and its opportunities, in the future and its promises, and in the divine joy of living. Amen.

Edwin Osgood Grover

There are seven "I believes" in the above, and the credo seems complete. It seems to me that nothing should be added or taken away. A teacher believing and living such a creed in the country school will be an inspirational force to country children. The country school needs more of wisdom in human lives. Too often the wisdom as revealed in what men have said or done in the past, as recorded on the printed page, is considered the only educational material worth while. Such a teacher will teach by example the true dignity of "work with the hands," and banish the false idea that an education will somehow enable one to get a living without work.

A teacher living this creed will teach her children to see and appreciate the wondrous beauty of country life, — the country road, the cluster of oak trees, the clover field, the trailing wild grapevine, the wild flowers, the wild crab tree, and the babbling brook. She will help to spiritualize country thought and life, for she believes "in beauty in the schoolroom, in the home, in daily life, and out of doors." Such a teacher cannot be content with merely drawing her salary while the schoolhouse and grounds remain cheerless and desolate. In some way the forces of the district will be organized for better things. The parents will be reached through the children, for the teacher believes "in all ideals and distant hopes that lure us on." Her salary is

FIG. 16. A Country Road

what? you ask. I do not know. She belongs to that small class of public servants who earn a great deal more than they receive. It may be that in lives transformed by her influence is a compensation greater than gold. At any rate, in "the joy of serving another" there comes the hourly "reward for all we are and all we do." If every country school-teacher in the United States could only grasp the true significance of present conditions and future possibilities of the country school, could have faith in the inspirational power of a life illumined with "the divine joy of living,"— in short, if every country school-teacher would actually live the above creed for five years, the nation would witness the greatest change ever wrought in the history of the American public school.

For the last twenty years the interests of the city school have held the center of the stage. The deliberations of

FIG. 17. A New Schoolhouse with Trees

educational gatherings have been almost exclusively confined to the consideration of problems of organization and management of educational systems in great centers of population. The reason for this seeming neglect of the country school is not far to seek. The tremendous growth of the population in our cities, due in part to unrestricted immigration, made the problem of caring for these hundreds of thousands of children in these cities the most pressing problem of the hour. It was natural, then, that our efforts should be directed citywards instead of countrywards. Now that we have made progress in the solution, and are witnessing a remarkable reaction in favor of country life, due to increased ease of transportation and communication, the country-school problem is the one of prime importance. Until recently one might scan in vain any programme of a teachers' association for a " country-school section " or a discussion of some phase of the country-school problem.

There are still many good peo-ple who believe that all wisdom will die with the city-school man. It may be that the country-school man is to blame for the neglect of this most important part of the edu-cational field,

FIG. 18. Work in the New Schoolhouse

namely, the country school. Is there any considerable num-ber of children attending the country schools, — enough, at least, to make it worth while to consider them for an hour or so during a three days' meeting of a great state teachers' association; or to be considered worthy of a column in a school journal; or important enough for a two-line notice in the press dispatch? Let us see. In Illinois a graded school is one employing two teachers or more, while an ungraded school is a one-teacher school. According to State

Superintendent Bayliss's report for the year ending June 30, 1904, the enrollment in Illinois for that year was as follows:

Pupils in graded schools 660,336
Pupils in ungraded schools 318,218

Total 978,554

Further:

Number of graded schools (including high schools) . . 2,218
Number of ungraded schools 10,677

Total 12,895

Also:

Average number of days per year for each pupil in graded schools 158
Average number of days per year for each pupil in ungraded schools 94

Again:

Number of teachers in graded schools 15,174
Number of teachers in ungraded schools 12,297

Total 27,471

Other statistics will appear in their proper places. Enough are given here to show that, for Illinois, 318,218 pupils taught by 12,297 teachers in 10,677 schools do offer opportunity for educational study, especially as the country has not yet an equality of privilege as to length of the school year. Superintendent Bayliss adds, " But, notwithstanding this very considerable inequality of privilege and the number of lame districts, not all of the progress has been made in the more favored schools."

The conditions for Illinois are about the same as for the other states of the great Middle West. The United States Department of Education has not yet classified schools so as to show the number of one-room country schools in the United States, with enrollment, etc. Chart No. 60 — a part of the exhibit of the United States Department of

Education at St. Louis — was a comparison of the city and
country schools for the year ending June 30, 1902. But
on this chart "cities" meant eight thousand or more people,
while "country" meant everything below eight thousand.
This is not a very good division for the student who would

FIG. 19. Down on the River

like to know the number of children in the distinctively one-
room country schools. However, the chart is here given,
and the reader may judge whether in the nation at large
there is a country-school interest of sufficient magnitude for
a passing notice.

CHART NO. 60, ST. LOUIS, 1904

	PER CENT	
	CITIES	COUNTRY
Population	32.6	67.4
School enrollment	26.2	73.8
Average attendance	28.7	71.3
Teachers.	20.6	79.4
Buildings	3.7	96.3
Value of school property	59.3	40.7
Expenditure for teaching and supervision . . .	44.3	55.7
Total expenditure for schools	47.2	52.8

As was stated above, the column headed "Cities" included cities with a population of eight thousand or more. The report of the Commissioner of Education for 1902 gave five hundred and eighty cities as the number to be included in the first column. Study these figures.

Yes, this a big country; and the bigness of it flashed upon my mind at the closing meeting of the "Ohio River

Fig. 20. An Old Schoolhouse

Tour" in the educational campaign recently conducted by State Superintendent Miller in the Panhandle State. From that West Virginia town to my own home is four hundred miles to the northwest. Then go four hundred miles more to the northwest, and we come to the Falls of St. Anthony and the twin cities of St. Paul and Minneapolis. Here take the North Coast Limited on the Northern Pacific, and one must needs ride two thousand miles more before arriving at Portland, the place of the Lewis and Clark Exposition. This is a magnificent domain, into which are constantly coming men, women, and children less favored in educational advantages, and who must be provided for. Education is the open sesame to a happier life; and that distinctively

American institution, the free public school, is the only organized institution that can take the children of foreign lands and make patriotic American citizens of them. The country school must share the responsibility in this great test of national stability, though at present the foreign question principally concerns the city.

The three great forward movements in the evolution of the country school, the move-ments in the campaign for an equality of edu-cational privilege for the country

FIG. 21. A New Schoolhouse

child, are: (1) improvement of the educational plant; (2) enrichment of the course of study; (3) consolidation of country schools.

IMPROVEMENT OF THE EDUCATIONAL PLANT

The little schoolhouse at the crossroads shall be as well fitted for the purpose intended as is the most modern city school building. It shall be provided with the necessary apparatus for doing the best work. The grounds shall be neat and attractive, making this place the most beautiful in all the countryside. Hence we need the outdoor-art movement for trees, flowers, vines, shrubbery, and school gardens; and the indoor-art movement for tinted walls, harmonious colors in furnishings, choice pictures and casts, and neat library cases filled with good books. These are the country child's rights.

ENRICHMENT OF THE COURSE OF STUDY

The country child shall be put into sympathetic and intelligent relation to his environment. The country-school studies shall relate more to the life of the child, that this life may be rendered more significant. In an elementary way (quite elementary for a while) the scientific discoveries in the domain of the new agriculture, with reference to soil and plant and animal life, shall receive some attention from the older pupils at least. Our agricultural colleges and experiment stations are discovering valuable information for the farmer. These discoveries will greatly modify farm work and country life when the great mass of farmers appreciate their value; and the time for this appreciation to begin is when the future farmer is a child at school. This kind of training for real life will demand and secure better teachers. All these things also are the country child's rights.

CONSOLIDATION OF COUNTRY SCHOOLS

This is a more efficient organization and administration of country-school interests to decrease educational waste and increase the power of the country child for good. This takes the country high school to the fields and supplies the connecting link between the farm and college of agriculture. The country child has a right to secondary education without the necessity of leaving the farm home to get it.[1]

And so the battle is fairly on. Of the final outcome there is no doubt. But victory, complete victory, will not be won without great effort and sacrifice. The hardest of all educational problems is to reach the average farmer and to enlist his active coöperation for the betterment of the country school. He who enters upon this work must have courage, patience, enthusiasm, tireless energy, and a genius for hard work. However, this is true of any cause that is really worth while.

[1] See articles on "Rural High Schools" by Corbett, in *School Review*, Vol. VIII, Nos. 4 and 6.

CHAPTER III

In the country we do not yet appreciate fully the educational influence of environment. We rely too much upon books and do not pay enough attention to things. Various reasons why boys leave the farm have been assigned by

FIG. 22. Noble Elms spared by the Telephone Company

speakers at farmers' institutes. I have never heard any one claim that the cheerless, treeless, country school yard of itself had any power to charm and enthrall the average country boy. The daily routine of hard work is much harder to

endure when there are wanting those elements of soul development which inspire the youth with new ideals. Hence
he wishes to go where such things are, that his being may
be satisfied.

It is not strange that when a boy reaches the age of
fourteen he refuses to associate longer with the old schoolhouse with its blank
walls and desolate
yard. He feels the
restraint of his envi-
ronment. He is begin-
ning to see life in a
different light, and
quits school then for
good, or else the
father moves to the
city, where his chil-
dren may have better
opportunities both in
school and out. The
secret of keeping
more boys satisfied
with the farm rests
primarily with the
character of the coun-

Fig. 23. Trees should go with the Flag

try schoolhouse and its surroundings. Why do not trees
and fence posts grow in many country school yards, when
they thrive with great vigor around the farm home a few
rods away? Scientific agriculture tells us that soil may be
inoculated so that alfalfa, soy beans, cow peas, etc., will
grow and produce abundant crops. Some one will do us
a great service if he will tell us of the particular microbe

and its method of culture that will correct the unproductive character of the soil in so many school yards, with especial reference to trees, flowers, vines, shrubbery, etc. The peculiar kind of bacteria needed is the one that will induce the average school patron or director to connect himself gently but firmly with a spade and do some excavating in the hitherto unexplored country surrounding the crossroads temple sacred to the "three R's."

There is need of some kind of inoculation. The report of Illinois for the year ending June 30, 1904, shows 1766 districts without trees in the school yard, 3532 districts with not enough trees, and 3954 with well-kept grounds; that is, there are 5298 country school grounds in the great state of Illinois that do not exercise an influence upon young children that will lead them to see and love the beautiful in country life. Indeed, the effect is quite the contrary. The problem for Illinois may be stated as follows:

Given: Sunshine, rain, fertile soil, clouds, the blue heavens, trees, plants, and seeds.

Given also: 5298 school grounds blessed with sunshine, rain, soil, and clouds, but needing trees, plants, and seeds. There are 150,000 boys and girls (more or less) playing on these grounds and watched over by 5298 teachers and nearly 16,000 school officers.

To prove: Our faith in the possibility of the right kind of environment as an educational force in the lives of children.

To show: Our faith by our works, with the coöperation of 16,000 school officers, 5298 teachers, and 150,000 children.

How long will the policy of neglect prevail in 5298 school districts?

Let us observe Arbor Day in every school with appropriate songs and exercises; but let us not forget to *plant* when planting needs to be done. For schools whose premises are treeless the proper thing to do would be to *dig* rather than *sing*, if only one could be done in a day. What is the use of singing about trees and ending at that, when planting and caring for trees is needed?

No, Arbor Day has not been observed in the proper spirit when some afternoon a little boy recites "What Plant we when we Plant the Apple Tree?" and a class of girls sing "The Brave Old Oak," and then all go to work

FIG. 24. The Four Oaks

on the arithmetic lesson, leaving the grounds as desolate as before. What would be the effect if one of the beautiful trees shown in this chapter could be placed in each one of the 5298 school grounds? Why not begin? Trees do have an educational as well as an ornamental value. Country people as a rule do not realize how deeply children are impressed by the natural world around them. The school is or should be the center of the life of the community. This center of influence should be made as attractive and powerful as possible. A pretty and attractive schoolhouse and grounds are an incentive to good work. The greatest obstacle to be overcome is public indifference. Shall the improvement of the school grounds be left to a general and faithfully executed policy of neglect? Is the old weather-beaten schoolhouse on a barren spot of ground so insignificant that it is not worthy of attention? "It is the most tremendously significant thing in the whole history of the

FIG. 25. A Real Playground

United States. It is the cradle of American education, the nursery which has always fostered, and still fosters, the national doctrine of equal rights for all."

The practical question is how to overcome indifference and arouse a healthy public sentiment for attractive school grounds. This is a hard question, and its answer must largely be determined by local conditions. For the last six years I have found the following agencies to be very helpful.

1. Bulletins on tree planting and attractive grounds sent to all teachers, school officers, and hundreds of leading farmers.

2. Illustrated printed matter sent from the office of the county superintendent to all the schools. This was an attempt to reach the

parents through the children. This literature showed the condition of all kinds of school grounds in the county. Illustrated articles were also furnished the local press. A picture tells its own story.

3. Books on trees, flowers, etc., and all that pertains to the beautiful in country life are placed in the seventy-three traveling libraries, so that the children and teachers in the one hundred and sixteen districts may form higher ideals of beauty in outdoor life.

4. Discussion of school improvement at our teachers' meetings and the annual institutes. These latter are held the last week of March, thus enabling teachers to carry out plans while interest and enthusiasm

FIG. 26. Standing by their Colors

are on. The general subject of beautifying school grounds was made the theme of the Union Township graduation exercises held in June, 1903. The subject for that year was "Outdoor Art for Home and School." Typewritten material was given the sixteen different programme committees — one set for each township — during the annual institute the last week of March. The material comprised such selections as the following:

1. Song of the Brave Old Oak.
2. Birds of Killingworth.
3. The Country Schoolhouse and its Grounds.
4. The Vine on the Schoolhouse.
5. The Black Walnut.
6. The White Elm.
7. The White Oak.
8. The White Ash.
9. The Shellbark Hickory.

From *Among Green Trees*, by Rogers.

10. How do the Robins build their Nests?
11. Arbor Day Song (air, Battle Hymn of the Republic).
12. Value of School Garden.
13. Why improve School Grounds?
14. Arbor Day Anthem.
15. Dear Dandelion.
16. Daisy Fair (motion song).
17. The Flower's Mission.
18. From my Armchair.
19. Why plant Trees?
20. Under the Washington Elm, Cambridge.
21. To a Mountain Daisy.
22. The Little Brown Wren.
23. Hints on Country School Grounds.
24. Tree Planting on Country School Grounds.
25. Arbor Day.
26. Forest and Forestry.
27. The Forest and Man.
28. Landscape Gardening.
29. Clover (poem by James Whitcomb Riley).
30. Improvement of School Grounds.
31. The Trees.
32. Plant Trees and protect Birds.
33. Historical Trees (told in rhyme).

The educational character of the above material can best be judged by quoting entire one of the above selections. Here follows selection 30:

The editor of a well-known magazine recently asked five hundred business men all over the country whether, in their opinion, there is any financial value in attractive surroundings to a business plant. Ninety-five per cent of those replying declare that the product of a business concern or factory is much more valuable when the factory or office is clean, attractive, and beautiful, and when the employees can come in daily contact with orderly surroundings and see floral beauties on the grounds. Furthermore, they declare that such well-ordered business concerns are a decided commercial benefit to the community.

A question of equal significance might be asked of educators, preachers, and parents, — whether, in their opinion, there is any moral, intellectual, and spiritual value in attractive school surroundings; whether the children are happier and their work more efficient by daily contact with beautiful school grounds; whether the cultivated taste and appreciation of the beautiful would not find expression in

the improvement of the home conditions, thus making the school a
radiating center for civic improvement.

The great interest in public beauty which is manifested all over
the country is largely due to the efforts of the American Park and
Outdoor Art Association and the American League for Civic Improvement. They have done much public service by a process of organization and education, and there is no better place to begin than in the
public schools. The most efficient way of reaching the parents is
through the children.

The greatest need and greatest opportunity is in rural districts;
and, alas! too often there is only bleakness and barrenness. The
school directors
seem to have set
apart the poorest
ground in the dis-
trict for the school
yard. Will nothing
grow? There are
no flowers, and only
some weak grass
and a few starved
trees. By a little
effort the unattract-
ive surroundings
could be made
pleasant and beau-
tiful. Children
should be led to

FIG. 27. A Shrubbery Detail

study Nature's method, and to examine her manner of planting flowers
beside the road, grouping trees and shrubs along the fences, in the
woods, and upon the banks of streams. The wind, the birds, and the
squirrels — Nature's agents — have no regularity in their seed planting.
The arrangement is an irregular massing of her trees, shrubs, and
flowers, and their struggle for existence produces pleasing variety
and effective results all the year round.

For inspiration in my efforts to create a new ideal with
reference to the beautiful in country life I am indebted to

various agencies given below, though not necessarily given in order of importance.

1. Bulletins issued by the United States Department of Agriculture, especially the ones issued by the Bureau of Plant Industry and the Bureau of Forestry.

2. Publications of the American Park and Outdoor Art Association.

FIG. 28. The Treeless School Grounds

3. Literature and pictures given by the Youth's Companion Publishing Company.

4. Various magazines like *Country Life in America*.

5. Arbor and Bird Day manuals issued for the past six years by the state superintendents of Iowa, Indiana, Nebraska, Wisconsin, and Illinois. Those of Wisconsin have been especially helpful.

6. Books like Babcock's *Bird Day;* Ely's *A Woman's Hardy Garden;* Miller's *Children's Gardens;* Blanchan's *Nature's Garden;* Dugmore's *Nature and the Camera;* Hemenway's *How to make a School Garden;* Roth's *First Book of Forestry;* Roberts's *The Heart of the Ancient Wood;* Rogers's *Among Green Trees;* Miller's *The Brook Book;* Gibson's *Eye Spy;* Burroughs's *Pepacton;* and many others.

7. A closer study of road, stream, and field in my own county of Winnebago. There is much of beauty in each school district which

the children do not yet see. If they do see it, they are like the lad who said to me a few days ago (when we were discussing Bryant's " What Plant we when we Plant the Apple Tree? "), in answer to the question about the beauty of common things, " We may see the

FIG. 29. Why not on the School Ground?

beauty, but we don't think of it." This was from a boy ten years old. I feel sure that teachers can get an inspiration from some one or more of the above sources, which will lead them to see and think more of the beauty of common things.

It does not cost much to plant trees. The small item of expense may not be the reason why more planting is not done. Perhaps teachers, children, and school officers do not know what to plant, or how to plant, or why to plant.

The following bulletins cost nothing and should be in every country school and should be studied by teachers and pupils. In addition to this, copies should be mailed to the school officers of every district still without trees. The bulletins are issued by the Bureau of Forestry, United States Department of Agriculture, Washington, D.C. Send postal card for them.

1. Tree Planting on Rural School Grounds (Farmers' Bulletin No. 134).
2. A Primer of Forestry (Farmers' Bulletin No. 173).
3. What Forestry Means to Representative Men (Circular No. 33).

Bulletin No. 134 was sent to two hundred teachers, three hundred and fifty school officers, and several hundred representative farmers in our county. I wanted them to know that trees will grow in the soil surrounding the average schoolhouse. This is a very useful pamphlet and its value in stimulating interest in trees cannot be overestimated, provided, of course, that it is read and that proper action results from the reading. The table of contents is as follows:

Reasons for School-Ground Planting.
Arbor Day and School-Ground Planting.
Preliminary Arrangements for Planting.
What Planting to Do.
Kinds of Trees to Plant.
Obtaining the Trees.
How to plant the Trees.
Why Trees die in Transplanting.
Care of Trees after Planting.
Studies for the Teacher and School.
Facts about Trees.

Can any outline be more practical and to the point for the country school-teacher anxious to do something to beautify the grounds? The fact is that we have so long regarded books as the sole agent in the education of the country child, that as teachers we have become slaves of the text and feel lost when we try to teach something or do something for which we can find no rule in the text-book of sacred reliance. Can anything of educational value come from digging in the dirt and planting trees? Listen to what the author of this bulletin has to say about the educational value of trees:

It is money well spent to make the schoolhouse and everything about it attractive and beautiful. Here is one of the centers of the life of the community, the one in which is gathered its most impressionable element. The school is supported at public expense in order to make good American citizens. It

FIG. 30. Treatment of Outbuildings

aims at securing the highest possible development of mind and character. Every element of order, neatness, and beauty, every broadening influence, every appeal to the finer nature of the child, means better men and women and a more thrifty, prosperous, and attractive community. Americans are justly proud of their school system, and should be willing to support the schools not only with money but with time and labor.

Under "Studies for the Teacher and School" are given such important topics as Characteristics of Trees, Influence of Soil upon Trees, Composition of Soils, Influence of Trees upon Soil, Influence of Trees upon One Another, and Books and Trees. The bulletin is well illustrated. But perhaps enough has been said to interest many teachers to secure a copy, and at the same time to have copies sent to school directors and prominent patrons of the district.

The country children in planting and caring for trees become a part of the great forestry movement that is sweep-

FIG. 31. Treatment of Outbuildings

ing over the country. The older children of the school will appreciate Circular No. 33, — "What Forestry means to Representative Men." Says President Roosevelt:

I ask with all the intensity that I am capable of, that the men of the West will remember the sharp distinction I have just drawn between the man who skins the land and the man who develops the country. I am going to work with, and only with, the man who develops the country. I am against the land skinner every time. Our policy is consistent, to give to every portion of the public domain its highest possible amount of use, and of course that can be given only through the hearty coöperation of the Western people.

President Roosevelt would have scant sympathy with the people who would allow the country school grounds to remain "skinned" of trees, and would not "develop" the possibilities that even a school yard holds.

The *Youth's Companion*, Boston, Massachusetts, publishes two excellent illustrated pamphlets which every country teacher and school officer should read. One is " How to set out Trees and Shrubbery," by Professor L. H. Bailey, Dean of the College of Agriculture, Ithaca, New York ; the other is " Suggestions for beautifying Home, Village, and Roadway," by Warren H. Manning, Secretary of the American Park and Outdoor Art Association. To see and read these publications will surely give higher ideals of beauty.

FIG. 32. Improving Grounds of Consolidated School

I refer to this literature because so often teachers and children would do things if they only knew what is best to be done and the best way of doing it. Since as teachers we are so fond of confining our education to the printed page, why not know something about trees and flowers as well as about the elements of a complex sentence or how to extract the cube root to three decimal places ? The following is the opening paragraph of the pamphlet by Dean Bailey:

One's training for the work of life is begun in the home and fostered in the school. This training is the result of a direct and conscious effort on the part of the parent and teacher, combined with the indirect result of the surroundings in which the child is placed. The surroundings are more potent than we think, and they are usually neglected. It is probable that the antipathy to farm life is often formed before the child is able to reason on the subject. An attractive playground will do more than a profitable wheat crop to keep the child on the farm.

Dean Bailey, in his book, *The Nature Study Idea*, says the following with reference to the first thing to be done:

The first thing to do is to arouse the public conscience. Begin with the children. As soon as they are directed to see the conditions they will believe what they see. They are not prejudiced. They will talk about it; teacher, mother, father will hear.

I give these quotations because the value of the beautiful in the country cannot be emphasized too strongly if we hope to spiritualize country life.

The grounds of the first consolidated country school in Illinois in Seward Township, Winnebago County (see another chapter), are 3.6 acres in extent and cost the consolidated district a thousand dollars. It was part of a cornfield; hence not a tree or shrub was growing when the school opened, February 1, 1904. By permission of the school directors, I asked Professor J. C. Blair, Chief of Horticulture, College of Agriculture, University of Illinois, to prepare a design for the improvement of the grounds, with suggested planting, which would serve as an ideal for the people. He did so, and Arbor Day was then observed in earnest, April, 1904. A good beginning has been made, although much remains to be done. But here is an opportunity for growth. If the people in this consolidated district are true to the new ideal, what a contrast this school ground will be to those surrounding the old houses!

The diagram is given, with the details of planting. The varieties of trees, shrubs, etc., are given. It is quite possible that some one is asking for the specific names of things to plant. Observe that what will grow in the latitude of Illinois will grow in Iowa, Missouri, Kentucky, Indiana, Ohio, Michigan, West Virginia, Pennsylvania, New York, New Jersey, and the New England states. This is according to a district map of the United States shown on page 39 of the Farmers' Bulletin No. 218, — "The School Garden,"—prepared by L. C. Corbett, Horticulturist, Bureau of Plant Industry, United States Department of Agriculture, Washington, D.C.

Fig. 33. Vines on the Schoolhouse

In the following enumeration of the Seward planting, prepared by Professor Blair, the scientific names are omitted where the common name is given. The numbers here given refer to numbers in the diagram (Fig. 35):

1. Schoolhouse.
2. Front walk, 5 ft. wide.
3. Walks to well, 3 ft. wide.
4. Girls' closet.
4*a*. Walks to girls' closet, 3 ft. wide.

5. Walk to rear door.
6. Boys' closet.
6a. Walk to boys' closet, 3 ft. wide.
7. Drive to rear door, 6 ft. wide, of cinders or gravel.
8. Drive to horse shed, 6 ft. wide, of cinders or gravel.
9. Shed for horses, 20 ft. by 100 ft.
10. Shed for manure, 5 ft. by 20 ft.
11. Tennis court, 27 ft. by 78 ft.
12. Tennis court, 27 ft. by 78 ft.

FIG. 34. At the Well

13. School garden or experimental plots, each 20 ft. by 30 ft.
14. Well.
15–46. American Elm (White Elm or Water Elm).
47. Althea (Rose of Sharon) (red, white, blue).
48. *Hibiscus Syriacus.*
49. Colorado Blue Spruce.
50. Sugar Maple (Hard Maple or Rock Maple).
51. (*a*) Red Siberian Dogwood. (*b*) Golden-barked Cornel. (*c*) European Red Osier Dogwood.
52. Sweet Shrub (Spicebush).
53. (*a*) Garland Syringa. (*b*) Large-flowering Syringa. (*c*) *Philadelphus billardii.* (*d*) Golden Mock Orange.

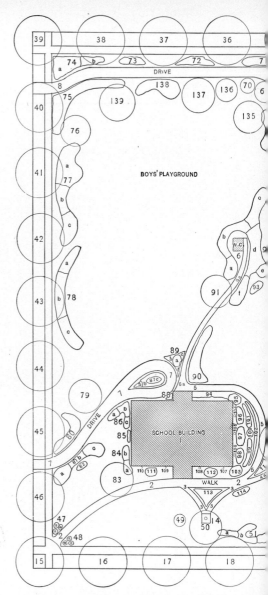

FIG. 35. A Design for the Improveme[nt]
Prepared by G. A. Crosthwait, under the directi[on]

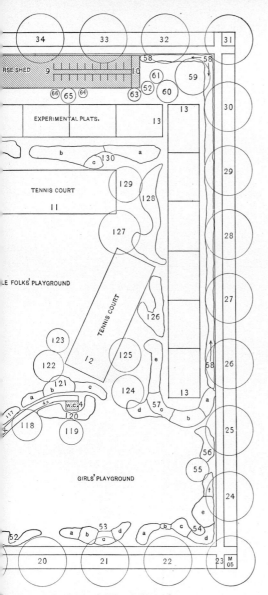

34   33   32   31

RSE SHED   9   10   58

58   61   59

66   65   64   52   63   60   30

EXPERIMENTAL PLATS.   13   13   29

b   c   130   a

TENNIS COURT   129   28

11   128

127   27

LE FOLKS' PLAYGROUND

126   68

123   TENNIS COURT   e   26

122   12   125

121   c   124   13   a

a   b   W.C. 4   d   57 c   b

117   118   120   119   25

56

55

GIRLS' PLAYGROUND   f   24

e

52   a   b   53   d   a   b   c   54   d

20   21   22   23   M 05

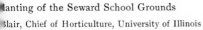

Planting of the Seward School Grounds

Blair, Chief of Horticulture, University of Illinois

54. (*a*) Japan Snowball. (*b*) *Weigelia candida*. (*c*) Wayfaring-tree. (*d*) Common Lilac. (*e*) Cranberry-tree. (*f*) Syringa *Vulgaris alba*.

55. Hardy Catalpa (Western Catalpa).

56. European Barberry.

57. (*a*) Common Elder. (*b*) Golden Elder. (*c*) Cut-leaved Elder. (*d*) Flowering Currant (Crimson-flowered Currant). (*e*) *Rhus glabra, Rhus copallina, Rhus typhina*.

58. American Arborvitæ (a hedge).

59. Basswood (Linden, Linn, Lime Tree, etc.).

60. European Larch.

61. Lombardy Poplar.

62. White-flowering Dogwood.

63. Red-flowering Dogwood.

64. Red Juniper (Red Cedar).

65. Nordmann's Silver Fir.

66. Red Juniper (Red Cedar).

67. Pyramidal Arborvitæ.

68. Pyramidal Arborvitæ.

69. American Arborvitæ.

70. Siberian Arborvitæ.

71. European Burning-bush (Strawberry-tree).

72. *Forsythia Fortunei*.

73. Dwarf Pink-flowering Almond.

74. (*a*) Cranberry-tree. (*b*) Japan Quince.

75. Hazelnut.

76. Kentucky Coffee-tree.

77. (*a*) Red Osier. (*b*) *Cornus paniculata*. (*c*) European Red Osier Dogwood.

78. (*a*) Mountain Sumac. (*b*) *Rhus glabra*. (*c*) *Rhus typhina*.

79. Norway Maple.

80. Flowering Raspberry.

81. (*a*) Van Houtte's Spirea. (*b*) Thunberg's Spirea. (*c*) Golden Spirea.

82. Tree Peony.

83. Tulip-tree.

84. Fortune's Pink Spirea.

85. *Spirea Bumaldi*.

86. (*a*) White Alder (Pepper-bush). (*b*) European Burning-bush.
     (*c*) Spicebush (Sweet Shrub).
87. (*a*) Dwarf Deutzia. (*b*) Common Mezereon. (*c*) English Fly
     Honeysuckle.
88. Hardy Ferns.
89. (*a*) Deutzia *Crenata candidissima*. (*b*), (*c*), (*d*) Dwarf
     Deutzia.
90. Hardy Roses of different varieties.
91. Basswood (see 59).

Fig. 36. A Row of Hard Maples

92. (*a*) Common Lilac. (*b*) Red Osier. (*c*) Purple Barberry.
     (*d*) Japan Snowball. (*e*) Purple-leaved Plum. (*f*) White
     Lilac.
93. Tartarian Honeysuckle.
94. Hardy Ferns.
95. *Forsythia Fortunei*.
96. *Lonicera Fragrantissima*.
97. Tartarian Honeysuckle.
98. White Tartarian Honeysuckle.
99. Indian Currant (Coral-berry).
100. Joan of Arc.

101. Snowberry.
102. St. John's-wort.
103. *Forsythia viridissima*.
104–110. Japanese Ivy (Boston Ivy).
111, 112. *Hibiscus Syriacus* (several varieties).
113. Great-panicled Hydrangea.
114. Flowering Currant.
115. Hardy Roses.
116. Oriental Plane-tree.
117. *Syringa vulgaris* (Charles X).
118. Maidenhair-tree (Gingks-tree).
119. Hackberry (Nettle-tree).
120. Japanese Sweetbrier.
121. (*a*) White Lilac. (*b*) Common Lilac. (*c*) De Markley's Red Lilac.
122. Scarlet Oak.
123. American Redbud (Judas-tree).
124. Pin-oak.
125. White Walnut (Butternut).
126. Silky Cornel.
127. Black Walnut.
128. Hazelnut.
129. Wild Cherry (Black Cherry).
130. (*a*) *Forsythia Fortunei*. (*b*) Japan Quince. (*c*) Pearl-bush.
131. Silver-bell.
132. White Pine (Weymouth Pine).
133. Hemlock (Hemlock Spruce).
134. Japanese Holly.
135. European White Birch.
136. Norway Spruce.
137. Black Pine (Austrian Pine).
138. Japan Corchorus.
139. Thornless Honey Locust.

In the accompanying plan (Fig. 35) no plants have been suggested besides trees and hardy shrubs. The idea is that in this way the most enduring and dignified planting can be produced. However, there are two great classes of plants which are of importance, especially in the earlier years of growth of our statelier plants. These are our herbaceous perennials and annuals.

Herbaceous perennials are easy to grow, and many may be planted in almost any place. They may be planted in the open or among or under trees and shrubs. In a naturalistic planting, however, they should not be planted in formal beds. They should be scattered about in a seemingly careless manner, and they should be found in the bays of shrubbery and in any nook that seems to need filling.

FIG. 37. The Results of Tree Planting

For quick effects the annuals come into play. What has been said of the perennials is true of the annuals as well. Whatever else is done in this planting, do not disfigure the landscape by digging up great spaces for formal flower beds. Let teachers and pupils have the privilege of noticing where the various perennials and annuals do well, and deciding among themselves where they are most at home. Our retiring flowers of the woodland would seem entirely out of place in a bed out in the lawn. A few perennials and annuals which may well find a home in some part of our planting are mentioned below:

Perennials. Anemone (or wind flower), columbine, asters, bluebell (or harebell), chrysanthemum, coreopsis, larkspur, foxglove, sunflower (especially the double variety), hollyhock, poppy, peony, phlox, goldenrod, trillium, bleeding-heart, iris, ornamental grasses, violets, spring-beauty, dogtooth violet, etc.

Annuals. China aster, alyssum, snapdragon, balsam, bachelor's button, coxcomb, pink, nasturtium, pansy, petunia, phlox, poppy, castor-oil bean, sunflower, verbena, zinnia, etc.

Bulbous plants. Crocus, dahlia, gladiolus, lily, narcissus, tuberose, tulip, etc.

Climbers. It is recommended that the outbuildings, horse shed, closets, etc., be covered as soon as possible with rapidly growing vines. If a latticework of some kind is built around the closets, they will soon be hidden. The slower growing shrubs will come on in due time. The American ivy, Dutchman's-pipe, bittersweet, virgin's-bower, trumpet-creeper, and wistaria are all hardy perennials. For the first year the climbing cucumber, hop-vine, or morning-glory may be used. There are many others from which to choose.

J. C. BLAIR

URBANA, ILLINOIS

Surely the excuse that we do not know what to plant is no longer a valid one. Our country schools should be centers of influence in the movement to make the country truly a country beautiful. There is great hope with the

FIG. 38. Where the Wild Crab Apple, Plum, etc., are Saved

rising generation. When the children of to-day become the men and women of a great to-morrow, if their education has done for them what it should do, they will "believe in beauty in the schoolroom, in the home, in daily life, and out of doors."

CHAPTER IV

SCHOOL GARDENS

The school garden in the country school is as yet an experiment. While this is true, it is nevertheless a movement which promises much, if properly directed, in the new education for the country child. Something more than talk is needed if our school grounds are to be made beautiful and if our children are to have elementary instruction in agriculture. Unless something is *done*, the grounds will continue to be desolate. The study of agriculture in the country school must lead the children to investigate for themselves with reference to soil and plant life. Hence the beginnings of the school-garden movement in the country school, though crude and unscientific to the expert, are to be commended, for they are a long advance over the do-nothing policy which has prevailed long enough. Let us have the courage to be pioneers in a movement that is right in itself, though we may not be able to see very far ahead. Manual training was held up to derision and laughed to scorn by those who were supposed, by themselves at least, to know all worth knowing in the theory and practice of education. Manual training flourished, however, and the school garden has at least a fighting chance.

We are slowly changing our opinions with reference to many things in the training of the child. To-day we are inclined to believe with John Dewey that education is not merely a preparation *for* life, but that it *is*, or should be,

life.   Professor Hanus of Harvard University, in his new
book, *A Modern School*, speaks as follows with reference
to the kind of education demanded by democratic society.
He says:

Now the only real preparation for life's duties, opportunities, and
privileges is participation in them so far as they can be rendered intelligible, interesting, and accessible to children and youth of school
age ; and hence the first duty of all education is to provide participation
as fully and as freely as possible.   From the beginning such an education cannot be limited to the school arts, — reading, writing, ciphering.

FIG. 39. A School Garden in Winnebago County (1903)

It must acquaint the pupil with the material and social environment
in order that every avenue of knowledge may be opened to him, and
every incipient power receive appropriate cultivation. Any other
course is a postponement of education, not education. Such a postponement is a permanent loss to the individual and to society. It is
a perversion of opportunity, and an economic waste.

And so the education of the country child for life's work
"cannot be limited to the school arts," — the "three
R's" of blessed memory ! What is the "material and social
environment" of the country child, — this educative material which is to assist in cultivating his "every incipient

power"? It seems that "appropriate cultivation" is not to come alone from reading some text-book on soil and the planting of seeds, but that there shall be "participation" in educational processes, so far as these processes can be "rendered intelligible, interesting, and accessible to children and youth of school age." Well, the school garden surely can be made accessible to most of the country children; and the boys and girls will gladly "participate" in soil experiments and plant growing, if a real live teacher will make the participation "intelligible and interesting." So, fellow-teacher in some remote district school, if you are teaching your children to *do* things as well as to study *about* things, be of good cheer, for you are in accord with educational thought and progress. Harvard University is pointing the way.

It would seem that the school garden in cities should, of course, be a very rational means of supplementing the study of books, to say nothing of its æsthetic value in beautifying grounds. Also many of the conditions there make it much easier to have successful school gardens. The school year is longer, and there are trained teachers with better salaries, teachers who have a high appreciation of beauty and the value of nature study from nature. This sympathetic attitude is the result of their Normal training, where, in a course covering two or three years, they are told how, in the most effective manner and with a minimum of "economic waste," they are to cultivate the child's "every incipient power." The city child does not come in contact with nature as does the country child; hence it is much easier to interest him. Also there is a much more enlightened public sentiment in the cities, with their public libraries and art galleries. Public-spirited men and women give time and money to encourage the return to nature. Perhaps there is a greater need of this in the artificial life of cities. The school garden is not likely to suffer during dry summer vacations, for there are the janitor and the hydrant. And it is not surprising that such cities as Boston, Yonkers, Cleveland, Philadelphia, St. Louis, and others should achieve such great results when there are salaried expert supervisors, who direct the work even in vacation time. And

FIG. 40. A School Garden in Winnebago County (1903)

this work is of the highest educative value. Instead of cities building larger jails and pointing with pride to such structures as the solution of the bad-boy problem, let more money be spent in farm schools, where the boy can get away from the slum back to the brown earth. Garden work is better than "bummin'."

I have before me a late bulletin on the Philadelphia school gardens. This is a joint report of the Civic Club, the Civic Betterment Association, the Public Education Association, and the City Parks Association. With a single

quotation from this valuable pamphlet I will drop all
consideration of the city-school garden and devote the
remainder of this chapter to the garden in the country
school. With reference to results the report says :

They [the gardens] have taken the children of their neighborhoods
off the street, even the big boys, at that formative period between
twelve and sixteen, when so many begin to go to the bad. Unless
there are public playgrounds and gardens, they have little else to do.
The gardens have given the children something to think about and
work over, and the product of that thought and work has been gathered by each child for his own. The experience has taught them
that work is worth something ; that results come from it ; that what
is taught in school is not something intangible, "highfalutin," im-
posed by some superior, earnestly soulful person, who was never
young, but instead is directly useful in everyday ways. Nature study
is changed from dry investigation of the causes of plant growth into
a lively, careful and scientific observation of the steps by which a
harvest is gradually prepared.

It was a happy thought to bring the plots together in big gardens.
Some dry-as-dust pedagogue might have reasoned from Jevons's logic
that a garden plot is a garden plot, even if not alongside of others,
and so have tried to induce each child to have his or her little plot at
home, — logic, but not human nature. Competition, good-fellowship,
the desire for companionship, all contribute to the success of the
school garden. The children are drawn by other children. They are
learning when they don't know it. The open air and sunshine are
enabling them to learn, to comprehend, more. It is a positively good
thing for their health to get their hands in good rich earth, — that old
mother earth from which we have all come. "Hands in the earth"
is now prescribed by doctors as a cure for lack of vitality, just as
fresh air and sunshine a-plenty is prescribed for consumption, and the
school garden compels all three.

To contemplate the difficulties in country-school gardening is to do nothing. I am aware that the average country
school-teacher is not as well trained as she should be,

and she is generally underpaid. The school year is short. The average for the country child in Illinois for 1904 was ninety-four days as against one hundred and fifty-nine days for the average city child. This is not what you might call an educational "square deal." Then, too, the neglect during vacation and the indifference or hostility of patrons make the problem of country-school gardening quite different from that in the cities. But a meek, submissive attitude towards obstacles that may lie in the way

FIG. 41. A School Garden in Winnebago County (1903)

of "participation" in vital educational processes in doing things, accompanied with increased devotion to "'rithmetic and spellin'," is not putting the country child into sympathetic and intelligent relation to his "material and social environment." We must be able to figure and spell, of course; but may we not be optimistic enough to hope that when we have passed through the crude experimental stage of country-school gardening there may result some material that will afford quite as much value and discipline for the country child as that now acquired from his joyous participation in alligation, foreign exchange, and marine insurance? But as a last argument it is said that country children have enough garden work at home. Yes, such as it is. But my observation leads me to the conclusion that there is vast room for improvement in the home garden of the average American farmer; and the right kind of training in the experimental garden at school will make the child a more efficient factor in the garden work at home. This has a dollar value, if you must look at education from the dollar point of view. But it has a culture value as well.

One purpose of the school garden in the country school should be to help in beautifying the grounds. Flowers should abound, for they are educators and make us sensitive to all that is lovely, whether in the field, along the roadside, or in the deep woods. To beautify the school grounds with the flower garden does not mean that all the wild vines, wild shrubs, or wild flowers are to be eliminated and a straight row of geraniums planted across the front of the yard, or a bed of nasturtiums made in the middle of the open space of the school grounds. Save all that is of a wild nature. Study how nature plants and imitate her example. Leave the open spaces for the playground and plant along the fences, walks, or at the base of the school building. I visited one of my schools recently where the directors are allowing the wild grapevines, wild blackberry and raspberry, wild flowers, etc., to flourish. Thus a bit of wild woodland is available for observation work. Here birds may nest and sing their songs, and the modest wild flower find a refuge and protection. Here children may learn lessons about animal and plant life in a very practical way. I visited another school which had some grand forest trees in the back part of the yard, with clumps of hazel bush interspersed among them. The hazel had all been cut down and put in neat piles ready for the torch. The trees were still standing. If fuel becomes scarce, it will be the proper thing, I suppose, to cut them down for firewood and save a few dollars in taxes for a year or two.

There is plenty of good literature available for the asking, which will tell school officers and teachers what to plant and how to plant. "How to set out Trees and

Fig. 42. A School Garden at Home (1904)

Shrubbery" (already mentioned, page 47), by Dean L. H. Bailey, is a valuable pamphlet published by the *Youth's Companion*. There are numerous diagrams in it which are very suggestive. I give one quotation only to interest the reader and cause him to read the entire pamphlet :

Next comes the planting. Let it be irregular and natural, and represent it by a wavy line. First of all, cover up the outhouses. Then plant heavily on the side, or in the direction of the prevailing wind. Leave openings in your plan wherever there are views to be had of fine old trees, attractive farmhouses, a brook, or a beautiful hill or field. Throw a handful of shrubs into the corners, by the steps, and about the bare corners of the building.

Besides the plan for improvement of the Seward school ground (see Chapter III), with suggested list of trees, shrubs, and flowers, as prepared by Professor Blair, the Farmers' Bulletin No. 218 gives some most helpful suggestions. This bulletin, " The School Garden," is prepared by Professor L. C. Corbett, Horticulturist, Bureau of Plant Industry, Washington, D.C. A postal card will get it. Eight pages of this bulletin are given up to the subject of the decoration of school grounds. Illustrations abound of plans for planting, and of walks, lawns, and annual plants, trees, and shrubs suitable for school grounds, with cultural directions. This bulletin should be in the hands of every country teacher and school director in our land. At least, our teachers should not plead ignorance of the most valuable and helpful literature along this line. Farmers' Bulletin No. 185, " Beautifying Home Grounds," is also by Professor Corbett. It is valuable, and it seems to me that the country school-teacher who is not inspired by these two bulletins and does not do some one thing to better conditions in the average farm home and country school has missed her calling. She (or he) is hired to teach geography and arithmetic to boys and girls, but Professor Corbett says in " The School Garden" (Farmers' Bulletin No. 218):

The plans of the grounds will serve as an exercise both in geography and in arithmetic, and if the pupils are encouraged to make such designs, their interest in the work will be assured, and a practical application of the principles taught in the schoolroom will be a result of no little value.

Is it possible that there is educative material in the environment of the country child that is not found in a textbook? Note that Professor Corbett says, " if the pupils are encouraged." Who is to be the One Courageous, the

Leader Inspirational, in this great new true educational uplift for the country school?

The second purpose of a garden in the country school is to utilize it for specific instruction in plant growth and soil treatment. If the elementary instruction in agriculture in the country school is to be of any value, the children must do some practical work instead of memorizing a few pages of some text-book, no matter how fascinatingly it may be written. A school garden, if only a bed four feet by six feet, under the direction of an earnest, enthusiastic teacher, will afford an excellent field for

FIG. 43. A School Garden at the Seward Consolidated School (1904)

training children in experimental and observation work. A farmer of the future in Illinois, who expects to make five per cent clear profit on an investment in land costing one hundred and twenty-five dollars per acre, will have to do some thinking; and the place for the thinking to begin is in the district school. Our higher institutions of agricultural instruction are discovering much that will be of great value to the future farmer. The problem is how to make this expert knowledge available for the country child. The school experimental garden promises much, if teachers and school officers will coöperate *with the children.*

Notice that I said an " earnest " and " enthusiastic "
teacher. Of course it would be better if she were " well-
trained " also. A boy, if "earnest" and "enthusiastic," will
learn to swim if you will only let him get into the water.
If we wait till the boys receive scientific directions at some
swimming school before they go near the river, not many
of them will ever learn to swim. This accomplishment,
however, may not be essential to the man's success in life.
There does come a time when most of us must either sink
or swim, regardless of rules or formulas. My point is that,
if we wait till all the country school-teachers know all about
plant growth or soil before they attempt a garden, the prob-
abilities are that the harvest will be over and the summer
ended before they get ready to dig and plant. This is what
I would say to teachers : The thing *now* to *do* is to dig and
plant and to learn by doing these very things with the
children. This will reveal to you your limitations, and if
you have the spirit of the true teacher and mean business,
you will find a way to attend a summer session for country
teachers such as the University of Illinois conducted for
the first time in June, 1905. To be sure, it is easier to
sit in the schoolroom and hear the children call over the
words in McGuffey's reader, the one you used when you
were a pupil a few short years ago. But are you seeking
the *easiest* or the *best* thing to do ?

The movement to instruct our children in the simplest
facts with reference to the science of agriculture will be
a failure if confined to a printed page. A school garden
affords opportunity for watching the growth of plant life,
and at the same time teaches one how to treat the soil so
as to retain moisture in case of drought, how to remove
injurious insects from plants, how to know the proper time

to harvest, and many other things pertaining to agriculture. Good reference books and bulletins of the state experiment station should be found in every country-school library. There is no excuse for not having the bulletins, since they may be had for the asking. But these are not the only things needed, nor indeed are they of first importance. The first and most important thing, it seems to me, is for each child to plant a seed of some kind and begin to care for a plant. To do this is to come in contact with nature in a practical and sympathetic way that cannot be attained through books. The Honorable James Wilson, United States Secretary of Agriculture, says :

The young farmer attending the district school could readily be taught what a plant gets from the soil and what it gets from the air. The several grasses could be planted, and their office in filling the soil with humus, enabling the soil to retain moisture, could be explained. The legumes — peas, beans, clover, and alfalfa — could be grown in the schoolhouse yard, and during recess or at the noon hour the teacher could interest the students by digging up a young pea or clover root and showing the nodules, whose office it is to bring free nitrogen from the atmosphere and fix it in the soil.

The best way to have a school garden is to have it. To be sure, there is inertia to overcome and prejudice. We get so in the habit of doing nothing, and our success in this direction is so phenomenal, that it requires some energy to make a new departure. We are afraid that people will say: "The school garden!—another fad. It's all froth and contrary to the sacred course of study." But if we wait till every one agrees with us, no progress will ever be made. The guiding principle should be, " Is the thing right and expedient ? " If so, make an effort to do it, and in such a way as to show results, no matter what may be the difficulties to be overcome.

There are to-day a hundred thousand school gardens in Europe, and the progress of the recent movement in America is encouraging, as many of the leaders in educational matters show a disposition to look upon this study as the basis and beginning of all nature work. This is the case in other countries, among them Russia, where no school can receive state funds unless it has a garden connected with it. The idea is a sound and healthy one, since sixty-five per cent of our exports are farm products; yet

FIG. 44. A Desolate Schoolhouse

thousands of children grow up without knowing anything at all of agriculture.

School gardens began with us in 1903. At my request a plan or model garden was prepared by Professor J. C. Blair, Horticulturist of the Illinois College of Agriculture. I think it a good thing to put our country teachers in touch with the state College of Agriculture and to get the children, and through them the parents, to begin to read and think about the most important, perhaps, of our state institutions, namely the College of Agriculture and the work of the experiment station. So we call on the various departments for help, and are making an effort to have all the principal bulletins form a part of the country-school library.

The model designed by Professor Blair called for a garden twelve feet by thirty-six feet. I believe this is too large to begin with, especially if the school has but eight or twelve pupils. The size is left to the judgment of the teacher. For three years now between seventy and eighty districts in Winnebago County have been doing garden work to a greater or less extent, as the illustrations in this chapter will show. We do not claim for these plots of ground results equal to those attained in the great city

FIG. 45. A Farm Home near the Desolate Schoolhouse

garden, with its expert supervision and trained teachers; but we claim that the spirit of the movement is all right, and what has been already accomplished affords no cause for discouragement or regret for the undertaking. It takes time to create sentiment for what is really worth while; and to make the school garden a permanent educational factor, the experiments must continue until the present school children become the teachers and school officers of the great to-morrow.

The plan prepared by Professor Blair was made the subject of a week's study at the annual teachers' institute, which is always held in March. Thus the teachers can at once put into practice what they have learned without waiting for six months to elapse before seeding time comes. The teachers and children have had to contend with dry weather, with the untamed character of the soil, and with the timidity that naturally goes with original experimental work not laid down in the school text-book of sacred

FIG. 46. A School Garden in Winnebago County (1905)

reliance. But, as said above, to contemplate the difficulties of school gardening is to do nothing.

Stereopticon lectures have been given at our teachers' institutes on the subject of school gardens, and the teachers thus catch the spirit of what progress is being made all over the country.

The agricultural editor of the Bloomington (Illinois) *Pantagraph* inspected some of our first attempts at gardening in 1903, and reported as follows in the columns of that paper:

The real measure of the work is not in pecks of potatoes and number of blossoms, — not in the commercial value of the products, but in its educative value to the child. A real beginning has been made, a general beginning, a uniform beginning, and this counts for a great deal. The thought and the work have been started in the right direction. It will be comparatively easy to increase the size and number of the gardens, the quantity and show of the products. It is only necessary to keep the matter moving next year and next.

The spirit of the work and the trend of public opinion seem to be of the favorable sort. And if this outdoor art makes as marked a transformation in the school premises as has been accomplished inside the schoolroom by the campaign for comfort, cleanliness, sanitary conditions, paint, proper wall colors, pictures and their artistic arrangement, libraries, organs, enthusiasm, etc., everybody will welcome it, fad or no fad. With such precedents in the accomplished fact of indoor improvements, and with such marked coöperation of teachers and pupils and patrons in this first season's work for school gardens, the outlook for their rapid development and complete success is good.

Doubtless there are teachers who wish suggestive outlines for school garden work. The following outlines were prepared by a highly competent teacher in the Rockford (Illinois) High School and used in the Winnebago County Annual Teachers' Institute, March, 1903.

The School Garden (General)

I. Diagram of the school garden (see page 77).

II. Present acquaintance with the plants of this garden. Of which plants can you recognize:
   1. The seed?
   2. The seedling plant and how it comes up?
   3. The blossom apart from the plant? If edible, what structure is used for food?

III. Plant relationships illustrated in the school garden.
   1. The monocotyledons: how characterized; families represented (grass family, lily family).
   2. The dicotyledons: how characterized; leading families.

IV. Soil : kinds of soil ; type represented in garden.

    1. Contrast lumpy and fine soils as to capacity for holding moisture.

    2. How the plant gets food from the soil.

    3. Conditions for germination and preparation of the soil to fulfill these.

    4. Cultivation after plant is established.

    5. Surface and deep tillage ; relation of root system to tillage.

    6. Depth to which roots penetrate in well-prepared soil. How smother the roots ?

    7. The plant foods supplied through soil water.

V. Propagation of plants.

    1. Seeds.

    2. Vegetative reproduction, illustrated by bulbs, tubers, cuttings, etc. Contrast the two modes. Which of the food crops are grown from seed, and which by vegetative reproduction ? Which is our chief reliance in agriculture ?

    3. Study of the potato.

        a. Food supply in tuber compared with that in seed. Nature of food.

        b. Modification due to underground habit.

        c. Advantages of underground habit.

        d. From what parts do the roots of a potato plant first spring ?

        e. Do the tubers grow above the roots or below them ?

        f. Are the tubers produced on roots or on stems ?

        g. When in the life of the plant do the tubers begin to form ?

        h. Does one stalk ever bear more than one tuber ?

        i. Do these stalks increase in length or diameter after the tuber begins to form ?

        j. How many kinds of stems has the potato ?

        k. Distinguish the feeding roots from the underground stems.

    4. Experimental work.

        a. Plant potatoes at different depths, from just under the surface to four inches. Which method gives best results ?

        b. Use seed pieces of varying sizes, from those with no eye up to the whole potato.

c. Any difference in value of cutting from stem to stem end
and bud end?

d. Which is better, one large piece or several small ones?

e. What is the order of sprouting of the eyes?

f. How prevent potato scab?

STUDY OF THE SEED

I. External structure : hilum (the scar) ; micropyle (little opening) ;
coats, texture, function.

II. Embryo : cotyledons (seed leaves) ; caulicle (little stem) ; hypo-
cotyl (part of the caulicle below the cotyledons); plumule
(little bud).

III. Food supply : where stored ; relative amount ; tests for starch,
oil, proteid.

KINDS OF SEEDS	BEAN	SQUASH	SUN-FLOWER	MORNING-GLORY
1. Sketch showing external features (name hilum and micropyle)				
2. Texture of coats				
3. Sketch embryo laid open, and name parts				
4. Texture of cotyledons				
5. Character of food; where stored				
Development of plumule				

IV. Escape of parts.
  1. Problems to be solved by the seed.
    a. Extrication of parts from the seed coats.
    b. Getting the first root started downward and fixed in the soil.
    c. Getting the stem started upward out of the soil and into the light without injuring the young leaves.
  2. Behavior while germinating.
    a. First visible phenomena. Illustrate differences in hardness by cutting dry seeds and soaked ones. Increase in

FIG. 47. A School Garden in Winnebago County (1905)

size. Sketch (1) dry bean, natural size; (2) bean showing wrinkling of coats (explain how this helps in the extrication of parts from the coat); (3) soaked bean when coat fits smoothly once more.
  3. Experiment showing expansive power of germinating seeds.
    a. First part to appear. From what part of the seed does it come? Advantage in being pointed at the tip.
    b. Direction taken by the root when it comes out. Observe direction taken by seeds placed in different positions in the germinator. Change the position of the seeds. Is there any advantage to the plant in having the first root grow downward?
    c. Growth of root. Where does it take place?
    d. Growth of stem. Where does it take place?
    e. Direction of growth of root and stem.

f. What part of the root bends when it turns from the horizontal position?

g. If the tip is removed, will the root turn?

h. Part first appearing above the surface. Reason for the manner in which the soil is penetrated by the rising stem.

i. How the embryo extricates itself from its coats.

j. Turning upward of the stem in the older seedlings.

STUDY OF PARTS	BEAN	SQUASH	MORNING-GLORY	PEA	CORN
1. Part first appearing above the surface					
2. How break through the soil?					
3. What parts extricated from coats?					
4. How extricated from coats?					
5. Do the cotyledons rise above ground?					
6. Changes in cotyledons as growth continues					

V. Conditions for germination.

The variance in conditions each time should involve but a single factor.

1. Germination dependent upon moisture.

  a. Blotting paper, wet and dry.

  b. Sawdust, wet and dry.

  c. Good soil, wet and dry.

2. Germination as dependent upon heat. Plant seeds in two pots containing similar conditions, but keep one indoors, the other outside. Try with (1) loam soil; (2) clay soil; (3) sand.

3. Germination as dependent on light. Keep soil moisture and heat constant, but place one pot in the light and the other in the dark.

The above represents most of the study for three days at the institute. In addition there was an outline for one day's work on trees and one day's work on birds.

In Vol. VI, Part III, of the *Proceedings of the American Park and Outdoor Art Association*, published March, 1903 (Charles Mulford Robinson, Secretary, 65 South Washington Street, Rochester, New York), is a very valuable bibliography of the school-garden movement in the United States. The list of articles is too long to reproduce here.

Circular No. 52 (revised by Dick Crosby), issued by the Office of Experiment Stations (A. C. True, Director)

FIG. 48. A School Garden in Winnebago County (1905)

United States Department of Agriculture, Washington, D.C., contains a list of a few good books and bulletins on nature study, school gardening, and elementary agriculture for the common schools. A postal card will get this valuable little circular. For the teacher or school officer who wants to know about the school-garden movement there is abundant valuable material now available and the supply is increasing. At the St. Louis Exposition last year there was a correlation chart on garden work, showing how garden work outdoors and indoors may correlate with the regular work of the school. This chart was a part of the educational

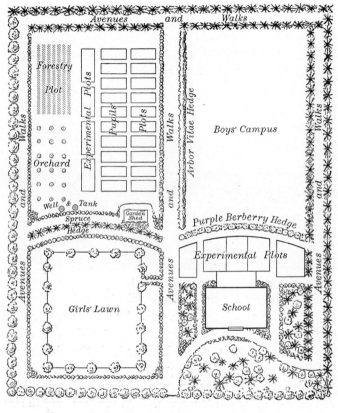

Fig. 49. Outline Plan of a Macdonald School Garden,
Bowesville, Ontario, Canada

exhibit of the Hyannis, Massachusetts, Normal School. It was reproduced in the pamphlet on Philadelphia school gardens mentioned in the first of this chapter.

True, if we could have such gardens as the Macdonald school gardens of Canada, better results would be obtained. If millionaires of the United States would find it possible to do as this man is doing, — doing something for the country child, — a great educational uplift would come to the agricultural interests of our country and, in fact, to all country-school work.

These gardens were started in the spring of 1904 in the provinces of Ontario, Quebec, Nova Scotia, New Brunswick, and Prince Edward Island. They are associated with Sir William Macdonald's plan for the improvement of the schools of Canada, and are a notable feature of the general scheme of Professor James W. Robertson, director of the Macdonald educational movement. Since these gardens are a factor in an educational movement, they have been placed under the Department of Education in each province, and not under the Department of Agriculture. The councils in the various provinces have passed orders incorporating the Macdonald gardens into the various educational systems. This places the gardens on a broader basis than in Europe or in any other country. They are attached to the ordinary country schools and are controlled by the local school authorities and by the taxpayers. The gardens vary in size from one acre to three acres or more. In general, the cost of maintaining them for three years is met by the Macdonald fund, as are also the expenses of the traveling instructor.

From a report on the Macdonald school gardens for the county of Carleton, Ontario, issued by R. H. Cowley, Inspector of Public Schools, the following is taken:

While the plan of laying out the gardens varies according to soil, surface, and location, the accompanying outline of the Bowesville garden suggests the general features that have been kept in view. These include a belt of ornamental native trees and shrubs surrounding the grounds; two walks each, about one hundred yards long, between rows of trees; a playground about half an acre in area for the boys; a lawn of about a quarter of an acre for the girls, bordered with some light and graceful shade, such as cut-leaf birch; a small orchard, in which are grown a few varieties of the fruit trees most profitable to the district; a forest plot, in which the most important

FIG. 50. A Model for a Country School

Canadian trees will be grown from seed and by transplanting; a plot for cultivating the wild herbs, vines, and shrubs of the district; space for individual plots and special experimental plots; an attractive approach to the school, including open lawn, large flowering plants, foliage, rockery, ornamental shrubs, etc.

The special experimental plots are, as a rule, larger than the individual plots. They are used for such purposes as the study of rotation of crops, values of fertilizers, effects of spraying, selection of seeds, merits of soils, productiveness and quality of different varieties of crops, and many other similar subjects. At one school a special study was made of corn, clover, tomatoes, and cabbage; at another beans, peas, beets, and potatoes occupied the experimental plots ; at still another some extra attention was given to plots of pumpkins, squash, cabbage, and cauliflower. At all the gardens special plots will be devoted to small fruits, such as strawberries, raspberries, gooseberries, currants. The experimental plots vary in area from two hundred to two thousand square feet, but where the quantity of ground is restricted the experiments may be successfully carried out on plots of a much smaller average size.

With reference to the place of the garden in school work the report says :

The work of the garden is recognized as a legitimate part of the school programme, and is interwoven already with a considerable part of the other studies. The garden is becoming the outer class room of the school, and the plots are its blackboards. The garden is not an innovation, or an excrescence, or an addendum, or a diversion. It is a happy field of expression, an organic part of the school in which boys and girls work among growing things and grow themselves in body and mind and spiritual outlook.

Of the advantages, the following summary only is given here :

1. Educationally it affords a release from the dull routine of the schoolroom and puts the pupil out into the fresh air and sunlight. It is a means of help by affording scope for motor activities that are natural to growing children. The garden work is correlated with much of the formal work of the school, such as arithmetic, reading, composition, drawing, etc. It serves as an introduction to the development of literary appreciation, as the " ability to appreciate the charm of many of the best poems depends not a little on ability to form visual images of natural objects." In this respect, if the teacher in the country school is alert, the country child has the advantage over the city child ; for " the urban eye of the town-bred child, who has never been interested in garden or field, must fail to catch the imagery of our best nature poems."

2. Economically the school garden teaches the composition and care of the soil, the best conditions for plant life, the value of fertilizers, seed selection, and the like.

3. Nationally the school garden develops an interest in the fundamental industry of the country. There develops the sense of ownership and respect for property. " In the care of their own plots the
pupils fight common enemies and learn that a bad weed in a neglected
plot may make trouble for many others. The garden is a pleasant
avenue of communication between the school and the home, relating
them in a new and living way, and thereby strengthening the public
interest in the school as a national institution."

One more quotation must be given with reference to the
school garden during vacation :

The general adoption of school gardens may naturally bring about
a desire to keep the rural schools open all summer, closing them in
the winter when the roads are worst and the weather severe. The

Fig. 51. Another Model for a Country School

conveying of pupils to consolidated schools may also help to induce
an arrangement of this kind. In the meantime there is no insurmountable difficulty or very serious problem in keeping the school garden
decent during the long summer vacation. Even if the garden were
to deteriorate from neglect during holidays, the fact would be of
altogether minor consequence against school gardens, since a well-
ordered pupil rather than a well-ordered garden is the supreme end of
it all. If the pupils do not provide for their plots during vacation, by
all means let the weeds grow. The worst possible mistake in such a

case would be to pay a janitor or some other person to take care of the plots for indifferent and unmindful pupils. At some school gardens in Carleton County last summer some pupils returned after vacation to weed-choked plots in which their flowers and vegetables compared very unfavorably with those of their more diligent companions. Their silent observation of this fact, and their strenuous efforts to redeem their plots, impressed upon them a lesson of moral and material value.

Aside from the school-garden work in Winnebago County, Illinois, for the past three years, other counties in Illinois report as follows :

Marion has ten school gardens ; ten per cent of the schools in McHenry County have gardens ; Coles County had a garden of one acre for a graded school ; Peoria County had twenty-five gardens in country schools ; Griggsville, Pike County, has had a garden for several years ; and mention must be made of the school garden of the Cottage Grove school near Springfield. Mention of the work of this country school, with illustrations of the work of the children, is made in the chapter on manual training.

It is very gratifying to see the interest that normal schools are taking with reference to school gardens. It would make this chapter too long to give even a brief account of all that is being done by these institutions for the training of teachers. Only the work of two will be noticed here, namely, the movement at the Eastern Illinois Normal School at Charleston and that at the Central Illinois Normal School at Normal.

Professor Otis W. Caldwell, instructor in botany at the Charleston Normal School, has issued a valuable bulletin on the school garden, well illustrated. This bulletin is valuable because its contents are not based on theory alone. For several years a successful school garden has been carried on at this normal school. Speaking of the garden in connection with the country school, Mr. Caldwell says :

In rural schools it will probably be found desirable to grow things that require least care during vacation, — shrubbery and such things in general as will serve to beautify the school ground, rather than the economic plants that are of greater relative significance educationally to the pupils of the city schools. But besides these there should be some beds of flowering plants, and these should not be allowed to suffer from lack of attention. It should be an easy matter to find in the neighborhood school officers or young people interested enough in the school ground to give the small care requisite to caring for these things during the vacation time. In some localities there are magnificent farm-houses and barns standing in beautifully kept plots, emphasizing the fact that the places where children are educated are ugly with weeds and general negligence. A little care given to the school ground during vacation would enable teachers and pupils to make it beautiful and useful during school days. The lack of proper care during vacation time should not be used as an argument against any proper use during the days of school.

Fig. 52. Trees set out in 1905

It has been my great pleasure to inspect the gardens at the Central Normal School at Normal. If any one is in doubt about the place of the school garden in a system of education, his doubts must be removed after visiting this place and listening to an explanation by President Felmley as the various plots are visited. In this way you catch the spirit and significance that you cannot get by reading an account of it. President Felmley has issued an excellent bulletin on "Agriculture and Horticulture in the Rural School." In this publication is described the school-garden idea as it is at his school. One quotation is sufficient to show the author's ideal.

FIG. 53. Nature Study

The special instruction offered in this line is not merely to train skillful farmers. It is quite important that farmer boys and girls learn to appreciate and love the country. There need be here no division in material or method. The knowledge of soil and atmosphere, of plant and animal life, that makes him an intelligent producer puts him in sympathetic touch with these activities of nature. If the farmer as he trudges down the corn rows under the June sun sees only clods and weeds and corn, he leads an empty and a barren life. But if he knows of the work of the moisture in air and soil, of the use of air to root and leaf, of the mysterious chemistry of the sunbeam, of the vital forces in the growing plant, of the bacteria in the soil liberating its elements of fertility; if he sees all the relation of all these natural forces to his own work; if he can follow his crop to the market, to foreign lands, to the mill, to the oven and the table; if he knows of the hundreds of commercial products obtained from his corn or the animals that it fattens, he then realizes that he is no mere toiler; he is marshaling the hosts of the universe, and upon the skill of his generalship depends the life of the nations.

CHAPTER V

INDOOR ART AND DECORATION

One article of the Teacher's Creed given in Chapter II is as follows: "I believe in beauty in the schoolroom, in the home, in daily life, and out of doors." An attempt has been made in Chapters III and IV to show the value and the means of securing beauty in the outdoor life as far as the surroundings of the school are concerned. The aim of Chapters V and VI will be to point out some practical things to be done in order to secure a corresponding condition affecting the indoor life of the children in country schools.

It seems an almost impassable gulf from the modern sanitary city-school building, with its beautiful but simple architectural proportions, to the ugly, unsanitary, box-car structure of a building that has stood for over forty years in so many country districts. In the character of the building may be found one reason why so many country children are paying tuition in city schools.

It is true that better work may be done in a dilapidated country-school building than is done in the best up-to-date city building. But the likelihood is that poorer work will be done in the former than in the latter, to say nothing of the educational influence of surroundings; for the records do not show that live, enthusiastic, well-trained teachers are rushing to the neglected country-school building for a salary ranging from twenty-four to forty dollars per month for a year of five to eight months.

But a better day is coming for the country child. A central building to take the place of the time-honored but worn-out district schoolhouses will give some help; but consolidation will come slowly, and in the meantime we cannot sit and dream. Duty demands that something be done for the hundreds of thousands of boys and girls now sitting amid forlorn surroundings. Just what that something shall be will, of course, vary with the prevailing conditions in the various districts.

It would be a fine thing if, in every district, we could have an ideal school board that would provide ideal conditions so that first-class work could be done by teachers and children from the first to the last of the school term. But the average school director is about the same in educational ideals as the community he represents. A great work needs to be done to create a higher public sentiment among the country people as a whole. The county superintendent of schools can do much in this direction, and his most powerful aids are the camera and the printing press; but in an educational campaign of this character the results will come slowly. The best results will come when the children of to-day, who are getting new ideals, become the teachers, school officers, and patrons of a new to-morrow. Here is the great promise, and the person who has a real interest in the educational uplift for the country school must have patience and learn to labor and to wait.

School directors can do something. Instead of spending thirty-five or fifty dollars of the school funds for a wonderful chart portraying the whole scheme in the education of man from the cradle to the grave, why not use the same amount of money for paint? The chart stands neglected because the teacher cannot use it in the average school.

A planetarium advertised for thirty-five dollars, to "clearly illustrate and practically solve the difficult problems relating to celestial sphere, ecliptic, equinoxes, apogee and perigee, zodiac, the seasons of Venus, right ascension and declination, retrograde motion of the planets, etc.," may be a necessary piece of apparatus in the hands of a teacher who knows how to use it ; but country schools are needing shades for the windows, a hard-wood floor, paint for the walls, a towel rack, a water tank, a jacket around the stove, and many other things, more than planetariums and geometrical blocks. And yet the school officers are throwing away good coin of the realm in such purchases of apparatus beyond the use of the average country school. Rather use the money to purchase lumber, paint, blackboards, and soap.

FIG. 54. A Stove Jacket

If directors will do nothing to secure sanitary conditions to a moderate degree, then some responsibility must rest upon the teacher. A teacher ought not to be compelled to scrub the floor and wash the windows ; but rather than teach in a dirty building from month to month, I would clean it or quit the school. The teacher can organize a sanitary commission, with herself as president and chief of medical staff. The children will gladly enlist as members of the ambulance corps, for no doubt there are dead things to be removed from the schoolroom. One such instance I recall in a country school in Winnebago County in 1904. The teacher has now been promoted to the city schools of Rockford. She was determined to have a clean room, and she succeeded ; but (alas for the country school !) she was too valuable to be retained there.

After the house is cleaned, with the exercise of tact the coöperation of the children can be enlisted to keep it reasonably clean in all kinds of weather. But do not disband the sanitary commission, even if the house is clean. As chief of the medical staff, visit the school directors and ask for a bushel of lime, if the school funds will warrant such an extravagant outlay. Tell them you know where you can get a few gallons of water and you would like to put the lime in it. The average director may become alarmed over the possible use of so much limewater ; allay his fears by telling him that you do not intend giving it to the children, but that the plastering is old and discolored and you intend to give it a good coat of whitewash as well as to cover up some pencil markings to be found on the interior of the outhouses. These two things can be done, and other things will come in due time if we faint not. I am in sympathy, under proper conditions, with the movement to teach higher subjects in the country school ; but if it is a choice between higher mathematics and soap, and soap is needed, I choose soap. I do not care who makes it, so long as it is anti-dirt in its affections. And where cleanliness is lacking, instead of foreign-language work with a study of that wonderful pair of twins on the banks of the Tiber, let there be substituted the work of the " Gold Dust Twins." Many of our country schoolhouses need to be purified as by fire.

Perhaps the interior woodwork of the school needs to be freshened up with a coat of paint. About as nice a job of painting as I have seen done in a district schoolhouse was done by one of our teachers during her last term of school. She told the directors that if they would furnish the prepared paint she would put it on. Not that I believe that teachers should become scrub women, painters, and plasterers; but if school authorities would not do their duty, if I wanted to teach, and if I had to live in a room six hours of the day for twenty-two days in the month for six months of the year, then for the children's

FIG. 55. A Water Tank

sake I would cure some things rather than endure them, or I would get out of the schoolroom and stay out.

Then there is the stove, standing usually in the middle of the room. The teacher can, perhaps, do little with the stove except in the way of fuel or stove polish. No explanation has ever been offered why school stoves and stove polish are such hereditary foes. The bitter enmity has existed for years, and yet they were made for each other. Who is to blame for these long years of hatred and separation? With little effort an acquaintanceship could be brought about that would brighten into the closest friendship.

At a small expense the children can be protected from the direct radiation of a highly heated stove. This can be done by means of a sheet-iron jacket, leaving a distance of twelve or eighteen inches between it and the stove. Such a jacket can be made and adjusted by any good tinner. The teacher can get figures as to cost and present them to the directors, at the same time intelligently informing them as to the value of a stove jacket as a sanitary addition to the schoolroom.

Every teacher should know that the air of the schoolroom becomes foul in cold weather. It can be smelt, it can be tasted, especially if the windows have been well nailed down and the fuel is not spared. If directors manifest no disposition to furnish a simple ventilating system, there yet remain one or two simple things that the teacher can and should do. The windows may be lowered somewhat on the side opposite that from which the wind is blowing; or, better still, boards three or four inches wide may be fitted under the lower sash of the windows on each side of the room. Surely, as a last resort, the windows may be thrown up once an hour and the children made to march around while the air is changing. It is not a loss of time.

As a rule, the water pail is in one corner of the room on a small bench, almost lost among the dinner pails and wraps. A pail of fresh water is brought in before school begins in the morning, and that oftentimes ends the water question for the day. The highly heated, foul atmosphere of the schoolroom has its effect on the water as well as upon the children. A small expenditure of money will secure a galvanized-iron water tank with a cover, and a porcelain-lined sink with a waste pipe conducting to the exterior of the building. The cost of both need not exceed ten dollars. The tank should have a cover to prevent the water from absorbing impurities, and the sink should be porcelain lined to prevent rusting. A good stove jacket will cost ten dollars. Thus for an expenditure of twenty dollars — about half the cost of a chart or a planetarium — the sanitation of the schoolroom may be greatly improved. But school sanitation is not as attractive a subject as school decoration, though more important.

The report of the Art Education Society and the Home Gardening Association of the Cleveland public schools

FIG. 56. Studying a Traveling Art Exhibit

for 1904 shows what one city is doing, through an organization of teachers, to put good works of art into the schoolroom. The Cleveland Art Education Society was formed among the teachers of Cleveland in 1896. The purpose of the society was "to secure reproductions of the great pictures of the world, foreign and domestic views, for the use of the schools of the city, as a means of educating the children in the appreciation of the beautiful." As to results, the report states that "by means of teachers' dollar membership fees, entertainments, lectures, etc., $6000 was raised the first year. This movement has gained many ardent supporters among teachers, scholars, parents, and other public-spirited citizens, and the work has gone on steadily, until there are now about forty-one hundred pictures in the schools. The total cost of the pictures now in the Cleveland public schools aggregates $27,665.65." The report gives a list of the pictures, statuary, and casts that have been placed in the eighty school buildings of Cleveland. The pamphlet is well illustrated.

In October, 1900, on my return from a visit to the centralized schools of northeastern Ohio, it was my great pleasure to see some of the schoolroom decorations in the schools of Cleveland and Indianapolis. I then determined that something of art education should begin for the country children of my own county. Since September 1, 1901, there has been raised by teachers and children, by means of socials, entertainments, etc., the sum of $4165. Of this amount about $1600 has been expended for pictures; the rest has been used in the purchase of such schoolroom furnishings as books, organs, pianos, clocks, and apparatus. Besides this we are indebted to interested friends for a very generous donation of pictures and casts.

It was not expected that many of the country schoolteachers of Winnebago County, in the very near future at least, would be able to visit the art galleries of Europe and study pictures. The next best thing was, if possible, to secure reproductions that might be studied at the annual teachers' institutes. Such a loan was secured for three consecutive years: institute of 1901, pictures by the Prang Educational Company of Chicago; institute of 1902, the best reproductions by the Soule Art Company of Boston;

institute of 1903, excellent pictures by the Horace K.
Turner Company of Boston.

These pictures were hung in the assembly room and hall
of the Rockford high-school building, and thus for a week
the teachers could in a sense visit the great art galleries
and in a measure begin to know the old masters. The purpose of the county superintendent was to have the teachers
make some acquaintance with pictures, proper framing, etc.,
before buying for the schoolroom. One period (forty-five

FIG. 57. An Improved Interior

minutes) each day at these institutes was devoted to illustrated talks on Murillo, Raphael, Millet, Rosa Bonheur,
Corot, Breton, Michelangelo, Landseer, and Ruysdael.

In addition to the study of pictures for those three years
at the annual teachers' institutes an opportunity was given
to read about art and artists. The city library of Rockford kindly loaned all the books necessary to carry out the
course of reading. These books were placed in the assembly
room of the high school, and one hour each day was devoted
to reading. The list of books was printed, so that during

the year any country teacher might continue the reading if she desired. The following short list, prepared by an art expert, contains such books as are deemed by him to be most useful for school libraries or for individual purchase.

A SMALL WORKING LIBRARY FOR ART EDUCATION

Puffer's Psychology of Beauty.

La Farge's Considerations on Painting.

Brown's The Fine Arts.

Goodyear's History of Art.

Lubke's History of Art.

Ferguson's History of Architecture.

Warnum's Analysis of Ornament.

Tarbell's History of Greek Art.

Weir's Greek Painters' Art.

Berenson's Central Painters of the Renaissance.

Brownell's French Art.

Clement's Sacred and Legendary Art.

Clement's Painters, Sculptors, and Engravers.

Clement's Artists of Nineteenth Century.

Hoyt's The World's Painters.

Taine's Lectures on Art.

Emery's How to Enjoy Pictures.

Coffin's How to Study Pictures.

Poore's Pictorial Composition.

Hatton's Figure Drawing and Composition.

Sturgis's The Appreciation of Sculpture.

Ruskin's Modern Painters.

Moody's Lectures and Lessons on Art.

Meyer's Handbook of Ornament.

Crane's Line and Form.

Day's Ornament and its Application.

Mayeux's Manual of Decorative Composition.

Jackson's Lessons on Decorative Design.

Maginnis's Pen Drawing.

Cross's Freehand Drawing.

Cross's Mechanical Drawing.

Brown's Letters and Lettering.

Burrage and Bailey's School Sanitation and Decoration.

Sanford's Art Crafts for Beginners.

Periodicals

School Arts Book.

Masters in Art.

International Studio.

Two books in the above list were read thoroughly and discussed at local teachers' meetings for two years. They were Burrage and Bailey's *School Sanitation and*

Decoration and Emery's *How to Enjoy Pictures.* These two
books are especially commended to school-teachers for their
private libraries, and the first-mentioned should be read by
school officers, as it gives valuable suggestions in regard to
interior decoration.

A school social once a year, if managed properly, is a means
of uplift for the entire district. The programme should be
thought out carefully and should be of a simple educative

FIG. 58. Pictures and Books

These pictures and books were bought with the proceeds of school socials

character. Amateur theatricals should not be attempted
in the average country school. Suppose October to be
observed as a library and picture month. Literature and
art should go together. The following suggestive plan
and programme was given to our teachers at the beginning
of our campaign.

I. Harvest home social during the month of October, for the purpose of securing books for the school and one or two
choice pictures for schoolroom decoration. Admission,
adults, 15 cents ; school children, 10 cents.

II. Preparation of room : Decorate with autumn leaves, grasses,
    flowers, fruits, grains, etc.

III. Suggestive programme :

1. Song by the school : " Illinois."
2. Recitation : " October's Bright Blue Weather " (Helen Hunt
   Jackson).
3. Recitation : " When the Frost is on the Pumpkin " (James
   Whitcomb Riley).
4. Autumn flower exercise : Various school journals contain
   suggestions for this number.
5. Music.
6. Songs of Labor (Whittier).
   a. " The Huskers."
   b. " The Corn-Song."
7. Song by the school.
8. Short essay : " The Value of a School Library."
9. Short essay : " Schoolroom Decoration."
10. The pupils' reading circle : A brief statement by the teacher
    of the purpose of the organization and giving the list of
    books for the current year.
11. Music.
12. A picture study : Here is an opportunity to interest patrons
    and children in art and artists. Comments should not
    be too technical. A few good examples are given below.
    Suitable pictures for October are the following :
    a. Millet, " The Gleaners."
    b. Breton, " The Gleaners."
    c. Troyon, " Oxen going to Work."
    d. Breton, " The End of Labor."
    e. Adam, " The Haymaker."
    f. Le Rolle, " The Shepherdess."

Secure a penny Perry picture of Millet's "Gleaners," or
a larger one if possible, and place it on the front wall in
plain view. Have one of the oldest pupils read short
selections about this picture and the man who painted it
(see Hurll's *Millet*, Riverside Art Series ; see also Julia

Cartwright's *Life of Millet* and Wilson's *Picture Study in Elementary Schools* for material relating to Millet).

13. Interesting and instructive bits of history about a picture or an artist, as above.
14. Song by the school.
15. Harvest home lunch: Refreshments of some kind will be a pleasant feature and a means of revenue as well. A basket tastefully trimmed with autumn leaves and filled with lunch for two can be sold to the highest bidder, and the proceeds may go to the library and picture fund.
16. Closing song by all : "America."

Thornbury tells us that the subject of the "Téméraire" was suggested to Turner by his friend Stanfield, while they were on a holiday excursion.

It was at these times that Turner talked and joked his best, snatching now and then a moment to print on his quick brain some tone of sky, some gleam of water, some sprinkling light of oar, some glancing sunshine crossbarring a sail. Suddenly there moved down upon the artist's boat the grand old vessel that had been taken prisoner at the Nile and that led the van at Trafalgar. She loomed pale and ghastly, and was being towed to her last moorings at Deptford by a little fiery, saucy-looking steam tug.

"There is a fine subject, Turner," said Stanfield. Turner's picture represents the sunset of a great day in England's naval history, — departing of the wooden navy; day of steel and steam soon to dawn. While studying this picture let the pupils read or commit portions of Holmes's poem written when it was proposed that the American frigate *Constitution* should meet with a like fate.

The pictures of Millet appeal strongly to many who know but little about art. The artist sympathized with toil, and his great genius was used to ennoble labor. Millet's art reveals the dignity in country life and toil. He teaches an important lesson to every American. Mrs. Cartwright says:

> He knew, as few masters have ever known, how to put a whole world of thought into an individual action, how to express the lives and characters of bygone generations in a single gesture; and with true poetic insight he makes us realize the deeper meaning that lies hidden below the eternal destiny of the human race, — the age-long struggle of man with nature, which will endure while seedtime and harvest, summer and winter, follow each other upon the face of the earth.

FIG. 59. A Room in the Seward Consolidated School

" The Sower " is another picture which appeals to the many. The figure represents a phase of farming fast disappearing. The patent seeder with a team of horses is now regarded as indispensable in up-to-date farming. To compare thoughtfully the picture itself with such a description of it as this by Mrs. Cartwright is a practice to be commended:

> And as he meditated over these old memories the great picture grew into being, and he painted that wonderful form of the sower, striding with majestic tread across the newly plowed field, flinging the precious seed broadcast. Night is falling, the shadows are lengthening over the wind-swept fields, and scarce a gleam in the western

sky lights up the winter landscape ; but still he goes on his way, careless alike of the coming darkness or of the flocks of hungry crows that follow in his track. In that solitary figure, with his measured tread and superb action, the whole spirit of the peasant's calling is summed up with a power and concentration of thought worthy of Michelangelo.

Millet was ever true to his ideals. He was willing to suffer for them. Herein is another lesson our children need to learn. Moreover, he teaches us to discriminate between

FIG. 60. A Room in the Seward Consolidated School

conventional and vital beauty. When Sensier urged Millet to make his peasants more attractive, Millet's reply was :

That is all very fine, but you must remember that beauty does not consist merely in the shape or coloring of the face. It lies in the general effect of the form, in suitable and appropriate action. Your pretty peasant girls are not fit to pick up fagots, to glean under the August sun, or draw water from the well. When I paint a mother I shall try and make her beautiful simply by the look which she bends upon her child. Beauty is expression.

The great mass of country people should be led to appreciate the beautiful in art as well as in nature, and the place to begin is in the country school. A start can be made with the Perry pictures and the Prang platinettes.

In June, 1902, a friend from Boston visited our schools, and in token of his appreciation of efforts made to put good pictures into the schoolrooms he decorated a schoolroom at his own expense.

The pictures are fourteen in number, well framed. The following are the subjects:

1. Stuart's " Washington."
2. St. Gaudens's " Lincoln."
3. St. Gaudens's " Shaw Memorial."
4. Millet's " The Gleaners."
5. Turner's " Approach to Venice " (in colors).
6. Turner's " Fighting Téméraire."
7. William Morris Hunt's " Flight of Night."
8. Ruysdael's " Windmill."
9. Van Marcke's " Water Gate."
10. " Lower Falls, Yellowstone " (in color).
11. Raphael's " Sistine Madonna."
12. Mauve's " Shepherd's Lane."
13. " Portrait of Longfellow."
14. Birgel's " Twilight."

The same gentleman, with the same spirit of generosity, gave all the pictures and casts to decorate the first consolidated country-school building in Illinois, an account of which, with illustrations, is found in another chapter.

The Illinois Congress of Mothers is always ready to advise with teachers about schoolroom decoration, as the following announcement shows:

The Committee on School Decoration of the Illinois Congress of Mothers cordially offers its services to any one engaged in school beautifying.

1. The selection of wall tints.
    Give size of room, height of ceiling, and number and direction of windows. Samples of suitable tints will be sent.

2. Choice of pictures.

State amount to be expended and give dimensions of wall space on which picture is to hang ; also direction of light received and average age of pupils in room.

A number of suitable subjects will be suggested and Perry copies of same sent to assist in selection. When purchase is certain, pictures themselves may be sent on approval.

3. Selection of frame, mat, etc.

4. Choice of casts suited to schools ; also of effective pottery, with suggestions for placing.

Hoping in this way to make available to the smaller towns of Illinois, and to the country schools, the varied assortment and excellent values possible to a great city, the committee invites you to make free use of its offer.

In the matter of schoolroom decoration it is not to be expected that country schools can excel or equal city schools

FIG. 61. A Room in the Seward Consolidated School

like those of Cleveland or Indianapolis. But something can be done. The following, from the chapter "The Old

Country Schoolroom" in *School Sanitation and Decoration*, by Burrage and Bailey, is direct and to the point:

But suppose such things cannot be had. An old picture frame may be found, scraped, rubbed down with oil or shellac, a glass fitted into it, and a back made, which may be removed easily. A full-page engraving from a magazine, a half-tone reproduction, a Japanese print, an unmounted photograph, — such pictures anybody can procure in these days, — these may be mounted on gray cards of uniform size to fit the frame, and each displayed for a day or two, or a week or more.

In any event the teacher should decree that nothing but beautiful things shall be hung upon the walls. Better bare walls than debased and debasing art ; better nothing in the way of decoration than decoration which is worse than nothing. The following list may prove useful to the country teacher who wishes to be able to name one desirable work of art, and then another and another as the interest increases.

> Abbott Thayer's "Caritas."
> Millet's "Feeding her Birds."
> Raphael's "Madonna of the Chair."
> Barye's "Lion and Snake" (cast).
> "A Cathedral" (Notre Dame, Canterbury, or Amiens).
> Guido Reni's "Aurora."
> Corot's "Paysage."
> Regnault's "Automedon."
> Della Robbia's "A Bambino" (cast).
> Watts's "Sir Galahad."
> Turner's "Old Téméraire."
> Donatello's "Infant St. John" (cast).

Make a bold beginning and believe in your ultimate success in securing what you want for the children.

It is not necessary to move to the cities to have the children come in touch with literature and art.

CHAPTER VI

SCHOOL LIBRARIES

During the last two or three years articles have appeared in the leading magazines, and in the public press as well, describing the wonderful growth of public libraries. Millionaires are erecting buildings and endowing libraries and art galleries for city people and their children, but who is making an effort to supply good reading matter for the vast number of children in the country schools? In *The World's Work* for July, 1905, is an article, "Libraries for Everybody," by Herbert Putnam, Librarian of Congress. This article is well illustrated with charts showing the growth and distribution of public libraries in the United States. Just how many people living on farms are included in the word "everybody," the last word in the title of the article by Mr. Putnam, is, of course, a matter of conjecture. It is safe to say that there are thousands of homes and hundreds of thousands of children in the country districts to whom good books are practically unknown.

Before describing how good books are secured and teachers trained to use and take care of them in country schools, let us see what is being done, not by gifts of millionaires but through the public school, to develop libraries and to have children acquire the habit of reading good books. The reports for 1904, issued by the state superintendents of Wisconsin, Iowa, Indiana, Missouri, Minnesota, and Illinois, show that commendable progress is being made. The following summary is interesting, for it represents a movement and shows results that are not widely known to the general public. A fine building for library purposes standing on a choice site in a city can be seen of men, but the country-school library movement is not so conspicuous, though more far-reaching.

Wisconsin has a library law requiring the levy of ten cents per capita for each person of school age living in the school district for a library fund for that district. A list of books is carefully prepared in the office of the state superintendent. The inference from the state report is that every country school in Wisconsin has a library, thus representing a total of 817,075 volumes purchased by a tax of ten cents per capita. There are, in addition, in cities not under per capita tax, 125,000 volumes in school libraries, thus making a total of 942,075 volumes of good books in the schools of Wisconsin.

Iowa has a law requiring the purchase of good books for country children. The books are selected by the State Educational Board of Examiners; and 10,706 school districts have libraries representing 614,492 volumes, 73,479 of which were added for the year ending June 30, 1904. This represents an outlay for that year of $25,548.31 from district funds and $10,439.20 raised by voluntary efforts. Iowa has 6821 country schools with suitable library cases.

The Indiana report makes no specific mention of "district-school" libraries, but states that there are 517,543 volumes in the Young People's Reading Circle libraries. Of this number 81,273 were added the past year.

Minnesota has state aid to the extent of $15,000 annually for school-library purposes. State Superintendent Oleson reports this amount inadequate. For the year ending July 31, 1904, there were 587,299 volumes in school libraries, 69,400 of which were added during the past year.

Missouri has 468,905 volumes in 5696 districts. As there are 9974 school districts in the state, the inference is that 4278 school districts have no libraries. This is 28 districts more than in Illinois.

Illinois has no state school-library law or state aid, and no state list of books. The report for 1904 gives 7499

Fig. 62. A Country-School Library

school districts (city and country) having 896,251 volumes in libraries, 87,021 of which were added the past year. There are 4252 school districts (city and country) without any libraries.

Of the 4252 Illinois school districts without library books, it is safe to claim 4000 as being one-room country schools. Now not a single one of these 4000 schools is necessarily a poor school because of the absence of a library. I am willing to allow that a well-trained normal or university graduate is teaching in every one of those 4000 districts, and thus by the superior character of work done by the teacher the absence of good ·reference books on history, biography, geography, literature, and art is not as great a loss to the children as it might be. But in the great majority of cases such teachers are not likely to be found in such districts. If they were, there would be good libraries in 3999 out of the 4000 districts, because such teachers would find a way to get books and, what is better, would make such good use of them that the children's lives would be enriched ; and through the children there would be a higher ideal as to the character· of the literature to be used in the home, if any at all had been used there.

It is not for me to offer any explanation why the children of 4000 country schools of the great and wealthy state of Illinois have no libraries. In my own county of Winnebago two reasons are sometimes offered why books are not purchased by school officers out of the school funds, as the law allows them. The first is that the district is too poor, and the second is that the teacher does not see to it that the books are properly cared for and efforts made to have the children acquire the habit of reading good books. This last reason is more serious than the first ; and it must be confessed that the indifference of many teachers to the library offers good excuse for it. The plea of poverty can have but little weight as an excuse why at least five dollars' worth of books may not be added annually in every country district in Illinois. There are grounds for believing that school funds are wasted in some directions. Directors, and most often the ones who claim that taxes are already too high, become helpless in the presence of an agent with a wonderful chart, and sign away thirty dollars in the purchase of a piece of apparatus which the teacher cannot or does not use.

A few years ago such an agent came to Winnebago County, and fully a dozen boards of directors bought the chart. Let us see what thirty dollars would do towards a good school library :

1905 set (20 books) of Illinois Pupils' Reading Circle . .	$13.15
One Webster's International Dictionary	10.00
Four supplementary first readers	1.00
" " second "	1.60
" " third "	1.80
One year's subscription to the *Little Chronicle*	1.50
Total	$29.05

No, poverty is not a sufficient excuse. Even if the teacher paid no more attention to the above books than she does to the chart, still the books are a better investment, for some of the pupils will read in spite of the indifference of the teacher.

William Hawley Smith, in *The Evolution of Dodd*, says :

And for you, who send your six-year-olds to school with a single book, and grumble because you have to buy even so much of an outfit, what are you going to do about it when your boy drains all the life out of the little volume in a couple of weeks or a month ? He knows the stories by heart, and after that he says them over, day by day, because he must, and not in the least because he cares to.

As to the second reason, that teachers do not use the books and do not compel the children to use them properly, there is too much truth. For six years at the Winnebago County Annual Teachers' Institute, during the library hour,

an effort has been made to teach teachers how to care for
books and make them an efficient factor in vitalizing the
regular work of the school, and at the same time to teach
them how to interest children in books so that they will
want to read after they leave school.   This last accomplishment is by no means to be despised.   As a rule, I believe

Fig. 63. Library Case and Reading Table

that if teachers make the right use of library books and
apparatus, they will have but little trouble in inducing the
average board of directors to supply them.

On July 1, 1899, there were fifty-six districts out of one
hundred and eighteen in Winnebago County (outside the
city of Rockford) without school libraries.   September 1,
1899, began with us the Twentieth Century Forward Library Movement.   Teachers, children, parents, and county

superintendents coöperated to secure the following results
so far as the local district libraries are concerned:

Number of volumes		in 1899	. . . .	1386
" " "	added	" 1900	. . . .	1542
" " "	"	" 1901	. . . .	2483
" " "	"	" 1902	. . . .	1284
" " "	"	" 1903	. . . .	772
" " "	"	" 1904	. . . .	330
" " "	"	" 1905	. . . .	552
Total			. . . .	8349

The decrease in the number of volumes put into local
school libraries since 1901 is because of the growth of the
Winnebago Country District School Traveling Libraries.
The increase of books for local district libraries has been
largely the result of socials held by pupils and teachers.

Net proceeds of school socials, 1901	. . . . . .	$868.68
" " " " "	1902	. . . . . .	1072.09
" " " " "	1903	. . . . . .	805.15
" " " " "	1904	. . . . . .	526.13
" " " " "	1905	. . . . . .	935.85
Total		. . . .	$4207.90

Not all of the money so raised was expended for books.
Some was used for pictures, organs, pianos, curtains,
shades, clocks, maps, desks, globes, and the like.

Amount expended from school funds for books, 1901	$525.21
" " " " " " "	1902	120.96
" " " " " " "	1903	89.10
" " " " " " "	1904	12.13
" " " " " " "	1905	106.86
Total	. . . .	$854.26

The decrease in amount of our district funds expended
by school officers is due primarily to the notion that a few
books bought one year are sufficient for the next ten years

or so; and also to the fact that the Winnebago County District Traveling Libraries bring new and better books every year to each school district.

The traveling libraries for the district schools of Winnebago County began in 1901 and were a result of my observation of the helpfulness of the Rockford Public Library to me when a teacher in the high school in that city. As there were traveling libraries from the city library to the various school buildings of Rockford, I thought that something similar to this might be inaugurated for the country children. The only questions to solve were how to get the money and how to make the libraries travel.

For several reasons I thought it desirable to get all the schools of a township together at some central point in June each year, and have appropriate closing exercises. At these exercises diplomas were awarded to all pupils entitled to promotion to the high school, to pupils having read six books during the school year, and to teachers who had completed the professional study for that year. An admission fee of ten cents was charged, and the net proceeds went to build up a traveling-library fund; the County Board of Supervisors also made appropriations for two years. My county board has always supported my efforts to build up the schools.

For the first year forty boxes of books were available. In 1902 eighteen more were added, and thirteen more during the summer of 1905, making a total of seventy-three libraries, representing 4248 volumes at a cost of $2195.39.

The programme and all committees for township exercises are arranged for the annual institute the last week of March each year. For the first four years the county superintendent attended every township exercise, being out sixteen evenings in June. During June, 1905, the teachers, with great credit to themselves, assumed full control, and the county superintendent attended only one township exercise.

The aim of the traveling libraries is twofold : first, to furnish aids for carrying out the regular work of the school ; hence the presence of supplementary readers, works on geography, history, etc.; second, to take to the country school much of the valuable literature that is not found in the ordinary school library. A better idea of the character of the books will be had if the contents of two boxes are given (see Fig. 64). The small boxes are for the one-room country schools and the large ones for the graded schools. There are sixty-four boxes for one hundred and six country schools and nine boxes for the nine graded schools, all outside the city of Rockford. The contents of box 50 are as follows :

6 Cyr's Second Reader.
5 Cyr's Fourth Reader.
1 White's Court of Boyville.
1 Wilson's Division and Reunion.
1 Montgomery's Leading Facts of American History.
1 Under Sunny Skies (Youth's Companion Series).
1 Scudder's George Washington.
1 Hart's Colonial Children.
1 Hawthorne's Tanglewood Tales.
1 Chase's Birdland.
1 Carroll's Around the World.
1 Kingsley's Four American Explorers.
1 Werner's Primer.
1 Pratt's America's Story for America's Children.
1 Bolton's Poor Boys Who Became Famous.

1 Beal's Seed Dispersal.
1 Eckstrom's The Bird Book.
1 Miller's Second Book of Birds.
1 Lights to Literature (Reader).
1 Guerber's Story of the English.
1 Barnes's For King or Country.
1 Long's Secrets of the Woods.
1 Arnold's Primer.
1 Brooks's True Story of George Washington.
1 Rorer's Good Cooking.
1 Clark's How to Teach Reading.
1 Wade's Our Little Indian Cousin.
1 McMurry's Robinson Crusoe.
1 Irish's American and British Authors.
1 Kupper's Stories of Long Ago.

The boxes for country schools are in groups of threes for circuits comprising six school districts. There are different books in each box of a circuit, though there are duplicates in the sixty-four boxes. For example, there are twenty copies of Thwaite's *The Colonies* and one hundred and sixty-four of Cyr's First Readers scattered among the boxes. But the plan of travel is such that it will be eighteen years before the same three boxes circulate among the same six

FIG. 64. Traveling Libraries for Country Schools: Plan of Disinfection

schools. If boxes 39, 40, and 58 are in Circuit B, comprising districts 24, 34, 22, 20, 21, and 23 for the school year 1904–1905, these three boxes are dropped to Circuit C for 1905–1906 and three boxes from Circuit S are advanced to Circuit B, and so on for eighteen years. Beginning with September, 1905, each box remains two months in each school. At the beginning of each school year the boxes are sent out by trolley lines, railway express, and in the county superintendent's buggy. In June they return to the county superintendent's office in the same way, where the boxes are checked up, books repaired and fumigated, and new books added. Every precaution is taken during the school year to guard against contagious diseases. If books are in a family where children are sick with scarlet fever, the teacher has instructions to require those books to be burned, and not to allow their return to the box in the schoolhouse. The children are urged to take books home with them while a box is in the district, so that the parents may become acquainted with good reading matter for children.

The large boxes for the graded schools each contain more books, of course. Box 5 contains the following :

12 Cyr's Fourth Reader.
1 Carroll's Around the World.
1 Parkman's Conspiracy of Pontiac (Vols. I and II).
1 Parkman's Count Frontenac, etc.
1 Blanchan's How to Attract Birds.
1 Coffin's Boys of '76.
1 Thompson's My Winter Garden.
1 Clark's How to Teach Reading.
1 Holder's Animal Life.
1 Greene's King Arthur and his Court.
1 Baldwin's Discovery of the Old Northwest.
1 Miller's First Book of Birds.
1 Plympton's Flower of the Wilderness.
1 Winship's Great American Educators.
1 Drake's Making of New England.

1 Tarr and McMurry's North America.
1 Drysdale's The Treasury Club.
1 Grinnell's Neighbors of the Field and Air.
1 Fiske's History of the United States.
1 Eggleston's The Graysons : a Story of Abraham Lincoln.
1 Fisher's The Colonial Era.
1 Seton's Krag and Johnny Bear.
1 Miller's The Second Book of Birds.
1 Barbour's For the Honor of the School.
1 Stevenson's Child's Garden of Verse.
1 Wilson's Division and Reunion.
1 Needham's Outdoor Studies.
1 Andrews's Seven Little Sisters, etc.
1 Baldwin's Old Stories of the East.
1 Menefee's Old Stories from the Masters.

1 Stoddard's Crowded Out o' Cro-
   field.
1 Blanchan's Nature's Garden.
1 The World's Work, November,
   1902, to April, 1903.
1 London's Call of the Wild.
1 Butler's Meaning of Education.
1 Riis's Making of an American.
1 Brooks's Century Book of
   American Colonies.
1 Deming's Indian Child Life.
1 Chenery's As the Twig is Bent.
1 Zollinger's Widow O'Galla-
   gher's Boys.
1 Arnold's Waymarks for Teachers.
1 Beard's American Girl's Handy
   Book.
1 Beard's King and his Wonderful Castle.
1 Allen's Navy Blue.
1 Robinson's Improvement of
   Towns and Cities.
1 True's The Iron Star.
1 Johnson's World's Discoverers.
1 Eastman's Indian Boyhood.
1 Henderson's Social Spirit in
   America.

1 Du Bois's Point of Contact in
   Teaching.
1 Burroughs's Pepacton.
1 Hancock's Life at West Point.
1 Stephens's Phelps and his
   Teachers.
1 Knapp's Story of the Philip-
   pines.
1 Barbour's Captain of the Crew.
1 Smith's Life in Asia.
1 Wade's Little Cuban Cousin.
1 Eckstrom's The Bird Book.
1 Smith's Under the Cactus Flag.
1 Brigham's Geographic Influences.
1 George's Little Journeys to
   Cuba.
1 Parkman's The Oregon Trail.
1 Chautauquan, January, February, March, 1904 (bound vol.).
1 The World's Work, January,
   February, March, 1904
   (bound vol.).
1 Country Life in America, January, February, March, 1904
   (bound vol.).
1 Holton and Rollins's Industrial
   Work in Public Schools.

Some of the above books are suitable for high-school pupils in villages, and some are for professional reading for teachers to enable them to do the work outlined by the county super- intendent for the current year. The township library lists of books issued annually by the state superintendent of Wis- consin for the past six years have been of invaluable assist- ance in the selection of books for the traveling libraries.

A school library, whether traveling or stationary, will be of little value unless teachers make right use of it. Indeed, it may do much harm. The average teacher in the country schools has much yet to learn about the use of the school library. They are not to be blamed, for they have never had books to work with or any opportunity to learn how to use them. The teachers need to be shown how to use books.

For six years we have had a library hour at the annual teachers' institute the last week of March. Several hundred volumes of books were generously loaned us by the Rockford Public Library, and an hour was set apart each day for reading. For the last two years the county superintendent conducted the daily exercise on library work. The following topics were discussed:

1. Value of different kinds of books.
2. The teacher and the care of books.
3. Are children interested in reading? If not, how to interest them.
4. How shall the teacher teach children to read?
5. Relation of library reading to school work.
6. How to become acquainted with books.
7. What does the teacher need to do to make better use of the library and to direct children?
8. Library reading in the district schools. When? Why? How?
9. Children's reports on books read.
10. Statements by teachers of work done the past year with library books in school.
11. Reports and discussions of work assigned various teachers by the county superintendent during institute week.

For the last topic the following outline was printed for each teacher as a guide when reading a book:

1. Kind of literature?
2. Suitable for what grade to read?
3. May be read to what grade?
4. General theme of the book?
5. Why is the book interesting to children?
6. What in the books is valuable for the child as literature?
7. Give a general report of the contents.

A recent library number of the *Outlook* says :

The teacher must be a constant and interested reader of the books he is demanding his pupils to read.   He must know and enjoy his *Robinson Crusoe* and *Alice in Wonderland*, his *Being a Boy* and *Little Women*.   His knowledge of juvenile literature should not be merely a shadowy reminiscence.   The teacher who has ceased to read the grade of books which make a normal appeal to the immature minds of his pupils is beginning to lose his usefulness ; for he owes it to his students not merely to tell them the titles of the books to read, but to stimulate them and sympathize with them from his own vital interest.   Many a teacher has been kept fresh for his professional work by his reading of children's books.

Libraries in country schools should aid in cultivating a taste for good reading and should supply material for supplementary study in regular school work.   But what is the use of all the energy and money expended in putting libraries into country schools if the right use is not made of the books ?   They should not be thrown about over the room or be tumbled promiscuously into the library case.   Every school should have a library case if possible.   I have seen books well taken care of in a common dry-goods box, with shelves and curtains arranged by the teacher.   Such an arrangement is infinitely better than nothing, and the cost is nominal.   The best library educational work that I ever saw was in a district school, where a good library case had been secured by the teacher and children as a premium for selling soap.   The books were nicely arranged on the shelves by grades, and a pupil was appointed librarian for two weeks.   It was that pupil's business for that period to see that the books were kept in good order and in their proper places.   At the end of two weeks some other pupil was appointed librarian.   Thus the children were made responsible, and they were receiving valuable training in the care of books. Here was positive direction for good results, instead of the negative "Don't misuse books," coming as a command from the teacher. And the principle is fundamental all through school work. Its successful application depends upon the tact and patience of the teacher.

In addition to instructing teachers how to make use of books and how to become acquainted with books suitable for children during the annual institute, another important phase of library work has been going on at the same time. Mention has been made of this feature in Chapter V, where a course in art reading was used in connection with picture study. For six years books from the Rockford Public Library have been used at the annual institute to carry out courses of instruction in other subjects, such as nature study, pedagogy, and United States history. The instructor in those subjects puts the references on the blackboard, and the student teachers have one hour each day to read them.

I shall not attempt to say what subject is most poorly taught in the country school. Enough to say that the teaching of United States history can be improved. This is doubtless true of other subjects. It is an easy and pleasant task to contemplate an ideal course in United States history, to be taught by a teacher who *knows* history, — a college graduate supplied with a number of library books and maps for class-room work. But to say the most helpful thing is not an easy task for a teacher who does not *know* history, who is not even a high-school graduate, whose school district has not a single library book or a wall map of the United States, and whose pupils are supplied with text-books a quarter of a century old. Every teacher should pursue a course of reading in United States history.

The following list, prepared by a noted author of school histories, is offered as containing a small number of what he regards as the most important and useful books for study and reference, most or all of which can be found in any good library:

A Short List of Books on American History

BIBLIOGRAPHY

Channing and Hart's Guide to the Study of American History (1492–1865).

HISTORICAL GEOGRAPHY AND MAPS

Hart's Epoch Maps of the United States (no text).
MacCoun's Historical Geography of the United States (revised edition).

GENERAL HISTORIES

Winsor's Narrative and Critical History, 8 vols. (to 1887, but not including the period of the Civil War).
Bancroft's United States, 6 vols. (revised edition) (to 1789).
Bryant and Gay's United States, 5 vols. (revised edition) (to 1896).
Higginson's Larger History of the United States (to 1903).
Hart's Epochs of American History, 3 vols. (1492–1889). The best single work there is.
McMaster's United States, 4 vols. (1784–1820).

Works of Reference

Harper's Book of Facts.
Larned's History for Ready Reference, 5 vols.
Hart's Source Book of American History.
Macdonald's Select Documents of United States History.
Hart's American History told by Contemporaries, 4 vols.
Wright's Industrial Evolution of the United States.
Johnston's American Politics.
Lossing's Cyclopædia of United States History (revised edition).
Bryce's American Commonwealth, 2 vols. (revised edition).

Boynton's School Civics.
Scudder's American Commonwealths (a series of volumes giving the histories of the states, by eminent writers).
Sparks's American Biography, 25 vols.
Morse's American Statesmen (a series of volumes by able writers).
Appleton's Cyclopædia of American Biography, 6 vols.

I. Period of Discovery (1492–1521)

Fiske's North America, 2 vols.

II. Period of Exploration and Spanish Colonization of America (1509–1587)

Parkman's Pioneers of France in the New World.
Cooke's Virginia.[1]

III. Period of Permanent English and French Settlements (1607–1763)

Fiske's The Beginnings of New England.
Parkman's The Discovery of the Great West.[2]
Drake's Making of the Great West.
Biography. See Sparks's American Biography for Lives of Nathaniel Bacon, Daniel Boone, Lord Baltimore (Calvert), Jonathan Edwards, John Eliot, Patrick Henry, Anne Hutchinson, John Ledyard, Cotton Mather, Governor Oglethorpe, James Otis, Sir W. Phips, William Penn, Count Rumford (Benjamin Thompson), Captain John Smith, Roger Williams, Governor Winthrop; Bigelow's Benjamin Franklin, 3 vols.; Montgomery and Trent's Franklin's Autobiography.

IV. The Revolution and the Constitution (1763–1789)

Lodge's American Revolution, 2 vols.
Lossing's Pictorial Field Book of the Revolution, 2 vols.
Fiske's American Revolution, 2 vols.
Scudder's America One Hundred Years Ago.

[1] In Scudder's American Commonwealth Series.
[2] This work deals, more or less directly, with our relations with the French and the Indians in the colonial period.

Fiske's Critical Period in American History.

Biography. Parker's Historic Americans, Bigelow's Franklin, 3 vols.,
Hosmer's Samuel Adams,[1] Morse's John Adams,[1] Greene's General
Greene, 2 vols., Lodge's Washington, 2 vols.,[1] Fiske's Irving's Wash-
ington and his Country, Sparks's American Biography, Lodge's
Hamilton,[1] Gay's Madison,[1] Roosevelt's Gouverneur Morris.[1]

V. THE UNION. NATIONAL DEVELOPMENT (1789–1861)

Rhodes's United States, 3 vols. (1850–1861).

Lossing's Field Book of the War of 1812.

Johnston's American Orations, 4 vols.

Webster's Great Speeches (Whipple's edition).

Quincy's Figures of the Past.

Biography. See in Morse's American Statesmen Series, the Lives of
John Adams, J. Q. Adams, Benton, Calhoun, Clay, Jackson, Jeffer-
son, Madison, Monroe, Randolph, Washington, and Webster ; in
Sparks's American Biography, the Lives of Fulton and Rumford ;
Redpath's John Brown, Johnson's Garrison, Prime's Morse, Rice's
Morton, Abbott's Kit Carson, Upham's Fremont, Parton's Famous
Americans, Mrs. Stowe's Men of our Times, Hunt's American
Merchants, Lodge and Roosevelt's Hero Tales from American
History.

VI. THE PERIOD OF THE CIVIL WAR (1861–1865)

Greeley's American Conflict, 2 vols.

Dodge's Bird's-Eye View of the Civil War.

McPherson's Political History of the Rebellion.

Biography. Nicolay and Hay's Abraham Lincoln, Holland's Lincoln,
Herndon's Lincoln, 3 vols., Thayer's Lincoln, Carpenter's Six
Months in the White House, McClellan's Own Story, Roman's
Beauregard, 2 vols., Badeau's U. S. Grant, 3 vols., Grant's Personal
Memoirs, 2 vols., Sherman's Memoirs, 2 vols., Sheridan's Memoirs,
2 vols., Farragut's Life of Farragut, Schuckers's Life of S. P. Chase,
Cooke's Robert E. Lee, Cooke's " Stonewall " Jackson, Johnston
and Browne's Life of Alexander H. Stephens, Alfriend's Life of
Jefferson Davis, Pollard's Life of Jefferson Davis.

[1] In Morse's American Statesmen Series.

VII. Reconstruction. The New Nation (1865 to the Present
Time)

Andrews's Last Quarter of a Century (1875–1895).
Andrews's United States at the Present Time (1904), 1 vol.
Wilson's Lives of the Presidents (1789–1893).
Johnston's American Politics.
Bryce's American Commonwealth, 2 vols.

The study of United States history received much attention at the last annual meeting of our county institute.
The Rockford Public Library loaned the institute a large
assortment of works on history, — more than a hundred
and twenty-five volumes, — suitable for a study of the
development of the spirit of nationality. Mace's *Method
in History* had been used in local institute work in various
centers in the county during the months previous to the
annual institute.

As to the objects and results of the use of books on United
States history in connection with instruction in that subject
at the annual teachers' institute, Principal B. D. Parker
of the Rockford High School, who was institute instructor,
says in an article in *School and Home Education*:

The main objects were (1) to endeavor to bring to the minds of
the teachers of the county a realization of the wealth of material
upon the history of our country, and, by leading them out of the
brief text-book to the broader fields, to inspire them with the desire
to know and to teach real history rather than outlines, dates, and
memory devices; (2) that the teachers might get a start in a small
way toward seeing our history as a history of the growth of ideas,
instead of groups of events bound together by nothing but similarity
in time; (3) to provide a scheme of instruction which should appeal
to the one who had had little opportunity for historical study, be
interesting to him who had begun to see the possibilities ahead, and
give opportunity to the more advanced student teacher to revel in
that which he loved. (4) These objects were to be gained not

through lengthy discourses by the instructor, but from contact with the great historical writers of the world. The duty of the instructor was simply to act as the introduction committee and then to keep out of the way and allow the newly formed friendships to grow.

Of the results Mr. Parker says :

The first result was the enthusiasm and earnestness with which the teachers took up the work. The spirit shown by them was an inspiration. Each day from the time they entered the library room till

FIG. 65. The Winnebago County Board of Supervisors

the close of that period their attitude was one of work. The " Let us have a good time" feeling which mars some institutes had no place. A good time was had, but it was because of good work being done. The college graduate and the teacher from the country school were there, and each found something to his liking.

Under the new unification system in New York State the state library and the library school have been placed in charge of the Department of Education. The first annual report under the new organization, issued by Commissioner Draper, states that "it is fundamental that there should be in every class room a library or collection of at least a few good books suited to the intelligence and intellectual development of the children in that room."

There are 1,227,317 volumes in the elementary school libraries, an increase of 246,063 volumes for the year 1904. The state appropriates $55,000 annually for libraries, distributed among districts in proportion to money raised by the districts and under regulations established by the Department of Education. The following table is of interest:

Number of common-school districts sharing in fund	1206
Number of union districts sharing in fund	189
Number of cities sharing in fund	39
Amount granted to common-school districts	$10,503.48
Amount granted to union districts	4,236.29
Amount granted to cities	30,649.13
Number of books bought by districts	97,668
Number of books bought by cities	225,288

The school-library section added to the unification law of 1904 is designed to increase the extent and effectiveness of libraries for schools. The school library is the only library for many communities, and is a means of creating sentiment for new public libraries. One instance of this is where the traveling school library in the Seward Consolidated School in Illinois has led to the organization of the Seward Public Library of several hundred volumes. This fund was raised by private subscription, and the books were placed in the library room of the school building.

In New York each of the eleven thousand school districts is urged to send its list of books to the Library Bureau of the Department of Education, and every encouragement is given by the bureau to help along the library sentiment all over the state. The teachers' library of six thousand volumes has been combined with the traveling libraries, and thus good pedagogical books go out to the teachers in the country schools as well as in other schools.

The traveling libraries of New York began in 1892 with a half-dozen libraries as an experiment. Now there are one thousand traveling libraries, with a total of 67,753 books, which are sent to all parts of the state. They have ceased to be an experiment, and the "plan has been copied by almost every state in the Union, and is accepted as a regular form of library work yielding the largest returns compared to its cost."

The Library Bureau is also assisting in art education in New York State. There are traveling art exhibits of 1586 large pictures of "the finest subjects and the best edition"; also 21,069 mounted photographs. All these are loaned to libraries, schools, etc., for six months at a time, to be hung on the walls "with proper labels and notes to increase their educational value." And not the least of the great work done by the Library Bureau is the loaning of 24,458 lantern slides, together with the lanterns, screens, and attachments for oil, oxyhydrogen, acetylene, or electric light. The report of the bureau says:

The growing demand is less significant than the general acceptance by schools, libraries, and clubs of pictures as having a proper place beside books as a great factor in educational work. The library has been a pioneer in broadening this field, and its experience and methods are widely utilized by others.

Besides all the above the bureau sends out "house libraries." These are libraries of ten volumes each, loaned to any home for three months for a fee of one dollar to cover transportation both ways. This is the "plan for extending through traveling libraries the privileges of the state library to the rural population living too far from the nearest public library to make its contents conveniently available." These libraries are suited to the needs of the country home, and as far as practicable are made up from lists submitted by the home wishing one of the house libraries.

The state of Massachusetts publishes no specific literature on the improvement of the country school as such. In that state the district or town system of expert supervision is relied upon to raise the standard of the country schools.

The report of the Free Public Library Commission of Massachusetts for 1905 is crowded with data showing how the public library is aiding the work of the public schools. Weymouth reports that twenty-five to thirty books each "are now sent every two months to seven distant schools, whose pupils otherwise would receive little help from the public library." It is fair to presume that these "distant schools" are one-room country schools. Many cities report assistance rendered schools, presumably city schools, in the way of traveling libraries, special lists for children, special teachers' cards, and the like. As was said above, since there is no special literature published by the state on the country school, it is hard for one not acquainted with the town system of Massachusetts to tell accurately from the report of the Free Public Library Commission what is done for the country school as distinguished from the village or city school. This book concerns itself principally with the country school, as its title, *Among Country Schools*, would indicate.

Mention must be made of the work of the Women's Education Association in the way of increasing the library interests of Massachusetts. It now has fifty traveling libraries containing 1417 volumes, with libraries on such special subjects as Venice, Florence, Shakespeare, English architecture, Rome, Italian art, Egypt, French art, Spanish art, and religion. The number of localities receiving benefit from these traveling libraries is forty-nine, probably almost all being country localities too far removed from some public library situated in a city. Besides these collections of books the association has twenty-four sets of pictures which have been loaned for one hundred and forty-nine exhibitions at one hundred and four different places.

State Superintendent Miller of West Virginia writes of the work in that state regarding the effort to supply the country school with libraries :

For some years school libraries in the towns and cities of West Virginia have been growing quite rapidly, but not until recently has much attention been given to the question of furnishing good litera-ture to the pupils in country schools. Interest in this work has increased, however, and on last Library Day, which, in 1905, was observed on the second Friday in December, instead of the first as heretofore, it is believed that about fifty thousand volumes were added to the school libraries of country districts alone. This brings the number of books within reach of the pupils in the district schools up to about one hundred and forty thousand. In this reckoning no account is taken of high-school, city, or public libraries.

Various methods were used by which to raise funds for the pur-chase of books. In many places an admittance fee was charged to a little entertainment proposed for the occasion ; in other communities contributions of money and books were received, while, still further, boards of education duplicated the amount that was raised by the school. One country school reports one hundred and one dollars as the result of its own effort for books, while another in a remote interior section of the state raised fifty-nine dollars. Of course, in some of the towns and thickly settled communities the receipts were much larger. A very encouraging feature of the work is the fact that not only are pupils interested in the library effort, but the citizens are contributing liberally to it and heartily aiding the movement that will give our youth a better class of literature.

In the selection of books the aim has been, even with a small collection, to choose books suited to the needs and comprehension of pupils in the different grades. Neither are the young men and women out of school nor the fathers and mothers at home forgotten. The vocations of the people are also considered. For instance, books on elementary agriculture, fruit growing, poultry raising, etc., have been chosen for different sections where the people were especially interested in these industries. Not only are books obtained for the libraries, but good periodicals as well, especial emphasis being placed upon good illustrated magazines. While in many districts at first the smaller and cheaper books must necessarily be purchased, we feel that this is a good beginning, if the books are carefully selected, and that when the reading habit is once formed in a community the interest will increase, and books of a more valuable make-up and possibly of a higher literary character will replace those first introduced.

Since June 30, 1902, two hundred and sixty-seven country-school libraries have been established in North Carolina. These libraries contain one hundred thousand volumes and are valued at $40,000. The Woman's Association for the Betterment of Public Schoolhouses in North Carolina has had a great part in this work. The story of the work of this association is told in another chapter.

The legislature of North Carolina has passed an act to aid the country-school libraries. It provides that where the patrons and friends of a country school raise ten dollars for a library the state will give a like amount. Provision for this is by appropriation of the County Board of Education, which also looks after the selection of the books and their care after purchase. In one year after the passage of the act three hundred and fifty-five libraries were established in seventy-eight of the ninety-six counties of the state, at an expenditure of $3550 by the state and $7100 by the counties and local communities, making a total expenditure of $10,650.

A recent bulletin issued by the Southern Education Board gives an account of the establishment of country-school libraries in one county in Tennessee. This but illustrates the new day coming for the country child all over the South land. The county referred to is Polk County, where in one year, as the result of aggressive work of the county superintendent, thirty-nine country-school libraries were established at a total cost of $1857.50, to be paid in three annual installments.

In 1903 there were sixty-nine traveling libraries in Tennessee under the control of the Women's Federation. The South Carolina Federation of Women's Clubs has sixty-four traveling libraries which circulate in nearly every county of the state, the railroads furnishing free transportation. The Texas Federation has fifty-seven traveling libraries which are sent to the country schools of that state.

CHAPTER VII

A FARMER BOYS' EXPERIMENT CLUB

" Country-school extension work " is perhaps a new term, but some way should be devised to reach the great number of country boys and girls who for various reasons quit the district school when they are fifteen or sixteen years old and do not go to a city or village high school. Here is one strong argument for the consolidated school with its high-school course of at least two years. It is quite difficult for many adults on the farm, and even for those living in cities, to realize the changes that have come into the country school with reference to attendance. Invariably they think of the old-fashioned country school, with an attendance of seventy or eighty pupils, many of them being boys and girls over eighteen years of age. Large classes were the rule, and the school was generally taught by a strong man, morally, intellectually, and perhaps physically.

In another chapter will be found data with reference to the small country school in various states. It is sufficient to state here that about one half of the one hundred and six one-room country schools of Winnebago County for the year ending June 30, 1905, had a total enrollment of fifteen pupils or less. I was interested to know how many boys and girls over fourteen years of age were enrolled in those one hundred and six one-room country schools. For the month of December, 1904, the teachers reported the exact number. This month was taken, for if the big boys and girls are in school at all during the year, it is in December after the corn husking is finished.

The number of boys over fourteen years old was reported to be one hundred and sixty-three, or an average of one and one half to each country school. The number of girls was one hundred and twenty-two in the same number of schools, or an average of one and one sixth. A considerable number of the schools have no large pupils, and so the teaching of agriculture in the small school will not reach the class of pupils it should reach. Where are the big boys and girls? State Superintendent Riggs of Iowa reports that there are ten thousand country children of that state paying tuition to attend city schools. Why is this?

One object, then, of the organization of the Winnebago County Farmer Boys' Experiment Club was to try to interest the big boys in the work of the Illinois College of Agriculture and the Experiment Station. The membership is not limited to boys who have quit the district school, but includes any boy who wishes to join, whether in school or out of school. It is quite likely that there are many counties in Illinois and other states where the old-time country school obtains, with twenty or thirty large pupils in attendance for at least five months of the year, and all taught by a well-trained normal graduate receiving from sixty-five to eighty-five dollars per month. Pupils in such schools do not need to go to city schools for an education; but such schools with such teachers are not found in the country districts of Winnebago County or in many other counties, if the statistics of various state superintendents report the actual condition of things. However that may be, I felt it my duty to know the exact situation in my own county and then try to better the educational opportunities for the country children under my charge.

Our Boys' Experiment Club was organized in the office of the County Superintendent of Schools at Rockford on February 22, 1902, the day following the close of the state farmers' institute, which was held at Rockford that year. The charter members of the club number thirty-seven boys, who met in my office that morning and listened to brief talks by Professor Shamel of the Illinois College of

FIG. 66. Some Prize Winners, Members of the Winnebago County Farmer Boys' Experiment Club

Agriculture and Superintendent Fred Rankin of the Agricultural College extension work. The club is growing and now numbers five hundred boys between nine and twenty-one years of age. The expectation is to have an increase in numbers and interest.

The machinery of this organization is very simple. So far there is no elaborate constitution and by-laws to tell the boys why they are boys and what boys are for. The county superintendent has a list of them, with the post-office address of each. Superintendent Fred Rankin of the

Agricultural College extension work has a duplicate list, and from each office go circulars, bulletins, and literature of various kinds, the main object being to keep in touch with the boys, and to interest them more deeply in the beauty of country life and the worth, dignity, and scientific advancement in agriculture. Last year about four hundred young men from the various counties of Illinois were enrolled in the College of Agriculture in connection with the University of Illinois at Urbana. This is something of which to be proud. But they were only four hundred out of the many thousands of bright boys who never will attend the College of Agriculture. A boys' club with the educational excursion is one way

Fig. 67. A Prize Winner, Eleven Years Old

of giving help and inspiration to the thousands of boys who cannot get an education at an agricultural college or anywhere else.

The teacher in the country school can be a very important factor in this country-school extension work. The bulletins of the College of Agriculture and of the Experiment Station should be on the reading table or in the library of every country school. There are many ways of interesting the older pupils of the district in them, if the teacher herself is interested. Suggestions as to how this may be done, and as to the value of experimental and observation work, will appear throughout the next few chapters.

The work of the boys since the organization of the club has been as follows: in 1902, testing vitality of various seeds, investigations with reference to smut in oats, experimenting with sugar beets, and growing corn from seed furnished by officers of the Winnebago County Institute; in 1903, growing high-bred corn from seed furnished by the directors of the Illinois State Farmers' Institute at Springfield; in 1904, the same work as in 1903; in 1905, growing high-bred corn

FIG. 68. A Prize Winner, Twelve Years Old

from seed furnished by officers of the Winnebago County Institute, and experiments with sugar beets from seed furnished by the Rock County Sugar Beet Company, Janesville, Wisconsin.

The first year, 1902, the enrollment was not large, the experimental work being carried on by only a few boys; but it was a beginning. The boys tested various kinds of seeds, planting corn and noting growth. Professor Shamel sent each charter member an ear of high-bred corn. In making investigations with reference to smut in oats, each boy was directed to go into four different fields and make three different counts in the same field by dropping a barrel hoop over as many stalks of grain as the hoop might inclose, and then counting the number of sound heads and also the heads showing smut. The percentage of smut was determined by the boys. This was practical arithmetic, just as valuable educational material as calculating the percentage of the number of inhabitants of a great city who live in tenement houses. Two boys reported as follows:

First Field

	Average Number Heads in Hoop	Average Number Heads of Smut	Average per cent Smut
First boy	106	4	3
Second boy	157	5	3

Second Field

	Average Number Heads in Hoop	Average Number Heads of Smut	Average per cent Smut
First boy	203	44	23
Second boy	206	46	21

Third Field

	Average Number Heads in Hoop	Average Number Heads of Smut	Average per cent Smut
First boy	213	27	13
Second boy	181	18	10

Fourth Field

	Average Number Heads in Hoop	Average Number Heads of Smut	Average per cent Smut
First boy	219	12	5
Second boy	240	13	5

The Experiment Station at Urbana estimates two dollars per acre as the loss from smut to the farmers of Illinois. Two of the fields shown above will go far beyond that. One owner had never heard of treatment of oat seed before sowing to destroy smut, although the subject was fully discussed at the local farmers' institute. Such work will cause more boys to attend the farmers' institute.

The sugar-beet experiment for 1902 was under the direction of the Experiment Station at Urbana, and was for the purpose of seeing whether sugar beets can be grown with

FIG. 69. With High-Bred Corn

profit in Illinois. Only a few boys planted seed that year. For the year 1905 seventy-one boys volunteered to grow sugar beets, representing thirty-three acres. The seed, five hundred and twenty-five pounds, was furnished free by the Rock County Sugar Beet Company of Janesville, Wisconsin. The complete returns of this experimental work showed that thirty-eight boys stayed in to the end, and the total shipment of the beets raised by these boys was one hundred and twenty-eight tons net factory weight. For these beets the boys received $590.77, about fifteen dollars per boy on an average. The experiment demonstrated that the soil of Winnebago County is suitable for raising sugar beets; it also showed the value of intensive methods of agriculture. The largest yield was obtained from one acre of ground; it amounted to nearly eighteen tons, and the two boys received $71.19 for their work. Two other boys had

two acres and received the same amount. This illustrates the value of good soil and cultivation. A boy and his sister got $14.58 for beets raised on a plot of ground 50 feet by 275 feet. This last furnishes material for practical arithmetic. At this rate how much could be raised on one acre, etc.?

FIG. 70. With High-Bred Corn

The Agricultural College Extension Department, under the direction of Superintendent Rankin, at my request, in March, 1905, issued a very complete bulletin on "Some Facts about Sugar Beets and how to Grow Them." This was mailed to every member of the club. Here is illustrated how the College of Agriculture and the country school can do valuable work.

The bulletin gives very clear, simple directions to the boys about the soil and its preparation for beets, seeding, cultivation, bunching and thinning, harvesting, etc. The following quotation from the bulletin shows its high educational character :

The Sugar Beet a Factor in American Agriculture

Sugar beets need care. Culture is everything; in fact, more attention is required than for most crops, but they pay double or treble in return. The haphazard methods so often practiced in corn culture would prove disastrous in the care of beets. Beet culture means a higher grade of farming, — a more intensive agriculture. Through

Fig. 71. A Sugar-Beet Grower [1]

the most scientific methods of plant breeding the sugar in the beet has been increased from six to eighteen and twenty per cent in less than one hundred years. The sugar beet is a " thoroughbred," and, like a highly bred animal, will degenerate under unfavorable conditions. Two thirds of the sugar we consume comes from the sugar beet. The consumption of sugar in America is on the increase; each man, woman, and child uses about eighty-five pounds of sugar a year. It requires over $50,000 daily to pay for the sugar consumed in Illinois, and it takes the value of the average oat crop of the United States to pay our annual sugar bill. An average acre of sugar beets produces from fifteen hundred to two thousand pounds of sugar.

[1] This member of the club with his brother has six acres of beets (1905), with which they hope to pay high-school and college expenses.

A Personal Talk on Sugar Beets

By Fred H. Rankin, Superintendent of the Agricultural College Extension Department, Urbana, Illinois

The writer was recently associated for two years in the care of over four hundred acres in sugar beets in central Illinois, and from this practical experience believes that the difference between thorough, intensive, and careful farming, from the beginning of the plowing to the end of the harvest, and slipshod, half-hearted work, is emphasized more in successful beet culture than in that of any other crop.

This circular was prepared especially for the Farmer Boys' Experiment Club of Winnebago County, Illinois, and others who live near

FIG. 72. Sugar-Beet Growers [1]

enough to find a market for their beets at the Wisconsin sugar-beet factories, but we urge other young people to grow some beets or other roots for their live stock; it will pay you well for your time. Your milch cows and hogs will enjoy this variety in their feed and be much better for it, just as you enjoy a variety of winter vegetables. The growing of beets will not only help the cow and the pig but will help the boy.

Beet seed plus rich soil, plus moisture, plus good culture, plus a thinking boy equals sugar beets. Try a few rods square or a quarter of an acre in beets, following carefully the directions in this circular, and, my word for it, you will find it pays. You will be awakened to a

[1] These two boys and two older brothers have one acre of sugar beets.

new appreciation of the value of fertility in the soil. You will find that it is something more than "just dirt." You will go to studying the soils on different parts of the farm. You will want to get better acquainted with the soil. You will discuss it with those who can tell you how the different soils were made. You will discuss it at your club meetings. You will want to read Experiment Station bulletins and to come here to the Agricultural College, where they teach much that is known about soils, crop rotation, growing of corn, clover, etc. Then you will want to know how to feed these crops to your live stock to the best advantage, and you will want to learn more about judging the market grades and classes of live stock. In short, you will be studying agriculture, and be recognized as a leader in better agricultural methods.

Perhaps all the boys who receive this circular may not feel like undertaking to raise beets. Very well; some other crop can be tried, — a patch of potatoes, a piece of corn, or some garden vegetables. But do not be satisfied with an average crop. Practice some of the careful intensive methods of farming that the successful sugar-beet growers follow. Do your level best, and, as David Harum puts it, "do it fust."

Nothing reveals character so much as the way you do your work. A botched job shows a poor workman, while a good piece of work shows the honesty of your purpose, adds to your manhood, and secures the confidence of all who have to do with you. In this way success is not only won but, what is more, royally deserved.

Ask your father to give you what you can make from this plat of ground, provided you do not allow any weeds to go to seed. I think he will do it, and then you surprise him; I know you can do it. Then save the money you get from the sale of this produce as a fund with which to buy books. We shall have some suggestions to make in a later circular regarding the selection of books and how to use them.

I have taken more space in this circular than was intended, but many of you have written letters which have an unusual inspiration, and you are urged to write to this department at any time. It is the aim of college extension work to be practically helpful to the young people of Illinois. You are cordially invited to make inquiries concerning the work of the Agricultural College, to the end that you may learn more as to what it is really doing for the young people of the state.

If you should not be interested, kindly pass this circular to some young person. At some future time he may thank you. I do so now.

For the sugar-beet experimental work in 1902 one boy made the following report, which illustrates the possibilities of work of this character:

My plat of ground for the beets was 38 feet wide and 20 rods long, making 45 square rods of land. There were 26 rows of beets planted 17½ inches apart. The total expense of raising them is as follows:

April 23, plowing	$ .40
" 24, twice harrowing	.25
May 10, cultivating with seeder	.25
" 10, harrowing	.15
" 27, disking	.25
" 27, twice planking; planker weighed 600 pounds	.25
" 27, planting, 3 hours' work at 15 cents	.45
June 4, hoeing and straightening plants, 4 hours at 15 cents	.60
" 10, raking, 3 hours at 15 cents	.45
" 21, " 3 " " 15 "	.45
" 28, hoeing with wheel hoe	.50
July 7, thinning out, 20 hours at 15 cents	3.00
" 9, hoeing by hand, 12 hours at 15 cents	1.80
" 19, hoeing with wheel hoe, 3 hours at 15 cents	.45
" 28, " " " " 3 " " 15 "	.45
Aug. 9, " " " " 3 " " 15 "	.45
Sept. 13, weeding, 3 hours at 15 cents	.45
Nov. 10, harvesting, 40 hours at 15 cents	6.00
" 10, team work	1.50
Rent of land at $5.00 per acre	1.50
Total cost of cultivating and harvesting	$19.60

The yield of the plat was 12,500 pounds. Deducting 1500 pounds for dirt leaves 11,000 pounds of beets. Number of tons, 5½; number of bushels (60 pounds to the bushel), 183. Actual cost of production per ton, $3.58; cost per bushel, 10 cents. Chemical analysis was sugar in beets, 18 per cent; purity coefficient was 86.7 per cent. Beets were fed to stock.

Why should not the teacher in the country school encourage practical arithmetic work like the above instead of devoting so much time to foreign exchange?

The growing of high-bred corn by the boys is a movement to get both them and their fathers interested in improved types of grain. It is estimated that if every farmer
in the United States who is raising corn would raise one
bushel more to the acre, it would mean for every acre
planted an annual increase of $25,000,000 to the wealth
of the nation. This can be done by planting the improved
varieties of corn and by better methods of cultivation. For

FIG. 73. Brother and Sister among their Beets

three years various members of our Boys' Experiment Club
have been doing this and selecting ten of the best ears raised
from their experimental plats for exhibition at the annual
county farmers' institute, where prizes are given boys in
order of the excellence of their exhibits. For 1902 one
hundred boys experimented by growing corn, for 1903 one
hundred and twenty-seven boys grew high-bred corn, for
1904 the number was one hundred and forty-three, and
for 1905 there were one hundred and twelve boys.

The boys also make observations as to barren stalks of corn in plats one hundred hills square and compute the percentage. The time the tassel and silk appear on a stalk is noted. It is not expected that a ten-year-old boy will be equipped with a compound microscope of ten thousand diameters and will know the whole mystery of life from the study of a cross section of a grain of pollen, and that at a single sitting. Rather have him use his eyes, — a little observation this week, more next week, more

FIG. 74. This Boy Hopes Soon to Take a Course at an Agricultural College

next year, until the habit of observing is fixed and there grows silently within him the power to judge, and he becomes educated because he sees things with his eyes.

As with the sugar beets, so in the experimental work with the high-bred corn: the Agricultural College Extension Department lends great assistance to the boys. Superintendent Fred Rankin, in May, 1905, issued a forty-page illustrated bulletin on "Studies of Corn and its Uses." This most valuable circular is full of suggestions for young people's clubs and for instruction in agriculture in the

country schools. Copies were mailed to five hundred boys of
my club, and to two hundred country school-teachers, while
several hundred copies are in my office for distribution to
school officers and prominent farmers. The bulletin is
divided as follows:

Part I. Study of the Corn Plant.
Part II. Studies of an Ear of Corn.
Part III. The Corn Score Card.
Part IV. Studies of the Parts of a Kernel of Corn.
Part V. The Commercial Products of Corn.
Part VI. Suggestions for Corn Experiments.

Part I is here given entire to illustrate the value and
importance of this extension work. Note the practical
arithmetic in 17, 18, 19, and 20.

PART I. STUDY OF THE CORN PLANT

The development of the present breeds of cattle and other live
stock plainly shows how careful, systematic, and intelligent selection
has improved these animals. Plants respond to breeding and selection as readily as do animals, and there is no longer any doubt that
varieties of corn may be further improved by similar methods.
Experiments conducted by the Illinois Agriculture Experiment
Station and other similar institutions have conclusively shown that
the composition of the corn kernel may be varied at the will of the
careful breeder, — that it is possible to increase or decrease the amount
of oil or of starch or of protein by selection of seed. An explanation of the different parts of the kernel of corn is given later.

It is equally true that great variations may be made in the ears or
the stalks by selection. The amount of husks, length of shank, size
and height of stalk, position of ear on the stalk, the number of leaves,
and in fact every physical characteristic, can be varied in a short
time by simple selection. It is just as important to know the character of every part of the corn plant as to know every characteristic of
the animal. The size, shape, and characteristic of the stalk strongly
influence the development of the ear and kernel of corn.

STUDY OF THE CORN PLANT

Name of variety............................ Size of field............................

1. Date the corn matures : (*a*) roasting ear............................
(*b*) dented or glazed............................ (*c*) ripe............................

2. Height of corn: average of ten plants........feet........inches.

3. Total number of leaves on ten plants taken from different hills............................ Average number of leaves per plant............................

4. Total number of leaves below the ear on ten plants taken from different hills............................ Average............................

5. Figure the total leaf surface on five average corn plants (for each leaf blade take twice the product of the length and average width)............................

6. Length of ear stem, or shank (distance from joint, or node, to base of ear)............................ Average of ten plants............................

7. The ear stem, or shank, may be (*a*) large, or nearly or quite the diameter of the cob; (*b*) medium, or about half the diameter of the cob; (*c*) small, or one third or less the diameter of the cob.

8. Husks (abundant, medium, scarce)............................

9. Husks (close, medium, loose)............................

10. Measure ten hills square; give number of ears on these one hundred hills............................ Average per hill............................

11. Give number of stalks in the above area having two or more ears............................

12. Give number of stalks in above area without ears (barren stalks)............................

13. Give average height of ears in above area............................

14. Position of the ears on stalks (pointing upward, horizontal, pointing downward)............................

15. Distance apart of hills each way............................

16. Give number of hills per acre............................

17. Measure off one acre which represents a good average of the field ; husk one twentieth of this and after weighing same carefully estimate the average yield of field............................

18. If hills of corn are 3 feet 6 inches each way, how many hills to the acre?............................

19. If in a field of corn planted 3 feet 6 inches each way there is on the average 1½ pounds of corn to each hill, counting 80 pounds to the bushel to allow for shrinkage, what is the yield per acre?......................

20. If corn is planted 3 feet 6 inches each way, and when mature is cut and put into shocks, each shock containing the corn from an area fourteen hills square, how many shocks to the acre?....................... How many shocks are sixteen hills square?.......................

The following table will assist in making an accurate estimate of the amount of land in different fields or plots:

10 rods × 16 rods = 1 acre	220 feet × 198 feet = 1 acre
8 rods × 20 rods = 1 acre	440 feet × 99 feet = 1 acre
5 rods × 32 rods = 1 acre	110 feet × 396 feet = 1 acre
4 rods × 40 rods = 1 acre	60 feet × 726 feet = 1 acre
5 yards × 968 yards = 1 acre	120 feet × 363 feet = 1 acre
10 yards × 484 yards = 1 acre	240 feet × 181.5 feet = 1 acre
20 yards × 242 yards = 1 acre	200 feet × 180.9 feet = ½ acre
40 yards × 121 yards = 1 acre	100 feet × 145.2 feet = ⅓ acre
80 yards × 60.5 yards = 1 acre	100 feet × 108.9 feet = ¼ acre

Some teachers allow or require their pupils to commit passages about tropical fruits, and perhaps make a perfect (so-called) recitation about the banana or the cocoanut. But to investigate and study a plant growing just outside the school yard, — "why, that is not education." Yet there are more country children who will make their living by growing corn than by growing tropical fruits. Not less knowledge, perhaps, of things far away, but more study of things in the environment of the country child is necessary. Corn is almost a common cereal for the United States. Last week I received a letter from a gentleman in North Carolina who wished me to send him all the literature I could about corn, as the people of his county wished to begin corn growing and the farmers' institute movement. The same variety of corn will not do equally well in every part of the United States. Find out from your own Experiment Station what variety is suitable; get an ear or two, and begin some experimental work with your pupils. It will vitalize your language and composition work, your arithmetic, your drawing, your nature study, and will surely quicken the educational interest of the patrons of your district. It will require courage and some study on the part of the teacher to do this, for it is so much easier to go on asking questions from a book.

When the boys of our club receive their corn to plant, the Illinois score card (see p. 190) is sent along, so that the boys may know how best to select ten ears for the exhibit.

MEASUREMENTS FOR STANDARD VARIETIES

There are many standard varieties, or breeds, of corn in which we recognize distinct variety characteristics, just as we do in the case of the Shorthorn, Hereford, or Angus breeds of cattle.

When as a boy I plowed corn in central Illinois I thought of corn as something to be fed to hogs, and I also knew that whisky was made from it. The boys of the Winnebago County Experiment Club are learning what can be made from corn besides pork and whisky. Speaking of the commercial products of corn, in Superintendent Rankin's interesting bulletin, Mr. Roy B. Simpson of the Glucose Sugar Refining Company, Chicago, says:

Until recently corn has been considered only as of value for the making of corn bread and cakes, beef, pork, and whisky. However, when man comes to study this marvelous plant in a scientific way, science evolves other products in rapid succession. From it now come the finest qualities of oils for table purposes, for the mixing of paints, for lubricating purposes, for manufacturing soaps, and the

FIG. 75. Some High-Bred Corn [1]

FIG. 76. Bottles showing Chemical Analysis of Corn [1]

The first bottle at the left represents 100 ounces of shelled corn. The five bottles at the right represent the chemical composition of this corn as determined by analyses. The elements are as follows: carbohydrates, 80.35 ounces; protein, 10.92 ounces; oil, 4.70 ounces; crude fiber, 2.60 ounces; ash, 1.43 ounces

[1] By courtesy of the Illinois Experiment Station, Urbana.

like. It yields gum, sugar, and sirup which cannot be surpassed. From it is obtained vulcanized corn oil, or corn rubber, which is used in the manufacture of rubber goods and linoleums ; and from the stalk are made the finest grades of paper. The pith of the stalk is converted into cellulose, which is used to protect war ships from shot and shell.

For the last three years the boys of the Experiment Club have had a half-day session at the Winnebago County Annual Farmers' Institute.

The boys are encouraged to keep memoranda of their corn growing and to write letters about their experimental work. These letters are sent to the County Superintendent of Schools and are published in his annual report and sent into every country home. The teacher in the regular work of the school can make the experimental work a basis for letter writing and thus be of great assistance to the boys in improving their power of expression. There is abundant room for improvement in the mechanics of letter writing, such as the use of capitals, punctuation, and paragraphing ; but if the boy has something to write and is not merely required to write something, there is more likelihood of his taking greater interest in what he generally considers a nuisance. The trouble with so much of our school work is that the teacher is content with the pupil's recitation of rules from memory, without his *actually doing* the thing talked about. If the pupil does give to the teacher some written work, too often he is not shown his mistakes and required to correct them by rewriting the exercise. The complaint is made that our pupils do too much written work. There is truth in this. We need to do less and do it better.

Following are three letters from boys about their prize high-bred corn (1904). These are fair specimens of many that were received.

I

I am sending you a record of the corn I raised for the institute.

Plowed the ground seven inches deep one week before planting. Dragged twice the same day the corn was planted. The ground had had no fertilizer for two years. The previous crop was sweet corn.

Planted the corn two inches and a half deep, in rows three feet and eight inches apart, the hills the same distance apart in the row. It was planted on May 17 and came up on the 21st, with no cultivation before it came up. Cultivated three times and hoed twice, the last time on the 2d of July. The corn tasseled out on the 6th of July and silked on the 20th. On the 13th of September I gathered it and hung it in the corn crib to cure for about a month. I then took it down and put it up by the stovepipe to dry for a while, then picked out the best ears and rolled them in paper, packed them in a box so that they would not get shelled or damaged, and then picked out ten ears for the institute.

II

My experimental crop consisted of Leaming corn. First I plowed the ground and then I rolled all the lumps off, so it left it in good condition for planting. I took a hoe and dug the holes, so that I could put the corn in moist dirt. I put three grains in a hill and made the hills three feet eight inches apart. I planted five hundred grains. Twenty failed to grow. There was a good deal of smut and suckers on my corn. I cut the smut and suckers off.

This is the work I did on my corn :

Hauling one load of manure	. . . .	½ hour	$	.15
May 10, 1904, plowing, 6 inches deep	. . . .	½ hour		.15
" 10,	dragging	½ hour		.15
" 16,	planting corn	½ hour		.15
" 29,	cultivation	40 minutes		.20
" 31,	hoeing	40 minutes		.20
June 16,	plowing	40 minutes		.25
July 20,	hoeing	25 minutes		.10
Total .	. . . .			$1.35

My corn is worth $3.75, and the profit is $2.40.

III

. . . In conclusion I have added the most important things I learned, experimental and otherwise.

The first thing that took my notice was that there were no losses from insects or cutworms. Having heard that smut germs floated in the air and grew whenever they struck a bruise on a stalk, I determined to find out for myself. So I punctured three stalks, and in less than three days I was surprised to find smut growing there. I cut it off and it ceased to grow. Then when the corn began to silk I wondered how to prevent so many poor ears of corn from growing. At last the thought came to me that I would cut off the silks, which I did, and found a week later that the ears were all shriveled up, and still later were dead. Thus I found another way to prevent ears from fertilizing. In doing so I prevented the growth of many poor ears and helped the stronger ones.

Therefore, by raising corn on the scale given by Mr. Hostetter, I have learned enough extra to more than pay for all the trouble it gave me.

The organization of boys' clubs has spread to many localities in Iowa, Indiana, Illinois, Wisconsin, Ohio, and Texas. Doubtless other states have inaugurated this movement, but the data are not at hand to specify by name. In Ohio the boys' agricultural club movement started with Superintendent A. B. Graham of Springfield township, Clarke County. So successful was Superintendent Graham in this work that he has been elected to take charge of the extension work of the College of Agriculture of the state university at Columbus. In collaboration with members of the faculty he is issuing some excellent bulletins that are calculated to exert a great influence. The latest of these, issued March, 1906, on " The Centralized Schools of Ohio," ought to be put into the hands of every patron of country schools. Some of the photographs used in that bulletin are used in Chapter XII.

Superintendent Cap E. Miller of Sigourney, Iowa, has attracted national attention by his work for the country schools. His annual report for 1903–1904 shows that he is a man who brings things to pass. There is an account of a county spelling contest, a county educational rally, township historical contests, agricultural conventions for boys and girls, and an educational excursion to the Iowa State College of Agriculture, June 3, 1904, which was attended by nearly fifteen hundred persons. A school fair and a farmers' insti-

tute were organized. By combining his annual teachers' institute with the local Chautauqua Assembly his teachers were enabled to hear some of the best speakers on the lecture platform.

Miss Anna Lois Barbre, County Superintendent of Chris-

FIG. 77. Testing the Germination of Corn with Plates of Sand.[1] (For cross section of a kernel, see Fig. 98)

tian County, Illinois, has a large and enthusiastic boys' club. Two excursions have been made to the College of Agriculture at the University of Illinois. She is planning for five hundred boys to take part in the corn-growing contest of 1906.

Other counties in Illinois having boys' clubs, so far as I have been able to get information, are Johnson, La Salle, Marion, McHenry, Piatt, and Mason.

[1] By courtesy of the Illinois Experiment Station, Urbana.

In Illinois the latest development of the boys' work is the offering of free scholarships for the two weeks' short course at the College of Agriculture to the boys making the highest scores in judging corn at the local farmers' institutes in the various counties. This movement was started by Director A. P. Grout of Scott County. Last February

FIG. 78. Some Prize Winners of the Winnebago County Girls' Home Culture Club

his congressional district sent twenty-six boys to the corn school at the College of Agriculture at Urbana. In all, seventy-five boys were sent from twenty-nine counties, with all expenses paid for the two weeks. The attendance at the corn school of 1907 bids fair to show a great increase in attendance on the part of boys. Winnebago County is planning to send a dozen or more.

To Nebraska belongs the honor of doing a big thing and doing it in a most successful way. J. L. McBrien, State Superintendent of Public Instruction, gave to his deputy, Mr. Bishop, permission to inaugurate a boys' corn-growing and a girls' cooking contest that would take in the entire state, the sum of one thousand dollars to be given in prizes to the successful boys and girls. The work was systematically planned, and literature on the subject was scattered broadcast over the state. The contest closed at the state capital, Lincoln, in December, 1905, with a great meeting and a banquet. There were six hundred and twenty-nine boys and girls present from all over the state. The banquet was under the direction of a French chef and consisted of seven courses that exemplified the wonderful food qualities of Nebraska corn.

MENU

Corn Soup   Pop-Corn Float

Corn Relish

Hot Corn Tamales

Hulled Corn with State-Farm Cream

State-Farm Corn-Fed Beef à la Challenger

Nebraska White Prize Hot Corn Bread with State-Farm
Student Butter

Aunt Chloe's Corn Pone

Granulated Hominy Grits   Croquettes en Surprise

Reid's Yellow Dent Johnny Cake with Milk

Baked Indian Corn Pudding

Cream of Corn Sauce   Molded Corn Ice Cream

Corn Meal Wafers   Golden Corn Cake

Corn Coffee

" Corn toasts " were responded to by prominent men of the state and nation.

A good beginning has thus been made, and the purpose is to continue along more comprehensive lines. Local clubs will be organized with a constitution, and county organizations will be encouraged. Plans for 1906 are well under way and include the following departments:

For Boys

1. Corn growing.
2. Wheat growing.
3. Sugar-beet growing.
4. Potato growing.
5. Manual training, — making of articles, useful or ornamental, for the home.

For Girls

1. Cooking of corn products.
2. Cooking of white and brown bread.
3. Preserving of fruits and vegetables.
4. Needlework, including plain sewing, embroidery, crocheting, and fancy work.
5. House ornaments.
6. Sugar-beet growing.
7. Potato growing.

Mr. Dick Crosby of the Experiment Station, Department of Agriculture, Washington, D.C., has made a careful study of the boys' agricultural club movements. The results of his studies and investigations have been issued in bulletin form. The bulletin closes with the following summary:

Collectively the boys have learned the value of organized effort, of coöperation, and of compromise, and the social instinct has been developed in them, — a matter of great importance in rural districts, where the isolated condition of the people has always been a great drawback to progress.

The influence upon the communities at large, the parents as well as the children, has been wholesome. Beginning with an awakening of interest in one thing, better seed corn, the communities have rapidly extended their interest to other features of rural improvement, with the result that in the regions affected by the boys' agricultural club movement there has come about a general upward trend to the thoughts and activities of the people.

Superintendent G. F. Snyder of Baraboo, Wisconsin, has recently issued his yearbook for 1905 on the Sauk County schools, which gives interesting details of his work. It contains also many excellent illustrations of the most beautiful scenes in the Wisconsin lake region. Superintendent Snyder has been active in organizing boys' and girls' clubs and in awakening a general interest in agriculture. He conducted an educational excursion of fifteen hundred persons from his county to the Wisconsin College of Agriculture, June 10, 1905.

Many schools in his county have had school gardens with good results, and farmers' meetings have been held, at which school men and instructors from the College of Agriculture have talked on questions of vital interest to the country school and farm. Superintendent Snyder was instrumental in securing a county training school for his county, and will soon give up the duties of his office to enter upon the management of this training school for country teachers.

The following is an account of the work of County Superintendent H. T. Ports of Marengo, Iowa, as given by a Des Moines paper :

On April 8, 1904, at a county historical essay contest of the school children, the boys and girls were called together for the purpose of organizing two clubs, with the result that there were twenty-two charter members to the boys' club and twenty-four charter members to the girls' club. From this small beginning they have increased in numbers, until now they each have a membership of about three hundred.

The boys have been experimenting largely with farm industries, and the girls have been centering their efforts in the art of making the home beautiful and comfortable. Outlines for observation, study, and work have been furnished the club members from time to time by their superintendent, which have been the basis of all their operations. Plant life and animal life in all their phases have been the principal sources of study and observation. The girls have experimented in the growing of flowers and all kinds of garden products, while the boys have experimented in all kinds of field crops, as well as garden products, and have carefully studied all the domestic animals, and a great many things equally interesting and important to boys and girls alike have been studied in common. The girls have also followed a course of outlines on hygiene and health of the home, and have done much in the domestic-science department. They are taught to cook, sew, and care for the various departments of the home, from the most trivial to the most important. Boys have been encouraged in the use of all kinds of tools in the manufacture of articles and implements useful to the home and farm. Combined with the industrial work is the literary work. Language and mathematics are emphasized, and essay, declamatory, spelling, and other literary contests are always held in connection with the industrial contests. Excursions and picnics are frequently had for the purpose of encouraging the boys and girls, and to emphasize the different parts of the work. Two excursions have been made to the State Agricultural College at Ames. On the first about seven hundred went and on the second about twelve hundred. Township and county meetings have been held frequently, where boys and girls are allowed to take part, and where special instructions are given by men and women of superior qualifications.

County Superintendent John F. Haines of Hamilton County, Indiana, has organized a Boys' Corn Club of nearly three hundred members, and for two years the boys have been growing corn for the annual corn contest. Each boy was given twelve hundred grains of a good variety to plant in experimental plots of ground. Specific instructions were given with reference to cultivation, observation, etc.

In August, 1905, Superintendent Haines conducted an educational excursion from his county to the Indiana State

Agricultural College at Lafayette. More than three hundred boys and their parents went on this excursion, and all expressed themselves delighted with the trip. Mr. Haines conducted a scoring contest at the last annual meeting of the boys. He says:

It is safe to say that one hundred boys could be selected in Hamilton County whose knowledge of corn is superior to that of any one hundred men that could be selected in the county.

County Superintendent Bunnell of Laporte County, Indiana, has issued rules and regulations for a mammoth corn contest in his county for the year 1906. The first prize is one hundred dollars, the second seventy-five dollars, the third fifty dollars, etc. The boys must make a special study of the corn plant, must plant one acre, — no more and no less, — and each boy must attend the local farmers' institutes for two years unless prevented by sickness. Each contestant must take a bushel of his best corn to the institute for 1906, and from this bushel select the ears for the final contest. The boy making the highest number of points, not counting cash premiums, in each township will have all his expenses paid for a week to attend the corn and stock judging school at the State College of Agriculture.

As has been said before in this chapter, the work with boys needs to be followed up for several years. It takes about a generation to effect real permanent results in this line. The past has too often witnessed a movement of this kind flourish vigorously for two or three years and then die because the promoters were so busy keeping their halos in proper condition for public inspection that there was not time for the next forward step that must always be taken.

CHAPTER VIII

EDUCATIONAL EXCURSIONS TO THE COLLEGE OF AGRICULTURE

In my work as County Superintendent of Schools, in attempting a solution of the country-school problem it has seemed that the educational excursion to the State College of Agriculture and Experiment Station is a very important

FIG. 79. The Excursion of Winnebagoes (1903) in Front of the College of Agriculture, University of Illinois

factor in creating a new educational ideal among the farmers with reference to the training of their children. The excursion is supplementary to the printing press and the farmers' institute movement in putting the people, especially the boys and girls, of the country districts in touch with higher institutions of learning, and at the same time enlarging their views of life by a railroad trip. One of the hardest of tasks is to create a sentiment for better things in the average district school. The average farmer is quick to recognize the value of improved farm machinery, electric roads, and telephones; but when one begins to talk to him about corresponding improvement in the country school, its material equipment, surroundings, improved course of study, and better teachers with better salaries, at once he stops you with: "Why, when I was a boy I went to an old log house, sat on a long bench, and studied a spelling book. Now look at me and my farm. I have made a success of life." I don't pretend to say that we have found in Winnebago County the only way to create this new ideal. Hard work, infinite patience, steadfast persistency, and tact are some of the elements that must obtain

FIG. 80. The Illinois College of Agriculture

if efforts to create a spirit for better things in the country school, or any movement looking towards the spiritualization of country life and thought, shall be crowned with success.

Not all the education of the country child is acquired in the country school. It has been said that the farm educates the child as much as the district school. The time is at hand when we must teach more practical things in the district schools. The child should visit places and see things for himself. Children *see* things along the country road to school, but they are not taught to *think* about these things; we allow them to spend too much time in reading *about* things. The polar bear gets more of the child's attention in books than does the study of a noxious weed on the farm, and it cannot be doubted that he is more interested in the one than in the other. The reason for this preference is not far to seek. The weed is a thoroughly familiar object, and it is an unalterable law of psychology that we do not attend to that which is wholly familiar. What is needed is that the significance of that noxious weed should be pointed out, and its relation to the life of the boy and to his prosperity as a farmer indicated. Then he will attend because there is something *attractive* about the object. The average country child will hardly be called upon to study arctic animals in their native environment, but there are many things worth knowing in an excursion of an hour or so in the neighborhood of the district schoolhouse.

The educational excursion was planned by me shortly after my organization of the Winnebago County Farmer Boys' Experiment Club (see preceding chapter) in 1902. The following has been the result:

First Excursion : June, 1902 ; to Illinois College of Agriculture and Experiment Station at Urbana; persons going, 130 boys and girls and 150 adults (total, 280) ; fare, $2.50 round trip; time, two days ; distance, 214 miles.

Second Excursion : June, 1903 ; to Illinois College of Agriculture and Experiment Station at Urbana; persons going, 112 boys and girls and 93 adults (total, 205) ; fare, time, and distance the same as on first excursion.

Third Excursion : June, 1904 ; to Iowa State College of Agriculture and Experiment Station at Ames; persons going, 90 boys and girls and 111 adults (total, 201) ; fare, $4.00 round trip ; time, two days; distance, 318 miles.

Fourth Excursion : June, 1905; to Wisconsin State College of Agriculture and Experiment Station at Madison ; persons going, 156 boys and girls and 170 adults (total, 326) ; fare, $1.25 round trip ; time, two days; distance, 65 miles.

The grand total for four years was 488 boys and girls and 524 adults, or a complete total of 1012 persons; and each excursion was practically a new party. In the second excursion there were only thirteen persons who went on the first. Twenty-two school-teachers were among the number who went on the last excursion.

It has not been my effort to secure large crowds. The brass band and hurrah features have been entirely eliminated. The excursions have been strictly educational, and persons going were those most interested, — those who had eyes to see and brains to think, and used both. It is safe to say that each returning party has been an educational missionary force in behalf of better education for the

FIG. 81. The Cattle Barn, Illinois College of Agriculture

farmer. Estimating that each of the one thousand and twelve persons interested at least two friends on his return with an account of what *he saw*, then a total of three thousand persons were reached in a most effective manner. As the four annual excursions were ably and fully treated by the local press, as well as by illustrated printed matter sent by the county superintendent into every school in the county, it is a conservative estimate to claim that ten thousand other persons had their attention called in a very practical way to the work of one of the most important of our state institutions, namely, the work of the College of Agriculture and Experiment Station. Good results will come in time in a general educational uplift in the interests of the country schools of our county. If I hear of no other return, the following extract from a letter has amply repaid all my efforts to inspire the boys and girls with higher ideals:

. . . It is through the excursion to the University of Illinois that I am most indebted to you, as that kindled my desire for an agricultural education. As I could not afford a four years' course, I went to Madison the following fall (1902) and commenced the short course at the University of Wisconsin, and secured a position at the Experiment Station of that place during the summer of 1903, and last winter completed the course.

The writer of this letter, by working with his hands, obtained an education and secured an honorable position.

With these educational excursions the cost of success is plenty of hard work and earnest thought. An illustrated chapter about the excursion is printed in my annual report and sent into every country home in the county. The *Pantagraph*, Bloomington, Illinois, — a newspaper earnestly advocating improvement on the farm and in the country school, — very kindly spoke as follows of the McHenry and Winnebago County educational excursions :

They make careful plans and good ones and start them in operation, but do not stop with any mere theory or formal procedure, however perfect or unique, but get out in the field, see how their plans are working, and work them, revising where necessary, meeting any deficiency, putting the whole weight of their personality and influence into the project, meeting doubts, overcoming objections, securing personal pledges, absolutely doing things, — and then people wonder why they succeed.

Their spirit and methods should be studied, emulated, and adapted to local conditions by other would-be-successful workers in similar fields. The price of success seems to be devotion, work (plenty of it), and the ingenuity of plan that comes from great earnestness and continued brooding over things desired to be accomplished.

A detailed account of each of our four annual excursions cannot here be given. To Professor R. A. Moore and his associates of the Wisconsin College of Agriculture great credit must be given for a most perfect programme of visitation, which was carried out to the letter. A type-written copy of the programme for the two days' visit was given each member of our party of three hundred and twenty-six. This is reproduced here, so that the reader may know what the Winnebagoes are doing and seeing on these educational excursions.

ANNUAL EXCURSION OF BOYS' EXPERIMENT CLUB AND GIRLS' HOME CULTURE CLUB OF WINNEBAGO COUNTY, ILLINOIS, TO MADISON, WISCONSIN, FRIDAY AND SATURDAY, JUNE 2–3, 1905   A VISIT TO THE UNIVERSITY OF WISCONSIN

Friday, June 2

12.30 P.M.: Arrive at Madison *via* C. & N. W. Ry. Take street cars in waiting at the depot and go direct to Agricultural Hall and have photo taken in group.

1–1.20 P.M.: Address in auditorium, Agricultural Hall, by Dean W. A. Henry.

1.20–2 P.M.: Tour of inspection through Agricultural Hall. The various laboratories, lecture rooms, and library will be visited.

2–2.45 P.M.: Dairy building, — creamery, cheese room, Pasteurizing laboratory, separating rooms, dairy machinery, etc.

2.45–3.30: Horticulture, — physics building, greenhouses, laboratories, apparatus, etc. A visit to the orchard and nursery.

3.30–4 P.M.: Experimental plots, — one hundred varieties of grain and forage plants on experiment.

4–5.30 P.M.: Live-stock buildings, — horses, cattle, sheep, and swine on exhibition. An exhibit of farm machinery in sheep-judging building. Instructors will be in their respective departments to answer questions and give all the useful information possible.

5.30 P.M.: Take a street car for down town from University Farm. Meals at Central Hotel and Fess House. Rooms in the vicinity of the university, with private families to accommodate two hundred. Those desiring to get rooms near the university will take meals at 425 and 426 State Street. Cars will stop at these places. Guides will be on hand to assist visitors in securing rooms.

6–7 P.M.: Supper.

8–9 P.M.: Visit to the state capitol, senate and assembly chambers, offices, executive rooms, etc. Informal reception by Governor La Follette. Enter capitol at north door, where guides will be in waiting.

Saturday, June 3

6–7.30 A.M.: Breakfast, visit to university.

8–9 A.M.: Women visit domestic-science department, South Hall.

8–9 A.M.: Men at engineering building and machine shops.

9–9.30 A.M.: Men and women, — Science Hall, geological and biological museums.

9.30–10 A.M.: Gymnasium, — running track, drill room, ball cage, and natatorium.

10–10.45 A.M.: Joint Historical Library, — museums, reading rooms, book stacks, etc.

10.45–11 A.M.: Take cars for boat landing, foot of Carroll Street.

11–12.30: Boat ride on Lake Monona.

12.30–2 P.M.: Dinner at Central Hotel, Fess House, and One Minute Rest.

2.10 P.M.: Leave Madison for Janesville.

The entire trip was most profitable. Madison is a beautiful place, and the weather was that of "a day in June, when, if ever, come perfect days." On our return home a stop of one hour was made at Janesville to inspect the plant of the Rock County Sugar Beet Company. This is the company that so generously donated beet seed to the boys of the Experiment Club.

At the Illinois State College of Agriculture the Winnebagoes were warmly greeted by Dean Davenport and his faculty, and during the entire stay every courtesy was shown us and every effort made to make the visit pleasant and profitable. In the main, the tour of inspection here and at Iowa was the same as that described for Wisconsin.

At Illinois College and Station the men and boys spent one afternoon in walking over the experimental farm and listening to the explanations of the instructors in farm crops, dairying, live stock, horticulture, etc. Sugar beets, corn, soy beans, cow peas, oats, wheat, and alfalfa were inspected. Some roots of the alfalfa were pulled up, and

FIG. 82. Looking at the Live Stock, Ames (Iowa) Experiment Station

the boys were shown the tubercles in which are the bacteria that store the nitrogen from the air and thus serve to maintain the fertility of the soil. It seemed like a fairy story to the boys to be told that the soil must be inoculated by these bacteria, and a field was shown on the experimental farm from which this inoculated soil was being sent to various points in Illinois, so that the farmers might scatter it over their own fields to insure the growth of alfalfa, the multiplication of bacteria, the gathering of nitrogen, and the consequent enrichment of the soil.

Is not this knowledge worth while in the education of the farmer boy of Illinois? Does it not rank in importance with the fact which he commits to memory from his geography that the Nile River overflowing annually keeps up the fertility of the soil for the people of Egypt? Our fathers bought land from the government for $1.25 per acre. Providence furnished rain, sunshine, and a fertile soil, and rich fields of grain covered the face of the earth. It could not be otherwise with proper industry. Now science must go with industry if our boys expect to make five per cent clear profit on land costing not $1.25 but $125 per acre in northern Illinois, in this beautiful Rock River valley.

Following is an account, written by a ten-year-old boy, of his impressions of an excursion to the Illinois College of Agriculture.

The trip was a very enjoyable one, and I will try to tell you about some of the things that we saw there. We left Rockford June 5, at 4.30 A.M. on the Illinois Central Railroad. Between Rockford and Chicago I saw thirteen schoolhouses, none of which had any trees in the yard. At Chicago Superintendent Kern took us to see Logan's statue. We had time before leaving to get a general view of the lake front, Michigan Avenue, and to see the tallest mercantile building in the world. We left Chicago for Urbana at 8.30 A.M. In South Chicago I saw the drainage canal and the swinging bridges.

At Kankakee there are stone quarries, but soon after leaving there I saw no stone quarry and noticed that most of the foundations of the houses were brick. There was a noticeable change in the appearance of the trees. I saw no leaf-blighted branches nor half-dead trees. The groves which I saw looked thrifty. The country from Chicago to Urbana is very level and I saw many flooded fields.

On arriving at Champaign about noon we were conducted by Mr. Fred H. Rankin to specially provided cars, on which we rode to the university grounds. We were met there by the dean of the college (Mr. Davenport), who conducted us to the stock-judging pavilion, where we were served with coffee, sandwiches, and cake.

After dinner we were shown through the main agricultural building, each professor explaining his part. This is the largest building devoted to this purpose in the world.   Then Professor Shamel took us over the fields and showed and told us about the sugar beets, cow peas, soy beans, and the wheat which had been planted.

He showed us a piece of land that had been planted to corn for twenty-five years without once having been manured. He showed us a field of alfalfa, and pulled up one of the plants that we might see the tubercles that deposit the nitrogen taken from the air into the soil.

Here also they were experimenting on planting corn, oats, clover, cow peas, and soy beans at different depths. We were shown the horse department, where they have some fine specimens of the Morgan horse.

FIG. 83. At the Oats Breeding Plots, Ames, Iowa

We next went to the dairy barns and saw the herd of cows under a test. In the beef department they had three car loads of cattle feeding for a test. They also had some fine specimens of Polled Angus and Shorthorns. From the cattle department we went to the orchards, where the spraying of trees was explained to us. In the evening we were entertained at Morrow Hall. Each professor gave a short talk explaining his department and what was being done in it.

The next morning we met at the Armory and were conducted through the gymnasium and the engineering hall. . . . Some of the other buildings which we visited are the electrical and mechanical engineering buildings, the hydraulic building, the central heating plant, the natural-history hall, and the library building. The latter is considered the finest building on the grounds and contains fifty thousand volumes. Having some time left, I revisited the museum in the natural-history hall.

The electrical and mechanical engineering buildings seemed to be of special interest to the boys. One of the professors said he thought it was because the wheels went round. Perhaps he was right. But I, for one, would like to take a course in this or some similar institution and find out what makes the wheels go round.

The excursionists went through the laboratories, where they saw students at work on corn, soil, etc. Dr. C. G. Hopkins, Chief in Agronomy and Chemistry, of the Illinois

Fig. 84. Inspecting Alfalfa at Ames, Iowa

College of Agriculture, together with his assistants, has for seven years been investigating and breeding corn so as to increase the yield per acre and at the same time improve its composition or quality. Four different strains of corn have been developed, namely, the "Illinois high protein," "Illinois low protein," "Illinois high oil," and "Illinois low oil." Briefly, the work has been to breed up the average size of the ear, to eliminate barren and inferior stalks, and to increase the amount of oil and protein. The protein is the nitrogenous substance in corn, and is the fundamental food required by growing stock to produce muscle, bone, and tissue, while the oil is the fatty part of corn, which is wanted by the feeder of cattle and hogs; at the same time corn, having a high percentage of oil, has a higher commercial value for factory use.

Corn is king. The visitor who inspected the farm exhibits in the Palace of Agriculture at the Louisiana Purchase Exposition must have been impressed with the royal

Fig. 85. The Famous "Blue Grays" on Experiment Farm, Ames, Iowa

claims of corn above all the other grains of the field. But to my mind, after a study of the exhibits of corn there, the prodigal display of corn with its many manufactured products was not the most significant thing in this wonderful exhibition. Near the huge pyramid of golden ears raised by the farmer boys of Illinois, in the space allotted to the Prairie State, was a small exhibit that, perhaps, did not attract the attention of more than one out of every five

hundred persons who strolled through this fascinating building. It was an exhibit of the Illinois College of Agriculture
and Experiment Station, showing the results of seven years
of scientific breeding and consequent development of corn.
Here was an illustration of things done in the domain of
the new agriculture, a page from the scientific text-book
on the new education for the farm, — a book which in its
wonderful possibilities reads like some tale of magic. The
mastery of this book means greater power for the new
farmer, and our country schools must be able to teach the
country child how to read it. The educational excursion
will help to reveal to the country people the possibilities
of the new country school.

The excursion to the College of Agriculture at Ames,
Iowa, in 1904, gave most of the boys and girls their first
glimpse of the mighty Mississippi River. Many of them
had never been outside of their home county; a few had
never been on a railroad train ; but in this centennial year
of the Louisiana Purchase, while most of them did not go
to the St. Louis Exposition, yet they could say that they
traveled over a part of the Louisiana territory, which one
hundred years ago wise statesmen at Washington regarded
as a vast wilderness not likely to be settled for a thousand
years to come. It was a great excursion through some of
the finest portions of Illinois and Iowa. Surely this is the
garden spot of the world and worthy of all effort to dignify
the occupation of the people, to develop the science of agriculture, and to enrich the life and reward more abundantly
the labor of a people who till the finest fields ever showered
with sunshine or rain.

A raft of logs was seen while we were crossing the
Mississippi River at Clinton, Iowa. In their after-school

work this would serve to interest the pupils in the lumber industry and the reason of its decline along the river. Why does the state of Michigan have a forestry commission? Why teach forestry in the Michigan State Agricultural College? What is forestry anyway? Why plant trees? When school children plant trees on barren school grounds, are they having a part in the great forestry movement sweeping over the country? Connect the country school

FIG. 86. Winnebagoes "on the Trail" to Madison, Wisconsin, June, 1905

more with life. Plant trees and flowers, and in school gardens care for plants and learn of the soil.

Our boys and their fathers were much interested in the cross-breeding experiment in cattle going on under the direction of Dean Curtiss, Director of the Experiment Station. While looking at the famous "Blue Grays," Dean Curtiss said:

This is the first work of this kind to be taken up in America. In Scotland this system of producing cattle has been practiced for a number of years. The "Blue Gray" cattle produced by this cross are decidedly the most popular feeding Galloways on the market, and it is also claimed that their meat is superior to that of other stock.

Feeding experiments are being conducted with these cattle at the college, and at the conclusion of the investigations they will be slaughtered and careful block tests made to determine the relative quality of their meat and economy of production.

On our way to Ames we passed through an Indian reservation, and the boys and girls saw some of the descendants of the original inhabitants of the Louisiana Territory, leading much the same life as their ancestors of one hundred years ago. There were rude wigwams, with the squaws weaving bright-colored blankets. As the train whirled through this bit of uncivilized country small patches of corn were seen growing here and there. It was a far cry from the corn patches of these Indians to the corn experiments of the Ames Station and the corn train which ran throughout Iowa for four weeks in the spring of 1904 under the direction of Professor P. G. Holden of the Iowa College of Agriculture.

Professor Holden traveled through most of the state on special trains furnished by the railroads. His object was to interest the farmers in scientific methods of corn raising, especially in the matter of the selection of proper seed for the spring planting. This was Agricultural College extension work on a large scale. If his work should result in the increase of one bushel per acre on the basis of 1903 seeding, it would be an increase of 7,398,320 bushels in Iowa's corn crop. This means over two million dollars added to the wealth of Iowa.

The selection and testing of seed corn is one of the most important and at the same time one of the easiest ways for the country school-teacher to begin elementary work in agriculture. A box of earth in the schoolroom and an ear of corn from seed selected by some farmer in the neighborhood are all the material needed at first. Of course a sufficient amount of moisture and heat are necessary when the grains of corn are put into the box of earth. Moist sand will do as well as dirt. Put one hundred kernels into the box and see how many sprout. Once the work is started and the results begin to be known, the entire community

FIG. 87. The Arrival at Madison: in Front of the New College of Agriculture, University of Wisconsin

will soon become interested. This work can be made to correlate with arithmetic and language work.

A valuable bulletin for help and suggestion may be had of Dean Davenport, Urbana, Illinois. This bulletin, No. 96, "The Testing of Corn for Seed," issued by the Experiment Station, is written by Albert N. Hume, First Assistant in Crop Production. It is finely illustrated, and I know of nothing better of its kind for a beginning in the study of corn. Mr. Hume tells the simplest way of sprouting seed and gives two pictures to show all the apparatus necessary, — simply two dinner plates and moist sand.

To show the importance of testing seed corn before planting, the following quotation is given from the bulletin:

Granting, then, that 8.81 per cent of the seed planted failed to grow, and that there were 1,000,000 bushels of corn used for seed in Illinois, the amount of corn planted which did not grow was 88,100 bushels. Valuing it at $2.00 per bushel, it represented a dead loss of $176,200. This amount alone would pay for testing practically every ear of corn planted in Illinois, counting labor at $1.50 a day. The great loss, however, consists in the shortage of the crop, due to this poor seed. The valuation of the corn crop in Illinois, as given in the year-book of the Department of Agriculture for 1903, was $95,000,000. Counting the proportionate loss, therefore, which might have been prevented by proper testing of seed corn, we have $8,369,500. The data herein presented certainly justify the conclusion that such a sum could have been saved by Illinois corn growers the past year by properly testing seed.

The expectation is that the educational excursion for 1906 will return to Urbana to see the growth of the Illinois College of Agriculture and of the University of Illinois since 1903.

CHAPTER IX

THE COUNTRY SCHOOL AND THE FARMERS' INSTITUTE

At the Illinois State Farmers' Institute round-up held at Joliet, February 21–23, 1905, Professor Frank Hall, Superintendent of the Illinois Farmers' Institutes, gave an interesting report with reference to attendance for the institute season just closed. From reports of ninety counties out of one hundred and two, the attendance was as follows:

Farmers	20,000
Farmers' wives	10,000
School teachers	2,000
Pupils	20,000
Total	52,000

The word "farmers" stands for those directly interested in agriculture. There are at least five hundred thousand farmers in Illinois, so that by the above figures one farmer in twenty-five attended the institutes throughout the state. There are twenty-seven thousand teachers in the state. Thus one out of every thirteen teachers attended the institutes. But these two thousand teachers, allowing an average of twenty pupils to the teacher, come in contact with forty thousand pupils.

Superintendent Hall further reports that combination institutes were held in many counties, where at the request of the County Superintendent of Schools the schools were closed for Educational Day and teachers and pupils attended the sessions for that day.

The superintendent names thirty-eight school superintendents and prominent teachers who have appeared on the programme of the various farmers' institutes. In at least thirty counties the pupils of the eighth grade and of the high school in the city in which the institute was held were allowed to attend one or more sessions of the local institutes. Very interesting sessions of this kind were held in Christian, Jasper, Jefferson, Kendall, Knox, Macoupin, Madison, Montgomery, Piatt, Richland, Tazewell, and

FIG. 88. Country Children in School

Williamson counties. The report of the State Board of Directors of the Illinois Farmers' Institutes for 1904 states that about sixty county superintendents of Illinois are coöperating with the institute officials. Special mention by name is made of the county superintendents of Alexander, Boone, Crawford, Christian, Dupage, Dekalb, Edgar, Fulton, Franklin, Greene, Hancock, Henry, Jackson, Jersey, Johnson, Knox, Kane, Kendall, Lake, Lasalle, Marion, Mason, Mercer, McLean, Moultrie, McHenry, Ogle, Perry, Pulaski, Peoria, Rock Island, Schuyler, Shelby, Stephenson, Whiteside, and Winnebago counties.

Superintendent Hall further stated at the Joliet meeting:

The county superintendents of schools, of whom special mention
was made in my last report (1904) as zealously coöperating with the
institute officials, have been no less helpful and efficient in the institute work this year. It is through these men and women that we are
able to reach to some extent the country schools. It is quite within
reasonable bounds to say that thousands of young people, through
the efforts of these officials and the superintendents of city schools,
supported and encouraged by the State Superintendent of Public
Instruction, Alfred Bayliss, have this year been brought face to face,
for the first time, with some of the interesting revelations of the
new agriculture.

At the three days' session of the state institute held at
Joliet, Illinois, February 21–23, 1903, the three evening sessions were of an educational character. Of course this was
true of all other sessions, but these evening sessions were
devoted more particularly to educational problems of the
farm and the school. The subjects discussed were as follows : What the Country Schools should Offer the Country
Boy and the Country Girl ; Boys' Clubs and School Gardens ; The Farm Home ; Education as Related to Useful
Occupations. There were also lectures illustrated with the
stereopticon.

All the above is given to show how the farmers' institute is developing as an educational movement. It must
do that if it is to do any permanent good. The institute
programme as a means of entertainment — as an imitation
of the vaudeville — is fast disappearing. If the farmers'
institute movement is to continue, a class of young people
must be educated to attend and so become leaders when
the present leaders pass off the scene of action. In some
places, where no effort is made to interest the boys and
girls and young people generally, the officers seem to be

controlled by the thought that when they (the officers) die all wisdom is to die with them. So the sessions are not advertised or the programme thought out, and the attendance is made up of two or three dozen retired farmers living in the town where the institute is held. The meeting is held in a hall that is either cold and poorly lighted, or heated red-hot with a smoky stove, and no ventilation.

The leaders of the farmers' institute movement in the United States are quickly realizing the importance of the effort to interest boys and girls and the country school-teacher in the work of the institutes and in the possibilities of the new agriculture. Mr. John Hamilton, Farmers' Institute Specialist of the United States Department of Agriculture, in a recent letter, said :

I now think that the farmers' institute movement must take hold of the country boy and the country girl. We have been dealing with the fathers and mothers thus far, which was a necessity until the value of the institute was demonstrated ; but we have come now, in my opinion, to a time in which it will be possible for us, in many states, to go a step further and take hold of the young people who are living on the farm.

Your success in interesting those in your county is proof of the practicability of the plan if it is properly organized and enthusi-astically conducted. There is no reason why we cannot change the whole sentiment of our country in a comparatively few years, if we go about it in a systematic way. Agriculture can be made popular as well as profitable, if those of us who are interested in country life take hold of the work in the right way and present the features that appeal to young minds in an attractive way.

At the boys' session of the Winnebago County Farmers' Institute held in 1903 a programme was arranged which included reports of experiments by members of the Experiment Club, and addresses by teachers, school officials, and others, the proceedings being enlivened by music.

Such was our first programme, and the hall had standing room only, and not much of that. The boys' and girls' sessions have been crowded ever since. The work described by the boys was for 1902, the first year of the boys' club. It is worth far more to the reader to know what was said that morning than that I should theorize on the value of such meetings; hence I offer no apology for presenting here extracts from the papers of some of the speakers. Some of the addresses were printed in the local press and thus scattered over the county. The most significant ones were printed in my annual report and sent over the county also. Work of this character needs to be followed up till — well, I should say, *till these boys have boys of their own.*

Fig. 89. A Boy at his Desk in an Old-Fashioned Country School

The fault with us at times in movements of this character is that we make a great spasmodic effort for a year or so and then put on our halos and rest in perfect ecstasies of self-satisfaction. Then the interest dies out, and you would never know there had been a revival in the county. A good motto is, " Keeping everlastingly at it brings success."

Following are reports of three boys:

I

I grew one-tenth acre sugar beets; cultivated them four times and hoed once, making about two days in all. Yield, seventy-five bushels; sugar, twelve and nine-tenths per cent; purity, eighty and one-half per cent.

Planted seed corn May 12, away from any other corn, about two and one-half inches deep, with a drill. I cultivated it with an eight-shovel cultivator and went through it with a two-shovel plow once. I found about two suckers on each hill of my prize corn.

I did some of the observation work sent out by the state College of Agriculture. The average number of stalks on a plot ten hills square was three hundred and eighteen and the number of barren stalks was eight; per cent of barren stalks was two. There were twelve suckers and eight suckers with ears on, — that is, on the average of three tests. It was early yellow corn and was planted three inches deep.

The raising of corn and beets has showed me that corn or anything else cannot be raised without good cultivation and moisture, to make a profitable business. I have learned that corn needs medium rich soil, as corn raised on a stony soil will not amount to much without a good deal of rain. When a boy has a plot of his own and is working for a premium he is a great deal more likely to work harder on his corn; and if in the habit of doing his work well, he is going to make a better farmer.

I think work of this kind will make the farmer boy think and depend more on himself, as the corn is to be raised by himself. He will do it well. I would like to go on and do better work, as I have become interested in finding out who does the best work and who gets the premiums. . . .

II

I learned in cultivating my beets that thorough cultivation is necessary to get good results. There is not much sugar in beets grown in sand, but clay produces a better sugar beet. I found also that a beet entirely isolated did not do well at all. I do not find it a very profitable business even at six dollars a ton. I also raised forty bushels of carrots from a quarter of a pound of seed, and, carrots being worth about four times as much as beets, they are a great deal more profitable.

III

My experimental work began with the testing of seed corn and clover seed. My corn tested eighty-two per cent and my clover seed tested seventy-five per cent, which I considered a very poor test.

. . . I harvested my beets the first week in November and had about one hundred and forty-four bushels. I put them in the cellar and am feeding them to the cows. They make excellent cow food.

FIG. 90. Country Children in School

In my corn experiment I found out that thorough cultivation is not all. We must have plenty of moisture and plenty of sunshine to insure a crop. It has taught me to observe other farms, — those that have been poorly cultivated and those where the cultivation was perfect. I have learned that a clean cultivation is far the best. I have found out by testing oats for smut that a large proportion of the oats is spoiled in this way. One of our neighbors lost at least a third of his crop by smut. This could have been averted by a little treatment beforehand. This man had no idea there was any treatment of oats for smut. I am greatly in favor of keeping up with the experiments. I think I have benefited very much in my last year's experiments.

The four following papers were read by adults :

I

1. I think the better way for the fathers to help along the work would be for them to join the boys' clubs.

2. Let them meet with the club once a quarter or oftener and talk the work over with the boys.

3. They can help the work along by furnishing the boys a small plot of ground, the best there is on the farm, to carry on experimental work. Let the plot be not far from the house, nor in some corner where it will be shaded half of the time, but out in the open field where the sun will shine on it from sunrise until sundown.

4. When it comes spring and planting time the fathers can help along the work by having one of the boys get the ground ready for planting a week before they need to plant and see to it that they get it in good order.

5. The fathers can help the boys along by furnishing them a good set of garden tools instead of an old rusty hoe.

6. The fathers should see to it that the boys have good seed of whatever kind they wish to plant, and when they get ready to plant go along with the boys and teach them how to successfully plant and raise a crop of vegetables or melons or grain, as the case may be. Planting the seed is where most of the boys would fail by planting them too deep. Show the boys how to hoe and cultivate the crops, and the best way to care for them.

7. Let the boys know that you are interested in what they are doing. There is nothing that will encourage a boy so much as to know his father is interested in his work. Right here I would say : Don't expect too much from the boys at the start, as they have to learn a little at a time, as we did years ago. Don't expect that the rows in his garden will be straight or that the weeds won't grow there, for they will, just the same as they will grow in your garden.

8. Another way the fathers may help along the work of the boys' club is to give the boys the use of one half an acre of ground to cultivate and care for in their own way. Let them plant whatever they think would pay them best, and let them have the proceeds for their own individual use. In that way the boys will learn to work, and work

FIG. 91. The Boys' Session of the Winnebago County Farmers' Institute, 1904

183

will become pleasure to them, because they feel that they are earning something for themselves.

II

The time is not very many years back, certainly not beyond the recollection of us older ones, when on these broad and then fertile prairies of northern Illinois anybody who could tickle the soil with a plow could make it laugh with a harvest. And we, poor simple souls, thought it was inexhaustible ; and we burned our straw stacks, sending up in smoke millions of dollars of fertility that should have been returned to the soil. We plowed the little valleys that should have remained in grass to keep the soil from washing away, — we plowed them and made water courses, and the spring rains took advantage of it and carried other millions of dollars' worth of soil down the rivers to help fill up the Gulf of Mexico. What have we got for it all ?

We got some valuable experience. We found we needed agricultural colleges, and a farm, and a lot of intelligent men to experiment with the soil, with seeds, the various crops, farm animals, and insect pests. We 've got them, and they teach us something new every year. . . .

I think every father should encourage his own boys to join an experiment club. Having joined, he should give them every facility for carrying out the experiment selected for the club work. Give them a good plot of ground. Advise them, but, having done this, leave them to work out their own ideas, modified by your advice or not as they may think best. He should beget enthusiasm in them by being enthusiastic over the experiments himself.

Let him impress upon them this fact, that no matter whether their crop is a good or poor one, their experiment has not been a failure, for they have learned something they did not know before.

When fathers can do so they should offer prizes for the club exhibits. Let each offer what he best can, — a lamb, a calf, a pig, in fact anything of value to the boys. . . .

III

Some one has said, " Three things fix a man's value in life, — his knowledge, or what he knows ; his ability, or what he can do ; and his character, or what he is." The school is intended to help pupils in securing all three. We read books in order to learn what others have thought and done before us, but neither knowledge, ability, or character comes from books alone. We must also study the men about us, that we may learn what others are doing now; and we must study the things about us in order to learn how nature works and how we must take hold of things if we would succeed.

You notice what was said, — "We must study the things about us if we wish to succeed." Who needs to do that more than the farmer, or the boy who intends to become a farmer? Are we in our district schools teaching the boys to study the things about them? We should be, if we are striving to keep them on the farm. What could better rouse their interest or create a liking for the farm than the study of nature, or, as we may call it, the study of agriculture?

The Boys' Experiment Club, organized about a year ago, has begun to do something to interest the boys in farming and farm life. Effects of their work can already be seen ; but the boys need encouragement and help in their work, and the district school ought to give it. And how can the school do this? The first thing is to get the sympathy and interest of the parents ; then their encouragement and help ; and every parent ought to be interested and willing to help us in this, if he wishes his boy to remain on the farm, be contented with farm life, and at the same time make a success of it.

In order to encourage the boys in their experimental work the school should have an experimental garden. Here we can use the help of the parents and the directors. They should see to it that the ground in some parts of the school yard is plowed or thoroughly spaded. The pupils, under the direction of the teacher, would do the rest ; they could bring rakes, hoes, and other tools, and carefully prepare the soil and plant the seeds.

In time the seeds would begin to grow and of course the weeds also. Then the children could be taught how to keep their garden free from weeds. They could learn the names and habits of common weeds and the methods of ridding the soil of them, and could make experiments similar to those which the boys in the club are making.

Then all along they could be taught the value of tools and the proper way of taking care of them. Perhaps if the schools take up the study of agriculture in earnest and teach the boys some practical

things, when these boys become the farmers of Winnebago County
we shall not see, as we go through the country, valuable farm implements going to rust and ruin because the farmer is too shiftless or
careless or ignorant to put them under shelter.

These are some of the things we propose to teach the boys and
also the girls of Winnebago County, if the parents and directors will
first do their duty in the matter. Also the pupils could be taught to

FIG. 92. A Subject for Consideration at the Farmers' Institute

take pride in keeping the garden and the whole school yard neat and
clean. Then when these boys and girls get to be school directors the
teacher and the pupils will not be obliged to wade through weeds in
the school yard when they commence school in September,—weeds
so high that the smaller pupils can hardly see over them. This is
what some of us have had to do.

But some will say, "Will not all this interfere with the regular
work of the school?" It will take time, of course, but is not this as
important as the regular school work? What is the use of teaching
our boys how to compute compound interest if we send them from
school so ignorant concerning farming that they make a failure of it?
Then they will not need to know how to compute compound interest.

There are some things that can be learned better from experience than from books, and those are the things we propose teaching the coming farmers of Winnebago County, if parents and directors will help us.

IV

The degree of a man's success upon the farm depends more on himself than on the farm. His intelligence and ambition, the determination, energy, the brain as well as the brawn power which he puts into his work are the growth of habit, beginning with the primary education of the boy, and must necessarily begin where the boy begins.

The fact that the district school is the place where the boys begin makes it the most important factor to build up agricultural interest. The work at the beginning must appeal to the interest of the boys through practical work in observing and experimenting with soil, plant life, and the farm in general.

The school garden as a means to an end has a practical bearing in agricultural education,

FIG. 93. A Subject for Consideration at the Farmers' Institute

and is in the reach of every district school at a cost not to be considered. How will the boys become practical farmers by working in a school garden? They learn by practical experience how nature yields to labor under various conditions; they learn how to love and care for the things that are a source of profit to the farmer and give beauty to his home. Industry is the result of this practical work which is the propelling power of knowledge.

The schools of Europe are a proof of what the school gardens can do for agriculture if placed in the hands of the pupils and their teachers. Germany leads the world in practical and profitable methods in agriculture, and there the school garden is most highly developed.

The uncomfortable schoolhouse, the neglected yard growing weeds, shadeless and barren, can offer nothing to the farmer boy to inspire, to educate, and interest. To improve these conditions is a duty every farmer must make his personal interest if life on the farm is to improve. A little interest, a little work, a little financial help will set these silent and practical forces at work to interest the boys upon the farm through the district school. From the school the experimental club will be recruited. A greater demand for the experimental farm, the agricultural school, and the farmers' institute will be the result. . . .

The programme for the boys' session is varied from year to year. The expectation for 1906 is to have reports from different members of the club similar to those given above for 1903. These reports will be followed by a stereopticon address.

The following is self-explanatory:

OFFICE OF COUNTY SUPERINTENDENT OF SCHOOLS,
ROCKFORD, ILLINOIS, December 20, 1904

To the Schools of Winnebago County :

It is my wish that there be a close coöperation between the schools and the farmers' institute of our county. Teachers may tell school officers that I recommend that the schools close on the day of the boys' and girls' programme, and that teachers and children attend the institute on that day. The directors should give the teachers this day without loss of pay.

Do not forget the date, Thursday, January 12, 1905. Teachers will please have children distribute these programmes throughout their respective districts. Urge all to go and see the exhibits of corn, needlework, and bread, and listen to the speakers. Quite as much of an educational value will be acquired by attendance on the boys' and girls' day as in an ordinary day's work at school. Let every one plan to be present.   Sincerely,

O. J. KERN

The farmers of Winnebago County for the years 1905 and 1906 believe enough in the boys and girls to give their own money for cash prizes without asking the merchants of the city of Rockford to give collar buttons, link cuff buttons, whips, lap robes, and poultry food.

FIG. 94. Studying Corn

PREMIUMS FOR WINNEBAGO COUNTY BOYS' CORN-GROWING CONTEST

ALL PREMIUMS CASH

First prize . . . . Fifteen dollars ($15.00)
Second prize . . . . Ten dollars ($10.00)
Third prize . . . . Five dollars ($5.00)
Fourth prize . . . . Three dollars ($3.00)
Fifth prize . . . . Two dollars ($2.00)
Next ten prizes . . . . One and one-half dollars ($1.50) each
Next ten prizes . . . . One dollar ($1.00) each

To all others making an exhibit cash premiums will be awarded at the discretion of the Corn Committee.

NOTE. The three boys taking first, second, and third premiums will be expected to write an article for Superintendent Kern after the institute, telling about the preparation of seed bed, planting, cultivation, and harvesting of prize corn.

CORN SCORE CARD

(Revised January, 1905)

Entry No.........................

....County Farmers' Institute

SCALE OF POINTS		SCORE
1. Trueness to type	10	....
2. Uniformity of exhibit	5	....
3. Shape	10	....
4. Color	10	....
5. Seed condition	10	....
6. Tips	5	....
7. Butts	5	....
8. Kernel uniformity	5	....
9. Kernel shape	5	....
10. Length of ear	10	....
11. Circumference of ear	5	....
12. Space between rows	5	....
13. Space between kernels at cob	5	....
14. Proportion shelled corn to ear	10	....
Total	100	....

....*Judge*

Name and address of exhibitor to be added here after score is made.

Name ....

Address ....

STANDARD MEASUREMENTS

	LENGTH	CIRCUM-FERENCE	PROPOR-TION
Reid's Yellow Dent	10–11	7¼–7¾	88%
Leaming	10–11	7¼–7¾	88%
White Superior	10–11	7¼–7¾	88%
Boone County White	10–11	7½–8	88%
Riley's Favorite	9–10	7 –7½	90%
Golden Eagle	9–10	7¼–7¾	90%
Silver Mine	9–10	7 –7½	90%

Measurements for Varieties not named above and for Mixed
Varieties

	Length	Circumference	Proportion
Northern Illinois	9–10	6¾–7¼	88%
Central and southern Illinois	10–11	7¼–7¾	88%

In all exhibits made prior to November 15 of each year all standards of length
and circumference shall be increased one-half inch, and standards of per cent shall
be reduced two.

Exhibitors may remove two kernels side by side from the same row at the middle
of the ear for kernel examination.

Explanatory

1. Trueness to type: conforming to variety characteristics in variety classes,
and to the prevailing type in general classes.

2. Uniformity of exhibit: uniform in shape, length, and circumference.

3. Shape: ear cylindrical, with proper proportion of length and circumference.

4. Color: free from mixture and true to variety color. In judging color a red
cob in white corn or a white cob in yellow corn shall be cut ten points. For each
mixed kernel up to five a cut of one fifth of a point shall be made; for five or more
mixed kernels a cut of one point shall be made. Kernels missing from the ear may
be counted as mixed, at the discretion of the judge. Difference in shade of color of
grain or of cob shall be scored according to variety characteristics.

5. Seed condition: ripe, sound, dry, and of strong vitality.

6. Tips: oval shape and regularly filled out with large dented kernels.

7. Butts: kernels rounded over the end of cob in regular manner, leaving a
deep depression when shank is removed.

8. Kernel uniformity: kernels from the same ear and from the several ears
uniform in size and shape.

9. Kernel shape: kernels deep, wedge-shape, and full at the germ end.

10. Length: varies with the variety measure. The deficiency and excess in length
of all ears shall be added together, and for every inch thus obtained a cut of one
point shall be made. In determining the length measure from the extreme tip to the
extreme butt.

11. Circumference: varies with the variety measure. The deficiency and excess in
circumferences of all ears shall be added together, and for every inch thus obtained
a cut of one point shall be made. Measure the circumference at one third the distance
from the butt to the tip.

12. Space between rows: furrows between rows, and space caused by round
corners of kernels.

13. Space at cob: space in row between kernels at cob. To examine for "space
at cob" take out several kernels near the middle of the ear; then observe the
kernels of an undisturbed row near the cob.

14. Proportion: In determining the proportion of corn to cob weigh each alternate
in the exhibit; shell and weigh the cobs; subtract the weight of the cobs from the
weight of the ears, thus obtaining the weight of the corn; divide the weight of the
shelled corn by the weight of the ears, thus finding the per cent of corn. For each
per cent short of the standard for variety a cut of one point shall be made.

The following circular letter was mailed to every member of the Boys' Experiment Club:

WINNEBAGO COUNTY FARMERS' INSTITUTE,
ROCKFORD, ILLINOIS, April 4, 1905

To the Members of the Winnebago County Farmer Boys' Experiment Club:

We are pleased to be able to tell you that at a recent meeting of the officers of the Winnebago County Farmers' Institute it was decided to have a boys' corn-growing contest again this year, open to any boy in the county eighteen years of age and under, and it was also decided to offer all premiums in cash.

Reid's Yellow Dent Corn, grown in this county, will be furnished this year by the Winnebago County Farmers' Institute, and any boy wishing to enter the contest will receive a package of seed by writing to E. M. Breckenridge, County Secretary, Rural Route No. 3, Rockford, Illinois, inclosing four cents in stamps to pay postage on the corn.

FIG. 95. Studying Corn

Write your name and post-office address very plainly.

Each boy *must* write for his own seed.

The conditions on which the corn is sent and received to be as follows. A package of the seed will be presented on condition that the boy receiving same shall plant three hundred grains of it in a square, with the balance in two rows planted on the south and west sides to fertilize and protect the inside rows; that he will cultivate it and

FIG. 96. Pure-Bred Cattle

FIG. 97. Studies in Corn

harvest it and exhibit not less than ten ears at the Winnebago County Farmers' Institute, the ten ears or more for exhibition to be taken from the inside square, and *nowhere else*. It is further agreed by the boy receiving this corn that he will comply with the rules governing the exhibit of corn at the county institute, and that he will attend at least one session of the institute, and that he will follow as far as possible the suggestions sent with the package in regard to keeping the record of growing the corn.

Many of you entered the corn-growing contest last year and made exhibits at our last county institute, and we hope many more will try this year.

Remember the prizes will all be cash again this year.

Wishing you a successful year, we are,

Yours truly,

W. I. WELLS, *President*

E. M. BRECKENRIDGE, *Secretary*

After the corn is sent to the boys who ask for it, the following four-page folder is mailed to each boy :

REPORT OF CORN GROWN

BY

Name...

Address..

IN

BOYS' CORN–GROWING CONTEST

Winnebago County, 1905

Corn grown in...Township

REPORT OF CORN

(Report to pertain *only* to the hills in which the three hundred
grains were planted in the inside square)

1. Kind of soil...
2. Previous crop on lot...
3. Manure used, if any ....
4. Time and depth of plowing...
....
5. Cultivation of ground before planting...
....
6. Date when planted...
7. Cultivation before it came up...
....
8. Date when it came up...
9. Cultivations (times and kind)..
....
....
10. Implements used..
....
11. When laid by...
12. Date of tasseling...
13. Date of silking..
14. Date when gathered...
15. Number of hills...
16. Number of stalks...
17. Number of ears..
18. Number of barren stalks...
19. Total weight at time of gathering..
20. Injury from cutworms and insects...
....

Remarks..
....
....
....
....

To the Boys of the Winnebago County Corn-Growing Contest:

Two copies of these report blanks will be mailed to each boy to whom seed has been sent by the Winnebago County Farmers' Institute. Fill out both blanks just alike, and as carefully and accurately as you can. Keep one of the reports yourself for future reference, and about December 1 mail the other one to the County Secretary, E. M. Breckenridge, Rural Route No. 3, Rockford, Illinois, with a letter about how your corn did, and whether or not you are going to make an exhibit of ten ears at the next county institute, which we expect to hold January 16–18, 1906.

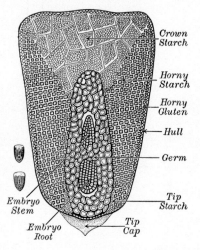

Crown Starch

Horny Starch

Horny Gluten

Hull

Germ

Tip Starch

Embryo Stem

Embryo Root

Tip Cap

FIG. 98. **A** Cross Section of a Kernel of Corn

The keeping of this record will be of equal value to yourself. Don't forget to mail one of them to the County Secretary next December.

We expect to be able to give a good cash prize to every boy who makes an exhibit of his corn.

Hoping you will have a very successful year in your work, we are,

Yours truly,

W. I. WELLS, *President*

E. M. BRECKENRIDGE, *Secretary*

In 1904 a Girls' Home Culture Club was organized in our county, and now numbers three hundred members. The Domestic Science Association is expected to take as great an interest in this organization as does the farmers' institute with the boys.

Premiums for Home Culture Club (1904)

Needlework Contest

The farmers' institute through the Domestic Science Association offers the following prizes to the girls of the Home Culture Club for sewing, patching, and darning, the work to be all done by exhibitor. The prizes in each case will be: first, $1.00 ; second, 50 cents.

Six prizes for girls of twelve years and under. Six prizes for girls from twelve to eighteen years of age, which for each class will be:

Two, — a first and second for best handkerchief made by hand.

Two, — a first and second for best setting in a patch in a piece of plaid goods.

Two, — a first and second for best darning a hole not less than one inch in diameter in either dress goods or table linen, darning to be done with either silk, linen, or cotton thread.

To the five girls doing the most skillful work, a gentleman offers five books, not less than $1.25 each, the girl doing the best work to have the first choice, the second best the second choice, and so on.

Bread-Making Contest

The Farmers' Institute also offers cash prizes to the girls of the Home Culture Club for bread, to be made according to requirements stated in a circular letter. Mrs. Mabel Howe Otis of Chicago will judge the bread by the Illinois Household Science Score Card.

For girls twelve years old and under, first prize, $3.00 ; second, $2.00 ; third, $1.00.

For girls over twelve and under eighteen, first prize, $3.00 ; second, $2.00 ; third, $1.00.

In addition to this, the very best loaf exhibited by any girl complying with requirements will receive a special prize of a Universal Bread Machine.

Bread must be brought in Wednesday, January 11, and each loaf accompanied with a written statement of : (1) how it was made ; (2) time left to rise ; (3) number of times kneaded ; (4) length of time spent in kneading ; (5) how long it was in the oven. Bread must be baked in pans approved by the Household Science Department of the University of Illinois, which measure nine inches by four inches by four inches.

BREAD SCORE CARD

Flavor . . . . 35 points
Lightness . . . . 15 "
Grain and texture . . . . 30 "

Crust { Color / Depth / Texture } . . . . 5 "

Crumb { Color / Doughiness } . . . . 5 "

Loaf { Shape / Size } . . . . 5 "

Moisture . . . . 5 "

                                                    _____
                                                    100 points

DIRECTIONS FOR MAKING BREAD

Sift and measure the flour; scald milk and put in bowl; add salt
and cold water, then yeast mixed smoothly in warm water; then add
flour to make a batter and beat until full of bubbles; gradually add
more flour; when too stiff to stir rub a little flour on molding board;
turn out dough and knead till it does not stick to your hands or
board and feels elastic; put back in bowl; set in a warm place to
rise about three hours, or until it is twice its original size; shape into
a loaf, using little or no flour; when again light bake fifty or sixty
minutes; take out of pan, but do not cover until cold.

We hope to have three hundred loaves from the three hundred
Home Culture Club girls, which will count ninety-eight points each,
and then Winnebago County can be registered as the banner county
of good bread makers for the state of Illinois.

MRS. W. L. FRISBE, *President*
HARRIET A. ENOCH, *Secretary*

The ladies of the Domestic Science Association very
wisely ignored fancy needlework and angel cake. The
chances are that if a girl can bake good wholesome bread

her cakes will be all right; and to be able to darn well is more important than Battenberg. The work for 1904 will be continued for 1905.

I have gone into detail in showing how the country school and the farmers' institute can coöperate, and I have done this because so many have written me for information with reference to *specific instructions for doing things.* In our

FIG. 99. The Cooking Class, Macdonald Consolidated School, Middleton, Nova Scotia, Canada

traveling libraries I put a number of books for teachers and pupils along the line of home, farm, and country-life interests.

It is far from my purpose to attempt to say how the farmers' institute movement can be improved. Abler men are at work on that. Valuable bulletins issued by the Department of Agriculture at Washington, D.C., are the following:

Proceedings of the Ninth Annual Meeting of the American Association of Farmers' Institute Workers held at St. Louis, Missouri, October 18–20, 1904, by W. H. Beal, John Hamilton, and G. C. Creelman.

Annual Report of Farmers' Institutes, 1904, by John Hamilton.

Farmers' Institutes in the United States, by John Hamilton.

Farmers' Institutes in the United States, by D. J. Crosby.

I will close this chapter by stating that too much must
not be expected of boys and girls at first. In order to get
things done one will need to camp on a boy's trail and
keep after him in a right way. In reading over the plans
of work given above one must read between the lines to
realize the constant hard work and earnest thought that

FIG. 100. Root Growth of Corn at Time of Tasseling

are necessary to make plans succeed. I do not pretend to
say the last word on this subject. There is a great field
for coöperation of the farmers' institute and the district
school in the direction of the material, social, moral, and
intellectual conditions affecting the country school and the
country child.

CHAPTER X

THE NEW AGRICULTURE AND THE COUNTRY SCHOOL

What place ought agriculture to have in the district school, and what kind of agriculture ought it to be? The following quotation from a prominent agricultural journal pretty nearly sizes up the situation:

Enough spasmodic theorization on teaching practical agriculture and æsthetic nature study has been expended to pay off the national debt. Let us pass into the next stage of the argument and get down to ways and means. If our children are to receive elementary instruction in chemistry, soil, physics, vegetable life, biology, botany, and all the rest of the list, some one must teach them. How many of them are really capable of teaching anything beyond the " a-b, ab's " with their hands tied behind them? It is not enough that a teacher may call up the class in geography and perfunctorily conduct a recitation with her eyes glued to a book. A teacher should inspire pupils with a love of study. She should make the recitation interesting. All this applies not only to the teaching of agriculture but to all branches taught in the country school, and serves to emphasize the need of adopting the central or township system. It is very difficult for any teacher to develop the proper interest and enthusiasm in the work of any branch with only an attendance of two or three pupils. On the other hand, it is a great waste to employ good teachers for only two or three students when they can better instruct several times that number. When the centralized plan is adopted it will be possible with the same outlay to supply a much better class of instruction in all branches.

Now an attempt will be made in subsequent chapters to discuss the small school, consolidation or centralization, and the preparation of country teachers to meet the demands of a new education for the country child. In this chapter the first two sentences of the above quotation will be considered, especially the second, namely: "Let us pass into the next stage of the argument and get down to ways and means."

The writer is of the opinion that, so far as one county is concerned (and there are others), the work as set forth in the chapters on School Gardens, A Farmer Boys' Experiment Club, Educational Excursions, and The Country School and the Farmers' Institute in this book does bear some relation to getting "down to ways and means," and shows a corresponding departure from "spasmodic theorization on teaching practical agriculture." The writer claims further that what has been said in those chapters is also "practical agriculture." He cherishes a hope that the same may be said of this and subsequent chapters on to the end of his story.

In the account of school gardens, boys' clubs, excursions, and the like, so far as this has any relation to the work of the district schools as they *now are*, nothing is said about pupils working with gang plows, harrows, and binders, or about silos, creameries, and separators. In short, nothing is said claiming that children in the country school should enter upon farm operations and raise crops to an extent that would make the teacher and pupils a very serious factor in crop production. It is at this point that there is much misunderstanding on the part of many farmers. They claim that they are able to "learn" their boys how to plow, and the mothers are equally confident of their ability to "learn" the girls how to sew and cook. What they want, they say, in the country school is some one to teach the "three R's, with plenty of time on 'rithmetic and spellin', like when we went to the district school forty years ago."

Now I firmly believe in the fundamentals, but my belief in them has not yet led me to an exclusive worship of them to the exclusion of other important educative material peculiar to the environment of the country child. This is a new scientific age of agriculture, and to meet the demands of a new age for the farmer with reference to two items only — the development of high-bred corn and the maintenance of soil fertility — better methods must come as the result of better education somewhere. It is just as reasonable to claim that, if the school of forty years ago with its curriculum then was all-sufficient and people were happy, and strong characters came from the country schools, so can the farmers get along without telephones, delivery of mail, self-binders, and other improvements. Then no one dreamed of soil exhaustion, and the good old times were the best.

Fig. 101. Corn and Soy Beans on Experiment Field, Winnebago County, Illinois

Northern Illinois and southern Wisconsin are great dairy regions. Now I suppose many people have the idea that if the country school is to teach agriculture for this particular region and an effort is made to put the country child into a sympathetic and intelligent relation to his environment,

the school officers must keep a cow on the school grounds ;
and when the time comes for the exercise in agriculture the
teacher must take the children out to the cow and give
instruction in milking, corralling the cow, etc. No ; the
children will learn how to milk at home. But if the very
valuable bulletins from either the Illinois or Wisconsin experiment stations on the dairy cow were in the schoolroom,
the children might acquire some useful knowledge about
such a common thing as a cow that would go just as far in
making a useful farmer and an intelligent citizen as what
children in the country schools are learning about the kan-
garoo and the cockatoo. But the cow and the hen as
subjects of study — perish the thought ! And yet, with
reference to the American hen the Secretary of Agriculture in his report for 1904 says :

> The farmers' hens are now producing one and two-thirds billions of
> dozens of eggs yearly, and these hens during their busy season lay
> enough eggs in two weeks, at the high prices of eggs that have pre-
> vailed during the year, to pay the year's interest on the national debt.

In my judgment the most important of the " ways and
means " asked for by the editor quoted above is some movement that will change the ideals of the great mass of the
country people with reference to education. The argument
must appeal to the farmer from his own point of view. And
this argument (too largely at present this is true) must be
a dollars-and-cents one. Will it pay ? How much will it cost?
The schoolmaster will have to learn how to meet the people
on their own ground.

Hodge, in *Nature Study and Life*, states a great truth
when he says :

> Cultivation of plants has indicated and developed elements of
> character fundamental to civilized life. Willingness to work for daily

bread, intelligent provision for the future, courage to fight for home, love of country, are a few among the virtues attained. When we consider its universal and fundamental character, the omission of soil lore from a system of education for the young is suggestive of a relapse to barbarism.

The average farmer, however, at this stage of the game is quite willing to risk the "relapse to barbarism." What he wants to know is, Will it pay? If educators can show him that a study of high-bred corn and soil will bring substantial returns, he is willing to spend more money on

FIG. 102. Soy Beans on Experiment Field, Winnebago County, Illinois

the country school and spend it in a better way. This putting of an educational system on so low a basis is highly repugnant to the "educator" who cherishes lofty ideals of "culture," "educational processes," "periods of adolescence," etc. But some of us who work in an atmosphere of real life in the fields have to meet conditions as we find them.

The following is a part of an address by Dean Bailey of Cornell to a body of New York farmers:

If there are one million people in New York State who are engaged in agriculture, and if that one million people must be lifted up into a newer and better life, then why not put before them knowledge of the subjects with which they have to do day by day, and put those subjects into such pedagogical form that they may be made the means of training the minds of the young people as well as giving them information?

It is interesting to observe how little relation the common schools have to the lives that men lead. The curriculum of our common schools is made from the curricula of our old universities and academies, made simple, and let down to the people.

In the beginning we must fasten the children's affections on the region in which they are. We must teach them the common things with which they live from day to day. That is the new idea in nature study that is coming gradually into our schools. If any one of you gentlemen were to be put into a new community, where you never had been, and where there was no school, and were asked to make a curriculum for a school, without thinking about it or being conscious of it, you would put into that school something having relation to that vicinity, to the soil and the animals, and those things with which that community had to do.

The common school is undergoing evolution, and gradually its point of view is being changed. The West, not fettered by tradition as we are in the East, is putting agriculture into its common schools, as has the South, having thrown off its old ecclesiastical traditions; and recently one little book along this line has sold in the South to the extent, it is reported, of fifty thousand copies. Up from the South and back from the West it is coming also into the East; and I predict that in the next ten years we shall see a tremendous revolution in the attitude of the common schools towards education.

In my humble opinion there has been no more important document issued by the National Educational Association than the Report of the Committee on Industrial Education for the Country Communities, July, 1905. The make-up of this important committee is this: Superintendent L. D. Harvey, Menomonie, Wisconsin, chairman; Dean L. H. Bailey, College of Agriculture, Ithaca, New York; State Superintendent Alfred Bayliss, Illinois; State Superintendent W. T. Carrington, Missouri; and Honorable W. M. Hays,

Assistant Secretary of Agriculture, Washington, D.C. This committee has been at work two years and has been continued for further investigation. This pamphlet should be widely read and discussed by country teachers, school officers, and members of farmers' institutes. One quotation here will indicate somewhat its importance:

> This committee does not hesitate to say that in its judgment the country schools, which train nearly one half of the school population of this country so far as school training goes, should definitely recognize the fact that the major portion of those being trained will continue to live upon the farm; and that there should be specific, definite, technical training fitting them for the activities of farm life. Such schools will not make farmers nor housekeepers, but they will interest the boys and girls in farming and housekeeping and the problems connected with these two important vocations.

After two years' work with school gardens, excursions, experimental club work, lectures, and instruction at teachers' annual institutes, and farmers' institutes as well, it seemed wise to us in Winnebago County to make use of one more "ways and means" of teaching "practical agriculture." At least, this might serve as a means to induce teachers, school officers, and patrons to change their opinion as to the new agriculture and the possibility of elementary instruction in the country school. For if we sit down and wait till teachers are trained or schools properly organized, nothing will ever be done. But a start can be made and the public sentiment educated to the possibilities of instruction in elementary agriculture. This last effort, beginning September, 1904, was to put the principal bulletins from the Illinois Experiment Station and the Department of Agriculture at Washington on the reading table or in the school library of the one hundred and sixteen school districts in the county outside of Rockford. The summary of the year's work, as taken from personal reports from teachers, gives for the year ending June 30, 1905, a total of eighteen hundred bulletins so placed. Of this number, one thousand are from the Illinois Station at Urbana and eight hundred from the Department of Agriculture at Washington.

The following are the principal ones from Illinois :

No. 66, Corn Experiments in Illinois.
No. 76, Alfalfa on Illinois Soil.
No. 82, Methods of Corn Breeding.
No. 87, Structure of the Corn Kernel and the Composition of its Different Parts.
No. 94, Nitrogen Bacteria and Legumes.
No. 95, The More Important Insect Injuries to Indian Corn.
No. 96, The Testing of Corn for Seed.

These are not all of the important bulletins issued by the Station, but they include the more important ones on corn and soil.

From the Department of Agriculture at Washington :

No. 79, Report of the Secretary of Agriculture, 1904 : Circular, Soil Survey, with map of Winnebago County, Illinois.
No. 134, Tree Planting on Rural School Grounds.
No. 94, The Vegetable Garden.
No. 173, Primer of Forestry.
No. 60, The Teaching of Agriculture in the Rural Common Schools.
No. 218, The School Garden.
No. 185, Beautifying the Home Grounds.

The expectation is to read and discuss some of the more important of these bulletins during the coming year in the teachers' institutes. Our country school-teachers need to know something of the great work going on at our higher institutions of agricultural instruction and investigation. The great majority of the country school-teachers are entirely unacquainted with the publications issued by these institutions. These bulletins, as a rule, are free, and a postal card will put one's name on the permanent mailing list of the state college and station. Through the teacher in the country school we hope to get the older pupils interested, and through the school the home. Thus this becomes an agent in assisting the farmers' institutes, the educational excursions, and the young people's clubs to bring about a different ideal with reference to the country school.

But the reader may say, "I don't live in Illinois, and we are not interested in corn or soil investigations in our state." Very well. Put yourself in touch with your own state

FIG. 103. A Traveling Library for District Schools Works on Agriculture and Country Life

College and Experiment Station, and find out what they are doing along the line of the particular crops peculiar to your state. The corn crop is the first in value in the United States, with cotton second, and hay or wheat third. Because of the writer's being on the list of speakers for the farmers' institutes of Illinois, as selected by the State Board of Directors, there are sent him, through Mr. John Hamilton, Farmers' Institute Specialist, Department of Agriculture,

Washington, D.C., bulletins from the Department and from all the principal state experiment stations. There is a great work being done for the farmer. The immediate problem is how to get the average country school-teacher acquainted with some of this work. If there is sufficient demand, I have no doubt that each state College of Agriculture will organize an Agricultural College Extension Department to help the teacher and children in the country schools. Illinois has had such a department for three years, and a most valuable factor it is, too. New York has one, and Ohio begins one with Superintendent A. B. Graham of Springfield as first superintendent. No doubt other states have a like department or will soon have one.

Besides the literature in the way of bulletins, our teachers, children, and farmers in general for the past two years have had the pleasure of hearing the following lectures, and all without any charge:

Corn Growing: Professor P. G. Holden, College of Agriculture, Ames, Iowa.

The Kind of School for Country People: Dean Eugene Davenport, College of Agriculture, Urbana, Illinois.

Birds and Their Benefit to the Farmer: stereopticon lecture by Ned Dearborn, Field Columbian Museum, Chicago, Illinois.

Industrial Education for Country Communities: Superintendent L. D. Harvey, Menomonie, Wisconsin.

School Gardens: stereopticon lecture by Professor H. D. Hemenway, Hartford, Connecticut.

School Gardens: stereopticon lecture by Dick Crosby, Department of Agriculture, Washington, D.C.

The Farm, Home, and School: stereopticon lecture by Assistant County Superintendent C. W. Farr, Chicago, Illinois.

The Newest Things in Agriculture: stereopticon lecture by Principal K. C. Davis, Dunn County School of Agriculture, Menomonie, Wisconsin.

Lest the reader may conclude that ordinary school problems are lost sight of, I give the following list of lectures given not on the same days as above but during the same period of two years :

Literature : Superintendent N. D. Gilbert, Head of Practice School, Northern Illinois Normal, Dekalb.

Eighth Grade Arithmetic : Professor George Howe, Normal University, Normal, Illinois.

Unwritten School Law : President David Felmley, Normal University, Normal, Illinois.

The Requirements of a Modern Teacher : Dr. John W. Cook, President of Northern Illinois Normal School and ex-President of the National Educational Association.

Arithmetic : Professor Frank Hall, Superintendent of Farmers' Institutes, Aurora, Illinois.

The Meaning and Scope of Education : Professor John Keith, Northern Illinois Normal, Dekalb.

Seventh-Grade History : Professor Edward Page, Northern Illinois Normal, Dekalb.

The Relation of Reading to Life : Superintendent W. L. Crane, Marshalltown, Iowa.

No ; the Winnebago County teachers are not devoting their entire time to corn. Many other things are discussed at the monthly teachers' meetings and at the annual institutes, and we still try to teach the fundamentals, as the subjects of two of the above lectures show, namely, reading and arithmetic.

In addition to bulletins from the Experiment Station an excellent text-book on agriculture was put on the teachers' reading course for Winnebago County. This book was read, and in many schools portions of it were discussed by teachers with the pupils. The book is *Agriculture for Beginners*, by Burkett, Stevens, and Hill ; it will be continued on our reading list for 1905–1906. Bailey's *The Nature Study*

Idea and Hemenway's *How to Make a School Garden* have been read by the teachers for the past two years.

In the seventy-three district-school traveling libraries there are books on elementary agriculture, trees, flowers, etc., and country life in general. In this way pupils, teachers, and parents, the school and the home, come in contact with the best of books. The following is a partial list. The numbers refer to the number of volumes in the seventy-three traveling libraries.

17 Burkett, Stevens, and Hill's Agriculture for Beginners.

4 bound volumes of Country Life in America (1903–1904).

6 Ely's A Woman's Hardy Garden.

3 Henry's Feeds and Feeding.

1 Miller's Children's Gardens.

3 Liggett and Hayes's Rural School Agriculture.

3 bound volumes of Review of Reviews (October, 1903–July, 1904).

2 Sever's Elements of Agriculture.

2 Sargent's Corn Plants.

6 bound volumes of The World's Work (St. Louis Exposition number).

4 bound volumes of The World's Work (August, 1903–July, 1904).

20 Bailey's The Nature Study Idea.

1 Blanchan's Nature's Garden.

6 Bailey's Plant Breeding.

20 Hemenway's How to Make a School Garden.

4 Roth's First Book of Forestry.

5 Rogers's Among Green Trees.

2 Thompson's My Winter Garden.

5 bound volumes of The World's Work (November, 1900–April, 1903).

6 Bradish's Stories of Country Life.

3 Bailey's Garden Making.

4 Maynard's Landscape Gardening as Applied to Home Decoration.

7 Shepard's Life on the Farm.

7 Stokes's Ten Common Trees.

3 Smith's Jolly Good Times on the Farm.

6 Weed's Seed-Travellers.

20 Ball's Plant Life.

20 Ball's Animal Life.

4 James's Practical Agriculture.

6 bound volumes of The World's Work (August, 1904–July, 1905).

6 bound volumes of Review of Reviews (August, 1904–July, 1905).

12 bound volumes of Country Life in America (August, 1904–July, 1905).

24 bound volumes of The World's Work, " The Wonderful Northwest" (Lewis and Clark Exposition number, August, 1905).

10 Eggett's The School and the Farm.

1 McFarland's Getting Acquainted with Trees.

1 King's The Soil.

1 Powell's The Country Home.

The above list of books in traveling libraries, with bulletins from experiment stations and the literature sent to children and teachers of our county by the Extension Department of the Illinois College of Agriculture, seems to me to be a departure from " spasmodic theorization on teaching practical agriculture," and an attempt to " pass into the next stage of the argument." We are trying to educate the teachers as well as the pupils. It is one thing to have books and bulletins and another thing to read them. The readings and discussions will be taken care of during the year at the monthly and annual teachers' institutes. I attend every one of these and help along the programmes. Everybody is busy.

In 1904 the sum of ten million dollars was spent in the United States by the Department of Agriculture and the various state agricultural colleges and experiment stations in the interest of higher education for the American farmer. It is money well expended. I spent nearly two months at the Louisiana Purchase Exposition at St. Louis trying to find out something about two things : (1) what is being done in the United States in the way of higher education for the farmer, and (2) what is being done to improve the country school, the place where all the elementary education, so far as schooling goes, is given to ninety-five per cent of the farmers' children. A study of the exhibits of

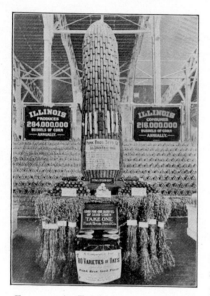

FIG. 104. An Exhibit of Corn and Oats at the St. Louis Exposition

the various experiment stations in the Palace of Education gave but a faint idea of the wonderful development of the science of agriculture, but the Palace of Agriculture revealed some of the results. The country-school exhibits in the various state educational displays were not very extensive, but enough was given to show that an earnest attempt is being made in several states to adjust the country school to the new agriculture and the new country life. Naturally the educational exhibits of great centers of population received most attention from the press, but the fact remains that nearly one half of the school population of the United States is being trained in the one-room country schools, whence will come the leaders of a great to-morrow in all lines of activity. At least ninety per cent of these pupils in the one-room country schools will remain on the farm and engage in a business that is the foundation of the world's prosperity, the importance of which can better be judged from the following statement by Secretary James Wilson in his Report of the Department of Agriculture for 1904:

An occupation that has produced such an unthinkable value as one aggregating nearly $5,000,000,000 within a year may be better measured by some comparisons. All of the gold mines of the entire world have not produced since Columbus discovered America a greater value of gold than the farmers of this country have produced in wealth in two years. This year's (1904) produce is over six times the amount of the capital stock of all national banks; it comes within three fourths of a billion dollars of equaling the value of the manufacturers of 1900, less the cost of materials used; it is twice the sum of our exports and imports for a year; it is two and a half times the gross earnings from the operation of the railways; it is three and a half times the value of all minerals produced in this country, including coal, iron ore, gold, silver, and quarried stone.

The efficiency of the country school must be increased in order to give the proper training to fit boys and girls to handle this immense business.

The state of Illinois, by appropriation of the legislature for the next two years, is expending *annually* the following amounts in the interests of higher agricultural education for the Illinois farmers:

College of Agriculture	$50,000
Live-stock investigations	25,000
Corn, wheat, oats, and clover	15,000
Soil investigations	25,000
Orchard investigations	15,000
Dairy investigations	15,000
Total	$145,000

And this money is well spent, as the results already show.

Mention was made in the chapter on Educational Excursions of the great work of Professor Hopkins in corn breeding at the Illinois Experiment Station. A study of his report and an inspection of the exhibit at St. Louis in the Palace of Agriculture is sufficient reason, I think, to maintain that the organization of a Boys' Experiment Club to grow high-bred corn, educational excursions to the Experiment Station, stereopticon lectures on corn at teachers' and farmers' institutes, and bulletins on corn studied by teachers and pupils, are all "ways and means" leading to the "teaching of practical agriculture." At least, work of this character will help to modify the viewpoint of the farmers with reference to the country school; and this is the most important thing now.

Mr. E. E. Chester, President of the Illinois Corn Growers' Association, reports as follows about the corn growers of Illinois:

The Corn Growers' Association has for its object the very careful and systematic selection of seed corn, and with this in view it has developed a system of measuring the good and bad features of corn, using this rule in their corn schools and in the selection of prize corn in corn shows.

The Corn Breeders' Association has for its object the increase of the yield per acre by breeding only from corn that has given a high yield, thus establishing an inherited potency towards increase in yield.

The rule for the Corn Growers' Association is the score card given in Chapter IX, page 190.

A large part of the twenty-five-thousand-acre farm of the Funk Brothers, in the richest portion of the corn belt of Illinois, is used for breeding plots in the production of high types of corn. Following is a single illustration showing the increase of yield per acre. On the Funk farm the 1902 breeding block record for ear No. 99, planted in a single row, showed a rate of yield of eighty bushels per acre of seventy pounds of corn, while the multiplying record for 1903, planted in five-acre plots, showed that plot No. 10, planted from the progeny of ear No. 99, yielded at the rate of ninety-nine and one-half bushels per acre of the same weight of corn. The boy of the Winnebago County Farmer

Boys' Experiment Club who won first prize in the corn contest of 1903 had a plot of corn which yielded at the rate of one hundred and twenty-five bushels per acre, while several others had plots that approached closely the hundred-bushel mark. These boys will be the farmers of the future and will raise greater crops than their fathers. The financial gains to the country at large will be measured by millions of dollars.

FIG. 105. A Little Literary Man studying Corn

The study of soil has begun in a practical way. In 1903 two experts from the Bureau of Soils, Washington, D.C., and three men from the Illinois Experiment Station spent several weeks in our county making a soil survey, noting every type of soil as small in area as a ten-acre lot. A valuable bulletin, with a map in various colors showing different types of soil, has been published and a copy put into every country school of Winnebago County. This map, with the soil bulletins issued by the Illinois station, supplemented by school garden work, will make a beginning. To be sure, the results will not be as valuable as they would be if the teacher had some knowledge of soil physics, but it is a beginning. If we wait till all things are ideal, nothing will be accomplished. Illinois is spending twenty-five thousand dollars per year in soil investigations. About twelve counties thus far are surveyed, and the expectation is that the good work will continue till every county in the state has a soil survey. This will take eight or ten years more.

I have tried to show the possibilities and practical ways of beginning the study of plant life and soil. The same will hold true with reference to fruit and dairy interests in various sections of the state. Southern Illinois is developing a great fruit industry. The state appropriates fifteen thousand dollars annually for orchard investigations, and a new horticultural building has been erected on the experimental farm at Urbana. Bulletin No. 98, "The Curculio and the Apple," is a valuable one-hundred-page pamphlet fully illustrated with several colored plates. This should find its way into the country-school libraries of southern Illinois, or of any part of the state for that matter.

So for animal life on the farm. Illinois is expending, under the direction of the College of Agriculture and Experiment Station, the sum of forty thousand dollars on dairy and live-stock investigations. New buildings have been erected for these departments on the farm at Urbana. To-day's mail brings all the latest bulletins issued by the Extension Department under direction of Superintendent Fred Rankin. The title of one is, "Testing Milk on the Farm, — Suggestions for Young People's Experimental

Clubs and Instruction in Agriculture in Public Schools."
Circular No. 84 is "Records of Dairy Herds" in northern
Illinois, by Arthur G. Glover, a field man connected with
the Dairy Department of the college. Bulletin No. 101
is "Crops for the Silo," etc. Bulletin No. 102 is on the
"Construction of Silos." If the teacher will but take the
trouble to write a postal card and have her name put on
the mailing list of the state Agricultural College and Experiment Station, she will receive the various publications as
issued. This is the first step towards "ways and means."
With respect to the bulletins of the United States Department of Agriculture, Secretary Wilson says : "The vast
majority of teachers in rural schools throughout the country
are unacquainted with the work and publications of this
department, and do not understand how these publications
might be utilized for instruction in subjects related to
agriculture." This is true with respect to the work and
publications of the various states.

Just how the particular bulletin will be used in the work
of the country school depends upon a great many different
things. This is a fertile field for discussion in the local
teachers' meetings and the annual institute.

The following is an editorial which appeared in the
Prairie Farmer (Chicago), July 13, 1905 :

" FADS " IN THE SCHOOL

Mayor McClellan, of New York City, took an extreme view of the
situation when he condemned industrial education without reservation on the Fourth before the National Educational Association. It
seems morally certain that neither the educator nor the general public
possesses a clear-cut idea of the turning point between what may be
called legitimate manual training and the "fad." Doubtless Mayor

McClellan was as much wrong when he dubbed manual training as a "get-wise-quick" scheme as was Commissioner Draper, of New York, when he branded the "three R's" as the plan of education that "tended to create a peasant class."

There is a middle ground between both extremes. We believe that the hand as well as the intellect should be educated, but it will be unwise to endeavor to develop one at the expense of the other.

The farmer is facing a form of manual training when the educator advises him to institute the study of agriculture and domestic science in the rural school. The *Prairie Farmer* is in full sympathy with both when properly applied, but we hope that the educator will be wise enough to fit the school for either of these innovations rather than attempt to fit them to the school. It is certain that if the educator is not wise and cautious in his progress, his systems for improvement will be kicked out as a "fad." Manual training needs sympathy rather than antagonism.

Many of our city schools have taken up manual training with entire success; others, like New York, have maintained their work only after most serious opposition. Obviously the former course is preferable. It would seem that if there be any explanation, it is simply that sane conservative direction forestalls the faddish criticism.

I quote the entire editorial for the sake of part of one sentence, with brief comment. The editor says, " But we hope that the educator will be wise enough to fit the school for either of these innovations rather than attempt to fit them to the school." So say we all of us. But the country-school educator in his attempt "to fit the school" for agriculture must have assistance from the public press in molding public opinion. The country school belongs to the farmers, and the farmers must move. Somebody must "fit them" to the new agriculture instead of trying "to fit" the new science to the farmer; but if we all wait till the "fit" is perfect in all details, many generations must pass away before the country child is allowed to find any inspiration in his environment.

The public conscience out in the field needs to be aroused
with reference to the country school. One prophet will
arise who will declare on public occasions that the country
school is all that it should be ; that it is the palladium of
our liberties, whatever that may mean ; that all the great
and good men in the history of our country came from the
country districts ; why should you wish to add anything to
a system of training
that produced a Lin-
coln or a Garfield ?
" If elected, I will
—" etc., etc. And
his reward is imme-
diate and abundant.
His halo rivals one
of the rings of Sat-
urn and can be felt
a great distance.

Another prophet
finds nothing good
in the existing order
of things. The coun-
try school costs too

FIG. 106. The Teacher's Corner in an Old-
Fashioned Country Schoolhouse

much ; taxes are too high ; consolidation is a fad ; it would
take all the horses of the state to get the children to the
school ; close the country schools and send the children to
town, etc., etc. He has his reward also, but his halo is
characterized by the diminuendo.

A third man, not gifted with prophecy or with wisdom
perhaps above the ordinary, believes in publicity with reference to the country school, — believes in taking the lid off
and seeing things as they are. He would give credit where

credit is due, censure when censure is deserved ; then sanely and courageously would he set about "to fit" the country school to the new conditions of country life. He holds to this as the sheet anchor, namely : "The farmers can't get something for nothing in the way of better schools. If they would have better schools, they must expend more money in a better way." There is no halo coming.

We need a general campaign for an educational uplift, to increase the usefulness of the country school.

In some states, it is true, an effort is being made "to fit" the country school to the new agriculture. I close this chapter with a part of the address delivered at the dedication of the first consolidated country school in Illinois, in Seward Township, Winnebago County, January 30, 1904. The address was delivered by Eugene Davenport, Dean of the Illinois College of Agriculture and Director of the Experiment Station. His subject was "The Consolidated Country School and the New Agriculture."

The consolidated country school is the only plan proposed that will keep intact the country home, educate the child within the environment in which he is growing up, and make him the intellectual equal of his city cousin. Any plan short of this is not only unjust to the individual, but it is disastrous to country life and to sound ideas touching the productive industries and the life of industrial people. Any plan that secures these educational advantages at the expense of the integrity of the home costs more than it comes to and leaves the family worse than it found it, because it uprooted it out of the country without planting it in the city, and henceforth it partakes of the life of neither. All this is bad enough for the family and the individual, but the damage does not end here.

There is an industrial side to this problem that is worth considering. The "new agriculture" means new conditions not only in the business but as to the people who follow it. The principles underlying agricultural practice are coming to be better known, and farming is growing constantly more difficult. The business is no longer limited to sowing and reaping and selling. Now things must be done with a view not only to economic production but also to sustaining fertility, to the end that the producing power of land shall not grow less, and we one day shall not find ourselves in the condition of modern Russia, — on the verge of starvation and in the throes of poverty, though inhabiting the best lands on earth. Yes, truly, agriculture considered from the modern standards is growing more difficult and will never be less so, for we do not intend in this country to trust the conservation of fertility, which is our natural life, to ignorant and untrained people. Agriculture is no calling now for the grossly incompetent or the hopelessly ignorant. It will never be better suited to the man of low capacity than it is to-day ; on the contrary, it will constantly demand more of him, and public policy will encourage that demand.

Accordingly our people must be educated, — educated not only as individuals and American citizens, but educated as farmers, not a few of them, but a lot of them ; not here and there one that has escaped, as from bondage somewhere, but whole communities of people, men and women together, bent not only upon getting the most out of our lands but also upon getting the most out of country life, by founding and maintaining homes wherein good men of the future may find a place in which to be born.

All this can never be done by the present system of weak and isolated country schools, not even with an agricultural college in connection ; neither can it be done indirectly by making use of the city schools for this purpose. City schools teach city life and the facts and atmosphere that go with city life. If we are to have a healthy country life and a normal country people, we must organize schools to teach country life and the facts of country life.

All people should be educated in two environments and from two standpoints. One is the world at large, — general and broadening ; the other is that in which his life has unfolded and his individuality developed, and in which in all likelihood his future will be cast. The only sufficient reason for changing one's environment at the school age is the certainty that the future calling is to be different from that of the family, and then something of educational value has been lost if the transplanting has taken place too early. It is better not to turn the back upon the things of childhood until we can look out upon the world through the eyes of a man. The consolidated school is the only solution for the educational necessities of country people.

This new agriculture, therefore, demands three new achievements in the way of education. One is a better training in the technique of the profession in order to make the best farmers possible of the individuals who occupy our lands ; the second is that this education shall be secured without disrupting the country home; and the third is that when it is over the product shall be a normal country child, to the end that if he remains in the country he will make a good countryman ; and that if he later goes to the city, he goes intelligently and for a purpose, in which case he will make a good citizen.

I hope now that you will meet these needs by doing the natural thing ; and what I mean is this, — I hope that this will not be a city school transplanted into a cornfield. I hope it will be a country school surrounded by all that will make it attractive, — yes, beautiful, and filled with all that will make it effective.

Why should this not be a city school? Is not a city school as good as a country school? Yes, for city people; but a city school for country people is as far from what is best as would be a country school for city people. It is not that one is better than the other, but it is that they are different. The city school has been long developing, and it is to be assumed that it has come to meet fairly well the conditions and needs of city people. Now the conditions and needs of country people are not less and they are not greater, but they are different. I would, therefore, have in such a school a good portion of agriculture, shop practice, household arts, and of science in general. Why? Because these are specially characteristic of country life. Some of them are also characteristic of city life, some of them are not, — the city people will look after that; but in the meantime it remains for us to put into country schools the things that are characteristic of country life, — those things that give it character, flavor, distinctness, — that make the differences by which we distinguish it as country life.

To summarize this chapter without claiming that the last word has been said, the following outline would seem to point the way to a movement from "spasmodic theorization" to the "next stage of the argument," which is designed to persuade country people to provide ways and means to fit their schools for the teaching of practical agriculture:

1. School garden work.
2. A Farmer Boys' Experiment Club.
3. Educational excursions.
4. Agricultural College extension work.
5. Bulletins and traveling libraries.
6. Coöperation of the country school and farmers' institute.
7. Discussions and illustrated lectures at teachers' institutes.
8. Consolidation of country schools.
9. Hard work and plenty of it.

CHAPTER XI

THE FINANCIAL PHASE OF THE COUNTRY-SCHOOL PROBLEM

There is a country-school problem.

Conditions vary so in different localities that it is extremely difficult to state a general remedy. This much is true, — that the solution of this important educational problem does not consist in abolishing the country school, but rather in studying how to increase the usefulness of this very important institution. The writer yields to no one in his belief in the value of the country school; but sometimes when one urges that the country school keep pace with progress along other lines, the cry of "Iconoclast!" is raised by those who believe "The present is good enough." Yet most of those who advocate the "let-alone policy" with reference to the country school do not so act with reference to improvement of farm machinery and the like. They want the best there is in a material way, and many of them send their children away to the cities for better educational advantages. At the same time, if those who must of necessity remain in the country begin to ask for the union of several weak small schools, and to build up a high school in the county for all, then comes the criticism that the country school is being destroyed. Or if the agitation is started for a better teacher, or to improve the old school building that has stood for forty years, then the cry is raised, "High taxes," "The country school costs too much as it is," "Leave things alone," etc.

It is seemingly hard for some people to realize the change that has come over thousands of country schools in the United States during the last forty years. If you talk with some of these people who always live in the past educationally, they will tell you about the country school of their youth, with its seventy-five or eighty pupils taught by a strong teacher in every sense of the term. I remember

FIG. 107. A Type of Small School in Winnebago County, Illinois

such schools and have no desire whatever to disparage their work or estimate lightly their output. No doubt there are in existence to-day many of the old-time country schools taught by well-educated teachers, men and women of strong characters, and receiving a salary of from seventy-five to one hundred dollars per month for teaching a one-room country school. But my observation leads me to believe that there are more of another kind.

In looking over various state educational reports of the great Middle West, I glean the following data. These figures

are for the year ending June 30, 1904, and show the enrollment for one-room country schools in Wisconsin :

Number of schools with 5 pupils or less 34
    "   "   "   "   more than 5 and less than 11 . . . 236
    "   "   "   "   "   "   10 "   "   " 16 . . . 527
    "   "   "   "   "   "   15 "   "   " 21 . . . 788

This gives a total of 1583 small schools out of a total of
6075 schools with one department.

Indiana reports 44 schools with an attendance of less
than 5 pupils, 243 schools with less than 10, 1085 schools
with less than 15, and 2006 schools with less than 20 pupils.
Missouri has 705 schools with an average attendance of
less than 12, and 2475 schools with an attendance of more
than 12 and less than 20.

Illinois shows the following with reference to enrollment :

Number of schools with less than 5 pupils 76
    "   "   "   "   "   "   10 "   525
    "   "   "   "   "   "   15 "   1150

It may be that each one of the small schools in the above
states is a good one, in charge of a first-class teacher and
doing excellent work,— but, after seven years of experience
with country schools, I doubt it. A small school at its best
is expensive, the per capita cost both on enrollment and on
average daily attendance being very high. But the solution
is not to cheapen instruction for the pupils in the small
school by hiring a poorly prepared teacher willing to work
for a minimum wage. The child in a small country school
is entitled to just as good an educational opportunity as
that enjoyed by the most favored child attending the public
school, whether in the city or country. There is a great
educational as well as financial waste in many hundreds of

the small schools. But economy in money expended does not necessarily mean *less* money expended. The country people can increase the usefulness of the country school by spending more money in a more economical way.

Strange as it may seem, the dollars-and-cents aspect of increasing the usefulness of the country schools is the first, last, and only phase that appeals to many country people. The question with them is, How much higher will the taxes be? not, Will the proposed improvement give us a better school and better returns on money expended, even if a few hundred dollars more are needed annually? The people and school officers need to study the financial phase of present conditions. Let us not cheapen educational opportunity for the country child. In our county I have tried to make a careful analysis of the problem as it is with us. Other counties may differ widely from Winnebago, but at any rate we need more publicity regarding the present situation. When we know the facts in the case we may reason more intelligently. In my annual report for 1905 I presented an array of statistics showing the cost of country schools in all the townships of Winnebago County. It is enough for present purposes to give the figures of two townships, comparing them with those of the city of Rockford. The table on page 230 will show the method pursued.

Now some observations as to the financial phase of the problem may be instructive. While it is true that the conditions of one county do not necessarily establish a general rule, yet they point to some things common to a great many localities, if the reports of state superintendents indicate anything.

There are one hundred and six one-room country schools and nine graded schools in Winnebago County. The

SEWARD TOWNSHIP

This is the township with the first consolidated school

Number of District	Census between 6 and 21	Total Enrollment	Average Daily Attendance	Number of Months of School	Boys over 14 Years	Girls over 14 Years	Total Expenditures	Per Capita on Enrollment	Per Capita on Daily Attendance
87	38	17	11	8	2	—	$387.02	$22.76	$33.36
88	27	17	10	8	—	—	299.63	17.62	29.96
117	28	8	6	8	1	—	292.39	36.55	48.73
89	18	13	6	8	3	—	338.55	26.04	56.42
92	29	15	13	8	4	—	460.34	30.69	35.41
144	39	34	23	8	6	—	390.01	11.44	16.95
121 (Consolidated)	139	134	88	9	19	3	2425.47	18.10	27.56
121 (Consolidated)	139	134	88	9	19	17	3824.05[1]	28.54	43.45

HARLEM TOWNSHIP

Number of District	Census between 6 and 21	Total Enrollment	Average Daily Attendance	Number of Months of School	Boys over 14 Years	Girls over 14 Years	Total Expenditures	Per Capita on Enrollment	Per Capita on Daily Attendance
48	10	5	3	9	—	—	$233.77	$46.75	$77.91
49	8	7	5	7	—	—	351.84	50.26	70.36
50	15	11	8	9	—	—	235.32	21.30	29.41
51	25	16	12	9	—	—	377.60	23.60	31.46
52	20	12	9	9	—	1	274.75	22.89	30.52
53	35	16	11	8	—	—	307.72	19.23	27.97
54	26	11	8	8	1	—	295.00	26.81	35.90
55	34	17	14	9	2	1	426.34	25.08	30.45
56	19	18	14	8	—	—	359.75	19.98	25.69

CITY OF ROCKFORD

Number of District	Census between 6 and 21	Total Enrollment	Average Daily Attendance	Number of Months of School	Boys over 14 Years	Girls over 14 Years	Total Expenditures	Per Capita on Enrollment	Per Capita on Daily Attendance
—	10,109	6773	5427	10	—	—	$122,634.95	$18.10	$22.59

[1] This amount of $3824.05 includes ordinary expenditure and $980 for first payment of bond and interest on new building erected last year; also $418.58 for painting, fencing, and gravel. See summary below.

expenditures for all educational purposes by the one hundred and six one-room country schools show the following with reference to the amount expended annually :

Number of country schools expending less than $300 39
Number of country schools expending more than $300 and less than $400 51
Number of country schools expending more than $400 . . . 16

As I have said before, the small school is expensive, as shown by the high per capita cost on both enrollment and average daily attendance. Again, the small school need not necessarily be a poor one. It is possible to have in each one of the small schools such a teacher as State Superintendent Bayliss describes, — one who is capable of instructing in an annual teachers' institute alongside of training teachers from our state normal schools. This teacher, a woman, has taught "the same country school for the last eight or nine years ; she has seven pupils enrolled this year, and her board of directors pay her sixty dollars per month." Superintendent Bayliss would hardly offer this one instance as indicating a general rule for the kind of teachers in the small country schools of Illinois. I doubt if this is the rule under like conditions in other states. However that may be, such is not the rule in Winnebago County.

If we are going to increase the usefulness of the small country school, we must increase the quality of the instruction. This means better-trained teachers at salaries ranging from sixty to eighty dollars per month. Hence country people can have better schools if they will expend more money on them and expend it in a better way. The money question is fundamental in the solution of the country-school problem.

It does not seem that the country children are getting a "square deal" under existing circumstances. Contrast the annual expenditures of the one-room country schools of Winnebago County with the pay of janitors in the city of Rockford for the same year. The lowest salary, three hundred and twenty dollars, is paid to take care of a four-room building.

SALARIES OF SCHOOL JANITORS, CITY OF ROCKFORD

NAME OF SCHOOL	AMOUNT
Lincoln	$550
Hall	590
Kent	550
Garrison	445
Kishwaukee	590
Nelson	320
Blake	445
Ellis	320
High School	1170
Henry Freeman	590
Brown	550
Montague	445
Church	550
Wight	550
Marsh	320
Haskell	320
Turner	590

As given above, the number of country schools expending less than three hundred dollars per annum is thirty-nine; the number expending more than three hundred dollars but less than four hundred dollars is fifty-one. The reader may say, "The above is not true of my county." I hope it is not; but I venture to say that if an investigation were made into thousands of country schools, and the exact figures given as I have tried to give them, we should find a similar condition of things. It is true that the prophet who says things are all right is the one who will be greeted with loud hosannas by the unthinking crowd, — by the people who don't know the actual situation.

Now the per capita expense in the country schools of Winnebago County ranges from $6.80 to $50.26 on enrollment, while on average daily attendance the cost per child ranges from $11.62 to $77.91. There are forty-eight country schools with a per capita cost of more than $20 on

FIG. 108. Another Typical Country Schoolhouse

enrollment, while eighty-nine country schools have a per capita cost of more than $20 on average daily attendance. There are forty-one country schools with a per capita tax of more than $30 on average daily attendance, and seventeen country schools with a similar tax of more than $40.

Bear in mind the most of these country schools are open only eight months and do not attempt any high-school work. The per capita for the city schools of Rockford for the same year is $18.10 on enrollment (same as Seward Consolidated) and $22.59 for average daily attendance.

Just one item more on school revenue in this connection. Many country people are afraid consolidation will increase the taxes to the extent of possible bankruptcy, and profess to be really alarmed on this score. By the statistics given in my annual report for 1905 (see page 229), sixty-three country schools are paying a higher per capita on enrollment, and fifty-eight of the same schools a higher per capita on average daily attendance, than the consolidated district is paying in Seward Township, *not counting the cost of a new building for the consolidated school;* and the omission of the cost of the new building is legitimate in making this comparison, for in total expenditures not a dollar is counted for new country-school buildings.

Better schools cost more money, to be sure ; but farms have increased in value and farmers have been receiving good prices for their products.

It may be urged that farmers cannot levy enough taxes on their valuation to support better schools. There may be instances of this kind, but this is not the rule. The following shows the tax rate, levy, and valuation of every school district in Winnebago County outside of the city of Rockford for the year ending June 30, 1904. Notice the inequality of taxation by the single-district system, as is the plan in Illinois. The school law of Illinois permits directors to levy two and one-half per cent per annum for general educational purposes and an additional two and one-half per cent for building purposes. Thus a total levy of five per cent is possible, if the necessity exists, on the assessed valuation. The "assessed valuation" as given below is the sum on which taxes are levied, and by the Illinois revenue law is supposed to represent one fifth of the fair cash value of the property of the district.

TABLE OF VALUATION, RATE, AND LEVY FOR YEAR
ENDING JUNE 30, 1904

No. of Dist.	Assessed Valuation	Rate per 100	Amount of Levy	No. of Dist.	Assessed Valuation	Rate per 100	Amount of Levy
1	$29,230	$1.15	$335.68	36	$22,978	$1.12	$257.34
2	15,978	1.94	309.68	37	22,941	1.80	412.92
3	104,411	2.00	1292.44	38	23,755	1.09	258.98
4	27,876	1.02	284.32	39	24,195	1.28	309.68
5	22,892	1.57	359.45	40	34,581	.89	307.67
6	43,308	.71	208.94	41	46,441	.78	362.34
7	15,277	1.85	282.61	42	70,378	.44	309.51
8	28,029	.55	114.11	43	57,625	.62	357.26
9	94,021	1.71	1077.38	44	33,081	1.09	360.39
10	28,149	1.55	436.32	45	65,743	.47	194.62
11	24,918	1.45	361.36	46	48,184	1.39	632.06
12	58,782	.70	281.28	47	48,564	.64	310.94
13	131,864	1.96	1872.00	48	45,856	.79	258.56
14	65,616	.55	299.34	49	41,200	.75	274.02
15	32,211	.96	309.21	50	40,671	.89	281.39
16	20,901	1.97	411.77	51	45,332	.91	412.51
19	18,463	1.95	360.08	52	37,333	.69	231.47
20	19,060	1.35	257.38	53	22,747	1.25	220.41
21	34,962	.88	307.64	54	69,557	.56	294.75
22	25,760	.90	231.85	55	54,582	.66	240.05
23	29,024	1.06	307.69	56	37,141	.90	285.25
24	24,520	1.47	360.50	57	73,859	.56	413.65
25	31,317	1.32	334.36	58	43,325	.60	259.95
26	35,448	.87	247.60	59	14,887	1.35	200.98
27	109,683	2.30	2420.09	61	66,811	.54	221.13
28	40,363	.90	315.15	62	32,996	.78	257.42
29	29,388	.96	260.25	63	63,503	.57	361.91
30	55,064	.65	357.91	64	38,190	.94	359.03
31	37,180	.76	282.59	65	35,046	1.03	294.72
32	32,863	1.48	362.88	66	79,155	.46	360.16
33	20,718	1.50	195.97	67	36,308	.74	268.63
34	15,325	1.69	258.97	68	160,989	1.72	2439.37
35	37,900	.68	169.29	69	129,251	2.08	2463.75

TABLE OF VALUATION, RATE, AND LEVY FOR YEAR
ENDING JUNE 30, 1904 — *continued*

No. of Dist.	Assessed Valuation	Rate per 100	Amount of Levy	No. of Dist.	Assessed Valuation	Rate per 100	Amount of Levy
70	$94,139	$0.11	$87.22	100	$37,694	$1.64	$618.18
71	67,200	.84	486.19	101	55,070	.75	344.71
72	75,065	.45	292.81	102	42,318	.98	414.27
73	33,320	.77	256.56	103	99,370	.40	319.57
74	38,399	1.07	410.89	104	24,781	1.25	309.82
75	30,717	.84	258.01	105	35,463	1.16	411.33
76	31,194	.91	283.89	106	22,786	1.47	335.95
77	26,810	.96	257.38	107	44,918	.52	180.37
78	29,620	1.30	385.09	108	29,195	1.32	385.39
79	34,650	1.19	412.34	109	49,439	1.08	406.71
80	23,815	1.08	257.17	110	17,539	1.17	307.86
81	32,597	.95	309.73	111	31,882	1.12	244.90
82	19,144	1.35	258.47	112	112,544	2.28	1738.14
83	41,596	.52	216.27	113	73,450	.35	117.97
84	35,092	.88	308.78	114	78,012	.33	163.28
85	57,639	.63	320.62	115	37,876	1.09	412.89
86	246,304	2.28	4608.98	116	29,335	1.23	360.82
87	60,619	.76	352.04	117	15,319	1.22	186.63
88	38,861	.80	310.86	118	24,074	.96	231.13
89	30,984	.83	257.15	119	32,572	.87	283.45
92	63,142	.57	275.87	120	24,426	1.05	255.43
93	58,620	.88	467.98	121	156,247	1.83	2425.10
96	44,403	.82	248.73	[Consolidated school]			
97	136,899	1.88	2198.54				
98	65,595	.71	243.96	144	16,279	.90	146.52
99	54,034	.38	161.13	202	27,671	1.56	417.48

The rate for the city of Rockford is $1.95 on a hundred dollars.

From the above table, it will be seen that out of the 106 country schools 63 levy less than one per cent for all educational purposes, while 94 country districts levy less than one and one-half per cent annually. A table of district-school tax and levy of Ogle County (adjoining Winnebago on the south), issued by County Superintendent Neff, has just been received. Out of a total of 162 one-room country schools in that county, 30 of them levied less than three hundred dollars, while 136 country schools levied four hundred dollars or less. The tax rate was less than one per cent for 97 schools, while for 155 districts the rate was less than one and one-half per cent, or $1.50 on a hundred dollars. As far as country-school revenues are concerned, it is fair to presume that Winnebago and Ogle counties, two of the best counties in northern Illinois, are fair representatives of that part of the state. The great bulk of school revenue for Illinois is derived from local taxation. The income from the state tax amounts to only forty-three cents for each person under twenty-one years old in Winnebago County, — not a very great sum.

HIGHEST AND LOWEST SALARY PER MONTH FOR COUNTRY SCHOOL-TEACHERS IN WINNEBAGO COUNTY, 1896–1905

HIGHEST SALARY			LOWEST SALARY		
YEAR	MALE	FEMALE	YEAR	MALE	FEMALE
1896	$42.50	$42.50	1896	$20.00	$18.00
1897	45.00	40.00	1897	23.00	18.00
1898	40.00	40.00	1898	22.00	20.00
1899	40.00	40.00	1899	25.00	20.00
1900	44.00	38.50	1900	25.00	20.00
1901	46.00	40.00	1901	25.00	20.00
1902	41.00	40.00	1902	25.00	20.00
1903	45.00	40.00	1903	25.00	20.00
1904	45.00	40.00	1904	25.00	20.00
1905	45.00	45.00	1905	25.00	22.50

Contrast the annual wage of the country school-teachers of Winnebago County with the annual wage of the janitors of the city of Rockford, as given in the table on page 232.

The number of small country schools in Winnebago County, as given by the first table in this chapter, is as follows:

Number of schools enrolling	5 pupils or less	. . . . . .	2
" " " "	10 " " "	. . . . . .	9
" " " "	15 " " "	. . . . . .	43
" " " "	20 " " "	. . . . . .	69

The real basis of comparison as to cost of small schools and consolidated schools is the average daily attendance. The unit is the day's work. On the basis of average daily attendance the number of small schools, as given above, shows the following changes:

Number of schools with average daily attendance of	5 or less	6
" " " " " " "	10 " "	41
" " " " " " "	15 " "	83
" " " " " " "	20 " "	92

And yet, after all that has been said in this chapter, some people wonder why I favor consolidation of country schools. I insist, however, that the consolidated school remain a *country school* and not become a city school. This is no reflection whatever upon the city school.

I have purposely dwelt upon the financial phase of the country-school problem, for it seems to me to be fundamental. Some would emphasize the poor teaching done in many country schools and the lack of efficient supervision. These are very important things. It is true that there are country school-teachers who do not earn the wages they now receive, but this can be said truthfully of other people. We shall have better teaching for the country child when the country people learn to appreciate what good teaching is. Then they will demand better teachers, and, what is of more importance just now, will be willing to pay a salary sufficiently generous to warrant a person's spending two or three years in preparation at a good normal school.

What is the plain duty of the country people? The country child is entitled to just as good educational advantages as those enjoyed by the most favored city child attending the American public school; and to have better schools for the country child, to increase the usefulness of the country school, and to meet the new conditions of country life, *the country people must not cheapen education, but more money must be expended in a more economical way.*

CHAPTER XII

CONSOLIDATION

In July, 1897, I attended the meeting of the National Educational Association at Milwaukee, Wisconsin, and there secured a copy of the Report of the Committee of Twelve on Country Schools. It was there I first heard

Fig. 109. The First Consolidated School Building in Illinois : Seward Township, Winnebago County

about consolidation, or centralization, of country schools. It seemed to me then to be a proper and sane solution of the country-school problem. I attended a country school when a boy and quit the district school when about sixteen years

FIG. 110. The Buildings abandoned for the Consolidated School

old for the same reason that hundreds of country boys are now quitting it. Now, after seven years' work as County Superintendent of Schools, I see no reason to change the opinion I formed at the Milwaukee meeting in 1897. Since then I have been privileged to visit the central-ized schools of northeastern Ohio. What I saw there but confirmed my conclusions formerly made, and after five years of educational effort we have succeeded in starting a consolidated school in Winnebago County, the first of its kind in Illinois.

I hope the preceding chapters of this book have shown that consolidation is not the only thing to be considered with reference to increasing the usefulness of the country school. It is only one phase of the work in Winnebago County, and a very important one, too, in view of the possi-bilities ; but we have not been content to wait till consoli-dation, in its own good time, should come and settle all our troubles. It will never do that. So in the meantime we organized the outdoor and indoor art movements, — that is, beautifying school grounds and school gardens, decorating the schoolroom, instituting traveling libraries, boys' and girls' clubs, educational excursions, and the like, in the hope of changing the attitude of the country people with refer-ence to the district school and leading them to see that the *consolidated country school*, in the true significance of that term, is the consummation of our efforts.

Consolidation, like other good movements, must pass through ridicule, reproach, and misrepresentation. At first the attitude of a great many country people is that of hostility. Innumerable, and to them insurmountable, objec-tions are given why consolidation " will never work with us." But time and reflection change the opinion of many. The

thing to do is to sow the seed, to inform the country people thoroughly as to the present condition of the country
school in all its relations, to inform them as to what consolidation really is, and then let them think the matter out
for themselves. In this educational campaign, which may
extend over five years, as was the case with us in Seward
Township, it must be the constant aim to reach the farmer
on his own ground. That which will appeal to the school-
man from a pedagogical or some scholastic point of view
ofttimes has no weight with the countryman. If you ask
me how to do this, my reply is, "I don't know." Local
conditions must be studied.

I am not in favor of consolidation if the consolidated
school is to be an imitation of a city school, or if it is
secured by telling the farmers that it will reduce expenses.
A great many of the country schools are too cheap now;
that is the matter with them. So far as I know, consolidation will lessen the per capita cost for education and
remove financial waste in the case of the expensive small
school. It is economy, however, for the country people
to expend more money in a better way, that will insure
greater returns to more children, and it may be that the
total school tax in time will decrease for the township.
Let us not cheapen educational opportunity for the country child.

The chairman of the committee that published the report
given at the Milwaukee meeting was Honorable Henry
Sabin of Iowa. Nearly six years later I received the following letter from him. It is given here because of the sound
judgment and sterling worth of the one who wrote it ; also
because it expresses so well what I had been advocating
before its receipt.

Des Moines, Iowa, February 16, 1903

Superintendent O. J. Kern, Rockford, Illinois

My dear Mr. Kern : I am greatly pleased with the tone of your articles in the *School News.* You seem to have gotten the idea that education is not entirely derived from books. I wish you success in working out your plans for better surroundings for the country schools, for more tasteful rooms, for well-cared-for school grounds, • for school gardens, and for better teachers. It seems to me that in our attempt to consolidate country schools we are giving altogether too much prominence to the intellectual work. We are holding out the idea continually that scholars will make greater advancement in their books if they can be brought to one large building and put through a graded course. This to me is the one great objection to consolidation. If we ever have time to do anything for the country districts, the first step must be to separate them from city schools, to give them a course of instruction especially adapted to country life, and to place in them teachers who are capable of giving that kind of instruction. As far as I know, there is not a normal school

Fig. 111. Transportation in Indiana

in the land making any attempts to supply teachers for country schools. If there is such a school, I should like to know where it is.

In my humble opinion the time has not yet come when we can dispense with the country schools. I can see great advantages in gathering the children from a few small districts into one large school, but with that change there should be the demand for at least three acres of school gardens and the attempt to make country life not only endurable but even attractive.

I cannot find this idea anywhere, except in Winnebago County, and the want of it I look upon as one of the great mistakes that we are making. If in every township there could be two or three schools of that kind, something like experiment stations, where children could

FIG. 112. Transportation in Indiana

be taught the rudiments of agriculture and the attractions of farm life, then there might be one school in the center of the township, something more in the nature of a high school; but even the object of that high school should not be to fit the child for college or the university, but to carry him farther along the same line in which he commences in the lower schools.

I am watching this matter of consolidation with a great deal of interest and, I confess, with some alarm. We never ought, in my opinion, to say or believe that consolidation will lessen the expense. If that is true, then I am against consolidation. What we need is to spend more money on our education, and I am fully in accord with President Eliot in this respect.

Perhaps this does not interest you particularly, and yet I think it will because of what I have seen of your articles in the papers. I am greatly interested in the country-school problem, but I want it to take the right direction. Simply to bring the country children into the city and make the country school an annex of the city school will be productive of evil and will intensify city life and degrade country life.

Yours very truly,

HENRY SABIN

I think all friends of the country school will agree that consolidation will lessen the per capita cost of education for small schools, but I agree with Mr. Sabin that we should not try to advance consolidation on the plea of less total cost to the territory consolidated. Country people as a whole, so far as I know, are not spending enough money in *the right way* for the education of country children. When farmers now in Winnebago County are offering from twenty-five to thirty dollars per month for hired help on the farm, while teachers'

Fig. 113. Going Home from School in Illinois: Temperature
Twelve Degrees below Zero

salaries are as low as they are, it would seem that there is much truth in President Eliot's contention.

Perhaps, however, the reader would like to know what consolidation is and to have a brief history of its progress.

Centralization or consolidation of country schools does not necessarily mean that all the schools of a township must be combined into one school located at the geographical center of the township. There may be a union of three or four district schools, making a two-room graded school, and there may be two of such schools in a single township;

or small schools may be centralized with an established graded school where conditions are favorable. Complete centralization, of course, means the union of all the schools of a township into one graded school, where conditions are favorable for such an arrangement. There may be a consolidation of the schools of two or three townships, just as there are now union districts.

Consolidation of country schools and the transportation of children are now going on in the states of Connecticut, Florida, Indiana, Illinois, Iowa, Kansas, Nebraska, New

Fig. 114. The New Way in Ohio

Hampshire, Maine, Massachusetts, Wisconsin, Vermont, South Dakota, Rhode Island, Pennsylvania, Ohio, North Dakota, New York, New Jersey, and California. These states represent over half of the population of the United States.

To Massachusetts belongs the honor of first developing the district system, and also the leadership in consolidation of school districts. By the act of 1869, any town in Massachusetts was authorized to raise money by taxation to enable the school committee, at its discretion, to provide for the conveyance of pupils to and from the public schools at public cost. Probably the first general statement in print of the results of the law of 1869 was a pamphlet prepared

by Superintendent W. L. Eaton, of Concord, for the Massachusetts public-school exhibit at the World's Columbian
Exposition. Superintendent Eaton says in part :

> At first the authority was used mainly to convey pupils to the high
> school. Within a few years, however, many communities have used
> this authority to increase the educational advantages of the children,
> constantly decreasing in numbers, who live in districts at a distance
> from the center of population. This has been accomplished by
> closing many district schools and transporting, at public expense,
> their pupils to the neighboring district schools or to the village.

The progress of consolidation and the amount of money
paid for transportation in Massachusetts is well set forth
in the table of expenditures for transportation published by
the State Board of Education :

YEAR	AMOUNT EXPENDED	YEAR	AMOUNT EXPENDED
1888–1889	$22,118.38	1895–1896	$91,136.11
1889–1890	24,145.12	1896–1897	105,317.13
1890–1891	30,648.68	1897–1898	123,032.41
1891–1892	38,726.07	1898–1899	127,402.22
1892–1893	50,590.41	1899–1900	141,753.84
1893–1894	63,617.68	1900–1901	151,773.47
1894–1895	76,608.29		

It would seem that the above amounts of public funds
expended for transportation is money well spent, if one
may judge from the following extract from the report of
the Massachusetts Board of Education prepared by State
Agent G. T. Fletcher :

> Whatever advantages a carefully graded system of schools, occu-
> pying a well-ventilated and well-cared-for schoolhouse, taught by a
> body of intelligent and earnest teachers, coöperating to secure the
> best discipline within and without the schoolroom, has over a mixed

country school, *such advantages are shared alike by all the inhabitants of this town. All are alike interested in all real progress in methods of discipline and instruction* and in improved appliances to aid instruction. Superintendents become more efficient. The introduction of new subjects of study and of drawing and music and nature study is made possible and easy. Appliances of all kinds and books of reference can be provided more extensively and at less cost. The history of this movement in Concord conclusively shows that the success of the plan was due to its intrinsic merit, acting upon the minds of an enlightened people desirous of furthering the true educational interests of their children.

From Massachusetts the movement spread through all the rest of New England. An idea of the significance and extent of consolidation in the great Middle West may be obtained from the reports of the State Superintendents of Public Instruction of the states of Indiana, Iowa, Illinois, Wisconsin, Michigan, Kansas, Ohio, and Nebraska.

Indiana reports as follows for the entire state :

Number of schools abandoned	783
Number of wagons used in transporting children . . .	378
Number of children transported	5396
Cost per day of transportation of pupils	$603.00
Cost per wagon per day for transportation of pupils . .	1.60

While at the St. Louis Exposition, in 1904, I tried to make a study of country-school improvement as shown in the various state exhibits in the Palace of Education. I was much impressed with the Indiana exhibit on consolidation. On my return home I wrote to various county superintendents for data and photographs, which I used in my 1904 yearbook for distribution into every country home in my own county. Part of the exhibit of Lagrange County, Indiana, is reproduced here, as follows :

FINANCIAL STATEMENT SHOWING SAVING FROM CONSOLIDA-
TION IN LAGRANGE COUNTY, INDIANA

SCHOOL YEAR 1903–1904

TOWNSHIPS	SCHOOLS ABAN- DONED	ADDITIONAL TEACHERS AT POINTS OF CON- SOLIDATION	SAVING IN NUMBER OF TEACHERS	SAVING IN SALARIES	SAVING IN FUEL AND REPAIRS	GROSS REDUCTION
Bloomfield .	4	0	4	$1,374.40	$300.00	$1,674.40
Clay . . .	4	0	4	1,374.40	320.00	1,694.40
Greenfield .	5	1	4	1,374.40	300.00	1,674.40
Johnson . .	5	1	4	1,374.40	260.00	1,634.40
Lima . . .	3	0	3	1,030.80	240.00	1,270.80
Milford . .	7	2	5	1,718.00	280.00	1,998.00
Springfield .	5	2	3	1,030.80	240.00	1,270.80
Van Buren .	5	1	4	1,374.40	320.00	1,694.40
Totals . .	38	7	31	$10,651.60	$2260.00	$12,911.60

From the above deduct the following additional expenses
incurred in transportation of four hundred and twenty-eight
pupils in twenty-nine hacks to fourteen different schools.
The difference, $6734.74, is the net saving by consolidation.

TOWNSHIPS	NUMBER OF HACKS	NUMBER OF PUPILS CONVEYED	COST OF ALL TRANSPORTA- TION FOR YEAR	NET GAINS
Bloomfield	4	73	$1017.00	$657.40
Clay	4	46	712.08	982.32
Greenfield	3	35	646.00	1028.40
Johnson	3	51	517.50	1116.90
Lima	2	30	583.00	687.80
Milford	6	117	1261.48	736.52
Springfield	4	43	873.00	397.80
Van Buren	3	33	566.80	1127.60
Totals	29	428	$6176.86	$6734.74

From this it appears that the transportation of four hundred and twenty-eight children made possible the closing of thirty-eight schools, a reduction of twenty-four teachers, and a net saving of $6734.74.

EDUCATIONAL STATEMENT

The following important facts are given with reference to service rendered in transportation :

1. The drivers carry watches and consult them while on the route.
2. Each driver keeps the time of the consolidated school, generally standard.
3. The rate of speed while on the route averages five miles per hour for the year.
4. The time of arrival varies from ten to fifteen minutes prior to the opening of the schools.
5. The more remote pupils ride about five miles, and sixty per cent ride three miles or less.
6. Children are kept comfortable by stoves, patent heaters, blankets, and soapstones.
7. The greatest advantage to the service is township ownership of hacks and the improvement of roads.
8. The drivers exercise due responsibility in promptly and safely conveying the children to school and returning them to their homes ; they also, by contract, prohibit questionable language, undue familiarity, and boisterous conduct in or about the hacks.
9. Eighty-five per cent of the patrons have reported the consolidated school as their preference in comparison with the "old way."
10. Decreased enumerations in eight of our eleven townships gave the system its initiative, and the better instruction and educational encouragement to the great majority of the conveyed pupils have strengthened the services of the schools and enhanced the local educational spirit.

In October, 1900, in company with State Superintendent Alfred Bayliss and Mr. John Black, Chairman of the Committee on Education of the Winnebago County Board

of Supervisors, I visited the centralized schools in Lake,
Ashtabula, Trumbull, and Geauga counties, in northeastern Ohio. In December of that same year I published
an illustrated report of that visit. This report has been
reprinted in part or entire by various school journals and
newspapers of the United States and Canada, and was also
reproduced entire, with illustrations, in the report of the
United States Commissioner of Education.

A small part of the account of our visit is here given.

*   *   *

. . . Madison Township, Lake County, presents an excellent illustration of what may be called partial centralization,
that is, a grouping of two, three, or four schools into one
without attempting to bring all the schools to the geographical center of the township. The latter method would not

FIG. 115. A Centralized Country-School Building, Green Township,
Trumbull County, Ohio

be practicable because of the shape of Madison Township.
It is one of the townships along the shore of Lake Erie
and is nine miles long by five miles wide. Most of the

townships of the Western Reserve are five miles square, while in other portions of the state, where centralization is successful, they are even larger than six miles square.

Centralization in Madison Township has been in successful operation since 1896. We visited the schools at Unionville

FIG. 116. School Building at Kingsville, Ohio, where Centralization of Schools began in 1892

and North Madison, and Superintendent J. R. Adams, principal of the Unionville school and superintendent of Madison Township during the months of December, 1901, and January, 1902, sent me the following facts and illustrations:

1. They have now only three one-teacher schools in the township.

2. Since centralizing the per cent of enrollment of children of school age, between six and twenty-one, has increased from sixty per cent in 1894 to eighty-six per cent in 1901.

3. For the year ending June, 1901, twenty pupils were taking high-school studies. (This is more than can be said of some Illinois townships.)

4. The total cost for the township for educational expenses in 1896 was $7555; for 1901, $7243.

5. The cost of transportation in 1896 was $332; for 1901, $1618.

6. The incidental expenses for the township in 1896 were $2509; for 1901, $902.

7. The total enrollment in 1896 for the township was three hundred and ninety ; for 1901, four hundred and fourteen.

8. The per capita cost for education for the township, based on total enrollment for the year, was $19.36 for 1896, and $17.50 for 1901.

. . . We next visited Kingsville in Ashtabula County, four hundred and one miles east of Chicago. This was our farthest point east. Kingsville is a small village with a township high school. To the school are brought all the children of the township, with the exception of two districts. Four wagons are used at a cost of twenty, twenty-four, twenty-five, and twenty-eight dollars per month respectively, for a month of twenty days. The school year is nine months. Five teachers are employed in the building. The testimony of the principal of the school, the town clerk, and Mr. Kinneer, of the Board of Education, was that there was an actual saving in the total cost to the township under the new plan ; and while money was expended for transportation of pupils, it was more than saved in the smaller number of schools operated; and as to the increased efficiency of the new centralized school over the scattered schools, that was beyond a question of doubt.

It was here that the Ohio plan of centralization had its origin in 1892. The erection of a new building in one of the districts of Kingsville Township brought up the question whether or not it would be better to abandon the school in that district and take the children to the village school at the general expense. In this first case of consolidation in Ohio the schools were centralized at the village school, a village situated about a mile and a half from the railroad. The results, educationally, in the small districts were far from satisfactory. In order to consolidate and transport children at public expense special legislation was necessary, and so the Ohio legislature passed the following bill, April 17, 1894 :

SECTION 1. Be it enacted by the General Assembly of Ohio that any Board of Education in any township which by the census of 1890 had a population not less than seventeen hundred and ten or more than seventeen hundred and fifteen; of any county which by the same census had not less than forty-three thousand six hundred and fifty, nor more than forty-three thousand six hundred and sixty inhabitants, may, at their discretion, appropriate funds derived from the school tax levy of said township for the conveyance of pupils in subdistricts from their homes to the high-school building of such township; provided such appropriation for any subdistrict shall not exceed the amount necessary, in the judgment of the board, for the maintenance of a teacher in such subdistrict for the same period of time.

The Kingsville plan proved such a success that on April 27, 1896, the Ohio legislature passed a bill for the relief of the counties of Stark, Ashtabula, and Portage, which provided that the Board of Education of any township of those counties may,

when in its opinion it will be for the best interest of the pupils in any subdistrict, suspend the school in such subdistrict and provide for the conveyance of said pupils to such other district or districts as may be convenient for them ; the cost of such conveyance to be paid out of the contingent fund of said district; provided the board of any special school district in any county mentioned above may provide for the conveyance of pupils out of the contingent funds, the same as townships aforesaid.

Since then a general law has been enacted, permitting the people of any township at the annual town election to vote yes or no on the proposition to centralize the schools of that township, — that is, to abandon the small districts and transport the children at public expense to the central school. Such, in brief, is the history of the legislation.

. . . But we wished to find centralized schools in a purely country township, where there was no village or village

FIG. 117. A Map of Ohio showing Centralized Schools, 1905

school, — a place where country life was being preserved. We went thirty-five miles south of Ashtabula and visited Gustavus and Green townships in Trumbull County. The first place visited was Gustavus. This township is exactly five miles square, as are all the townships of the Western Reserve, with the exception of those along the shore of Lake Erie. In Gustavus Township the townhall is situated exactly in the center of the township, as is the case in Green Township. Here was a church, the post office, a country store, and a few houses.

I had a picture of the centralized school of Gustavus Township and was anxious to see the real thing. We saw it, and all was as represented. The school building is located in the center of the township. The school has been in operation two years. It is a four-room school, having a principal and three assistants. All the children of the township are brought to this central school, and nine wagons are employed in the transportation.

The wagons are provided with curtains, lap robes, soapstones, etc., for severe weather. The Board of Education exercises as much care in the selection of drivers as of teachers. The contract for each route is let out to the lowest responsible bidder, who is under bond to fulfill his obligations. The drivers are required to have the children on the school grounds at 8.45 A.M., which does away with tardiness, and to leave for home at 3.45 P.M. The wagons call at every farmhouse where there are school children, the children stepping into them at the roadside and being set down upon the school grounds. There is no tramping through snow and mud, and the attendance is much increased and far more regular. With the children under the control of responsible drivers, there is no opportunity for vicious conversation or the terrorizing of the little ones by some bully as they trudge homeward through the snow and mud from the district school.

. . . While we were at the Gustavus school the principal advised us to drive five miles to the west into Green Township, where the people had centralized and put up a fine new brick building at a cost of over six thousand dollars. The people of Green Township had watched the

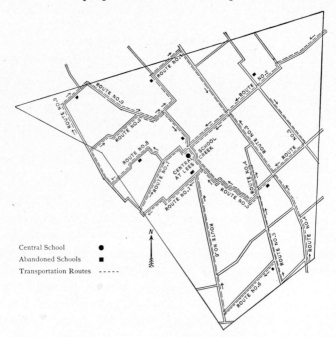

Fig. 118. A Map of Wayne Township, Clinton County, Ohio, 1905

school in Gustavus Township for two years, and believed so thoroughly in the new plan that at the last April election they voted to centralize and bond the township for a long term to erect a new building. The vote was overwhelmingly in favor of the new school. We drove west to the center of Green Township, which is five miles square. This

township is eleven miles from one railroad and six miles
from another; so it is distinctively rural. To be sure,
there is the townhall, a post office, a church or two, a
country store, and a few dwellings. That is New England

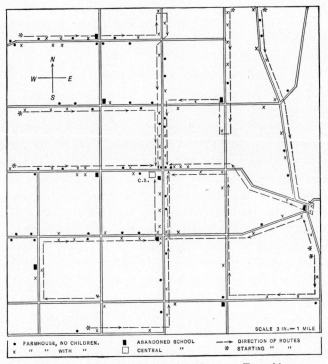

Fig. 119. Transportation Routes, Gustavus Township,
Trumbull County, Ohio

brought to the Western Reserve. We all were enthusiastic
over this building for country children. We never saw the
like before in the country, where miserable box-car, one-
room structures are the general rule. And the possibilities
of such a school — who can measure them?

This building stands in the center of the township in a community distinctively country. It was built in 1900 at a cost of six thousand dollars. There are six schoolrooms with two additional, one of which may serve as a library room and the other as an office and reception room. There is a basement under the entire building, part of which may be utilized for laboratory and gymnasium. The building is heated by steam.

They began this school in September last. The enrollment is one hundred and eighty against one hundred and fifty of last year in the scattered schools. Four teachers are employed. All the children of the township are brought to the school, and eight wagons are employed in the transportation. The campus has about three acres. Shade trees, school decoration, library, etc., will come. How easily that school can be made the social, literary, and musical center of the entire township! What an inspiration it must be to a corps of teachers to work in such a community as that!

In the primary grade were all the little ones of the entire township in a beautiful room, while in the high-school room were many large farmer boys getting an education they could not otherwise obtain. On the playground all the big boys of the township play baseball. Think what it is to get all the boys of a township — country boys, I mean — on one playground. There will grow up a unity, and each boy, having studied and played with other boys of the entire township, will be stronger for it. When the boys and girls of Green Township compete with those of Gustavus Township in football, baseball, or in literary contests, on athletic ground or in townhall, each team will have the backing of an enthusiastic township. In a great many districts there are hardly enough boys to play "two-cornered cat." Can you wonder that children get tired of district school after a certain age? I am not sure that I have grasped the full significance of what we saw here, but if that is good for Ohio boys, why not the same for Illinois?

At the Green Township central school, where the new six-thousand-dollar brick building has been erected, I asked a high-school class how the roads were when they were bad. A young lady said they were " real bad," while a young man

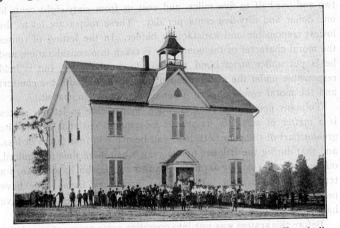

FIG. 120. The Centralized School at Gustavus Township, Trumbull County, Ohio

said they sometimes found it necessary to put four horses to the wagon. The principal said that the people were preparing to improve the main roads over which the wagons ran. Thus better schools bring better roads.

The day spent at Gustavus and Green township schools was by far the best one in the Western Reserve. As far as educational matters are concerned, the townships were far ahead of anything I had ever seen.

*   *   *

Mr. C. G. Williams, member of the Board of Education, Gustavus Township, Trumbull County, Ohio, in the September (1902) number of the *Ohio Teacher* has the following with reference to transportation :

Nine covered wagons, built expressly for this purpose, with a view to comfort and health of occupants and owned by the route contractors, call at the home of every pupil in the morning and return every pupil to his home after school. Our routes vary in length from two and one-half to five miles, and cost us from sixty-eight cents to one dollar and fifty-five cents per day. These routes are let to the lowest responsible and satisfactory bidder. In the letting of routes the moral character of the contractor is taken into consideration, and he is put under strict bond not only to do the work, but is held responsible under the superintendent of schools for both the comfort and the moral condition and order in his wagon in transit.

To many people the price at which we are able to let our routes is a matter of surprise. It should be remembered that during the greater part of the year both trips can be made in four hours or less, and that during the balance of the year, when more time is required, our contractors (usually farmers with few acres, who have to keep a team of horses anyhow) are not busy upon their farms. We have never yet had any trouble in letting our routes, and of late we have had enough routes to supply all who would like them.

Before this system was put into operation some prospective patrons worried a little as to what might happen should a child be taken ill at school, in some instances a long way from home. Our Board of Education has thought best to provide against that trouble by contracting with a man to take any pupil immediately to his home that the superintendent thinks should for any reason go home. We have not as yet had to expend over three dollars any year for this purpose. It surely is a comfort to a parent to know that his child will be brought home if occasion demands it.

Speaking of opposition, it should be recorded that when the proposition came before our voters for indorsement four years ago at our annual spring election, it was defeated upon a tie vote. Three weeks thereafter the same or a very similar proposition was submitted to our

voters, and, with practically every vote in our township cast, centralization was carried by a majority of only seventeen votes. It will be
seen that public sentiment was pretty evenly divided and that the new
system and the new school would have very many critics.

Illinois has been behind other states in the matter of
consolidation. It may not be too much to claim that our
visit to Ohio and the publication of the account of our

FIG. 121. The Centralized School at Lee's Creek, Wayne Township,
Clinton County, Ohio

investigations are the beginning of the renaissance of consolidation for the Prairie State. The first consolidated
country school in Illinois was dedicated in Seward Township,
Winnebago County, January 30, 1904. The second school
building as the result of consolidation is being erected in
Johnson County in southern Illinois, where William M.
Grissom, Jr., of Vienna, is county superintendent. The
expectation was to be ready for school November, 1905.
County Superintendent Dean, of Geneva, Kane County,
northern Illinois, reports that in the newly consolidated

district in that county the voters, by a vote of seventy-one for and twenty-nine against, voted to bond the district for six thousand dollars to erect a new building. The one in Johnson County costs five thousand dollars, while the one in Winnebago County cost six thousand dollars, with an additional expenditure of one thousand dollars for a site of 3.6 acres of fine land.

The first agitation for a consolidated school in Winnebago County was in Seward Township on February 22, 1899. At that time the writer gave an address in favor of con-

FIG. 122. An Abandoned Two-Story Brick Schoolhouse in Wayne Township, Clinton County, Ohio

solidation. The address was received with but little favor by the majority of the people. The new six-thousand-dollar building for the consolidated district was dedicated at the same place on January 30, 1904. This was one tangible result of a five years' educational campaign.

The Seward consolidation is a beginning in a small way. The beginning in Ohio was at Kingsville in 1892, by taking children from one subdistrict to the Kingsville school. No new building had to be erected. Even for this they had to get special legislation to allow the transportation, and so careful were they that the legislature said this could be done only in "any township which by the census of 1890 had a population not less than seventeen hundred and ten or more than seventeen hundred and fifteen." Seemingly the people could not be trusted, as some think they cannot be now in Illinois when it comes to the matter of spending their own money to provide better school facilities for country children.

The consolidated district in Seward Township, Winnebago County, Illinois, is made up of old districts 90, 91, and 93. In area it is exactly one third of the township, which is six miles square. The new consolidated district contains twelve sections of land, or 7680 acres. The assessed valuation of districts, as made by assessment in 1902, is as follows :

District 90	$58,399
District 91	52,790
District 93	35,126
Total	$146,315

The assessed value by the Illinois revenue law represents one fifth of the fair cash value. By that the value of the consolidated district is over seven hundred thousand dollars. Taxes are levied on assessed valuation, and since some of the land could not be bought for one hundred and fifty dollars per acre, it is not an exaggeration to say that the value of this consolidated district is nearly, if not quite, a round million of dollars.

The assessed valuation of this consolidated district in 1904 was $156,243, with a tax rate of $1.83 on the $100 to pay all expenses of the school and first payment of bonds and interest. The Illinois school law permits a total levy of five dollars on every hundred dollars of assessed valuation for this purpose. Thus the tax rate for this new school is exactly one third of what the law allows. *Country people may have better country schools by spending more money in a better way.*

The consolidated school has a school year one month longer, employs four teachers, and does two years' high-school work. But, as was said before, suppose the total cost is more, better returns will come for money expended.

The building has four rooms and a basement. In this basement, which extends under the entire structure, there are two large rooms which may, in the future, be utilized for a workshop and a manual training room.

All the walls have been decorated in color, and a friend from Boston, Massachusetts, very generously donated pictures and casts, so that art education is beginning for these country children. His gifts were the following:

Bust of Lincoln.
" Cherubs Singing "—two pieces.
" Morning."
" Night."
" Boys Playing Trumpets."
" Boys Playing Drums."
" Triumph of Alexander "— three pieces.

Alma Tadema's " Reading from Homer."
Bouguereau's " Homer and his Guide."
Breton's " Song of the Lark."
Corot's " Lake."
Douglas's " Ancient Britons."
Farquharson's " Over Snow Fields Waste and Pathless."
Hock's " Fishing Boats."
Homer's " Fog Warning."
Hovenden's " Breaking Home Ties."

Landseer's " Distinguished Member of the Humane Society."
Le Rolle's " By the Riverside."
Van Marcke's " Water Gate."
Millet's " Gleaners."
Murillo's " St. John the Baptist."
Plockhorst's " Guardian Angel."
Pyle's " Washington in his Garden at Mt. Vernon."
Raphael's " Sistine Madonna."
Raphael's " Madonna of the Chair."
Riecke's " Sunset Glow."
Ruysdael's " Windmill."
Turner's " Fighting Téméraire."
Volkman's " Waving Wheatfield."
Watts's " Sir Galahad."
Waterlow's " Nursery."
Portrait of Longfellow.
Arch of Titus.
Capitol at Washington, D.C.

By centralization all the children of the township have the same chance for those higher educational advantages which, under the present plan, only five or ten per cent are able to get by leaving home and going to the city. With a central graded school and a high-school course the children can be at home evenings under the care of their parents. The people of the country districts are entitled to receive the fullest benefits for money expended. Better means of education, better training, stronger characters, — the possibility of all these must appeal to every parent and to every public-spirited citizen of any community. The course of study may be so enriched that all the farmer boys may be taught some of the fundamental principles of agriculture, horticulture, etc., without sending them away to a university to learn what may be learned at home. Such a township high school, with good teachers, ought to be able to

FIG. 123. Abandoned One-Room School-house in Wayne Township, Clinton County, Ohio

teach the boys and girls something about the formation, composition, and care of the soil, rotation of crops, constituents of plants, and fruit growing. In compliance with the request of the State Farmers' Institute of Illinois, an elementary course in agriculture has been added to the state course of study for the common schools of Illinois. The farmers of Illinois are doing well in having a College of Agriculture at the state university at Urbana. Let the influence of that work extend to every township in the way of an enriched course of study in the township union graded school, and one result will be that more boys and girls will go to the College of Agriculture. Reference was made in Chapter XI to the number of boys and girls over fourteen years old in one county. Out of a school population (between six and twenty-one) of 2714, for 106 one-room country schools there were only 167 boys over fourteen and 121 girls of the same age enrolled for the year ending June 30, 1905.

FIG. 124. An Old Schoolhouse at Snow Hill, Hancock County, Georgia

Where are all the big boys and girls that used to be in all the country schools, as some of us used to know them? During the same year there were enrolled in the six village high schools and the city high school of Rockford 86 girls and 68 boys, a total of 154 country pupils paying tuition for high-school privileges.

The following table shows the amount of high-school tuition the country people of Winnebago County have paid for ten years to have a part of the children educated away from home.

These statistics are taken from the township treasurer's books :

Year	Rockford	Peca-tonica	Durand	Rock-ton	Winne-bago	Roscoe	Cherry Valley
1895	$1,523.21	$300.25	$229.93	$18.00	$204.00	$33.10	$21.00
1896	1,561.34	201.82	102.83	—	121.25	163.65	13.50
1897	1,500.00	313.89	88.84	58.00	424.61	137.06	36.00
1898	1,871.80	258.54	131.89	54.00	249.57	84.20	78.00
1899	1,655.61	364.68	112.02		279.93	135.20	27.00
1900	2,009.27	346.00	232.01	54.40	245.62	116.30	—
1901	2,429.01	346.00	216.50	33.20	185.00	62.10	61.00
1902	2,633.88	346.00	238.25	82.80	215.20	108.50	18.00
1903	3,902.72	340.00	147.50	56.60	115.16	63.00	—
1904	2,742.50	444.55	171.50	68.00	64.75	129.20	36.00
Totals	$21,829.34	$3,261.73	$1,671.27	$425.00	$2,105.09	$1,032.41	$291.00

Grand total for ten years $30,615.84

The above is not what the county superintendent says or thinks, but what treasurers' books show. This $30,615.84 will build four such buildings as the Seward Consolidated School building, with 3.6 acres for a site for each building, and enough will be left over to equip thirteen school wagons at a cost of $200 each. The Seward building cost $6000 and the site $1000. This makes a total of $7000. Multiply $7000 by 4, and the result is $28,000 ; subtract this amount from $30,615.84 — the amount of tuition the country people have paid for the last ten years, — and the remainder is $2615.84. This will equip thirteen wagons at a cost of $200 each. Are the Seward people wise in their day and generation ?

Or if each family provides its own transportation without public expense, as they do in Seward Township, this $2615.84

would give $653.96 as a fund for a small manual training equipment for each of the four buildings. It has been shown that in Seward Township nineteen boys and seventeen girls, each over fourteen years of age, a total of

Fig. 125. A New Schoolhouse at Snow Hill, Hancock County, Georgia

thirty-six large pupils, were enrolled in the consolidated school last year. There were twenty-seven nonresident pupils enrolled in that school, and their tuition amounted to $265.25, almost enough to meet the first annual interest of $280 on the bonded indebtedness of $7000 at four per cent.

It is not enough to consolidate. After that is done the school must be developed along the line of country interests. I do not want the evils of a graded system for the country consolidated school. If directed as it should be, the consolidated country school should offer the following advantages over the average country school :

1. There will result the inspiration and interest that always come from numbers. A school of eight or ten

pupils is not calculated to stimulate a boy or girl to do the best work. With only one in a class there is not that competition and rivalry which call forth all the powers of the child, — the preparation for the real struggle of life.

2. Stronger classes will thus be formed, giving the teacher more time for the recitation and for the necessary instruction.

3. There will be better trained teachers for the country children, and these teachers will command and receive better salaries.

4. There will result greater economy in school buildings and equipment. It will cost less to keep one central building than several scattered schoolhouses, the first cost of the one central building not being as great as that of eight

FIG. 126. An Old Academy at Snow Hill, Hancock County, Georgia

or ten scattered buildings. Besides, the children will have the influence of a modern, sanitary, well-ventilated, well-lighted, and well-heated building. The surroundings have perhaps quite as much to do in the education of the child as the subject-matter of the text-books.

5. The school year for the country child will be lengthened. There will be high-school privileges. The attendance will be more regular. More pupils will use the money expended for education, and thus the per capita cost will be reduced.

6. Such a school will afford time and opportunity for systematic instruction in the elementary principles of agriculture throughout the grades. With trained teachers working under the direction of the College of Agriculture, such a school will be able to meet the demand for instruction in things relating to the farm. Here can be taught something with reference to feeding standards and selection of stock, fruit growing and constituents of plants, rotation of crops, and composition and care of the soil. The consolidated school along these lines may become an experiment station, working under the direction of the expert investigators of the College of Agriculture.

7. Consolidation will help to bring better roads. As it now is with us, the farmers always get their milk to a central creamery, if it takes four horses. Is not a child deserving of as much consideration as a can of milk? It is not at all difficult to hear of objections to consolidation. These may be summarized as follows : (1) It will cost too much ; (2) the roads are not suitable ; (3) the roads and weather are often unfit to take out a team ; (4) it is better for the children to walk ; (5) it compels a cold lunch at school; (6) it will reduce the value of farm lands in the neighborhood of abandoned schoolhouses ; (7) there is sentiment against removing "the old schoolhouse "; (8) it will throw many teachers out of employment ; (9) it takes children too far from home.

Superintendent R. P. Clark, of Ashtabula, Ohio, at the Special State Conference in the interests of country schools, held by the University of Illinois at Urbana, June 26–30, 1905, discussed very fully the subject of transportation as it is in Ohio. They do not have hard roads there. A part of Superintendent Clark's paper is here given:

There is no phase of the question of consolidation of country schools that is the subject of so much controversy and criticism as transportation. Transportation is the rock on which the consolidation

FIG. 127. New Schoolhouse at Snow Hill, Hancock County, Georgia

idea is most often wrecked. It is the one phase of the consolidation question that the average farmer in the country districts thinks he fully understands. Approach him on the subject of consolidation and he immediately turns the conversation along the line of transportation. Show him the benefits in general to be derived from consolidation and he gives evidence by his reply that he only considers the fact that he lives five or four or three or two miles from the center of the township. Paint him a picture of a township as a social and intellectual unit and he will only look at it from a distance of five or four or three or two miles. Call his attention to the broader, humanitarian side of consolidation and his poor neighbor cannot be brought into nearer focus than five or four or three or two miles.

It never occurs to the average farmer that he is very likely preju-
diced beyond a reasonable degree. His life, perhaps, has been very circumscribed and his horizon narrow. He is conservative to a remark-
able extent. When any question is brought to his attention he at once, as does any other man, seizes upon that phase of it that is or seems most tangible and appeals most strongly to his interest. Therefore the average farmer sees in the question of consolidation of schools only one thing worthy of consideration, namely, transportation. Meet this question and almost invariably the battle is won. Make other considerations of greater importance, as indeed they are, and the heaviest gun of the opposition is effectively spiked. . . .

In the first place, it is necessary to say that in these discussions of consolidation of schools the townships considered are all five miles square, and while they present a variety of surface and soil, they are of the same size and are very similar in social conditions. They are in that part of Ohio known as the Connecticut Western Reserve, and the people are for the most part descendants of that sturdy New England and Pennsylvania stock that came into Ohio in the early part of the nineteenth century. The roads during a portion of the year are as bad as roads can be and still be roads.

Road improvement has just reached Ohio and there is good pros-
pect of better things, but in no township considered in reference to consolidation has the slightest attempt been made to improve the roads along the lines of modern methods. It is safe to say that the townships of northeastern Ohio can, in general, duplicate all the objec-
tionable features standing in the way of consolidation found in this (Illinois) section of the country. . . .

In a former chapter reference was made to a report of an important committee appointed by the National Educational Association at Boston, Massachusetts, July 9, 1903. This committee made a report in July, 1905. The report in pamphlet form is entitled " Report of the Committee on Industrial Education in Schools for Country Communities."

In this report W. M. Hays, Assistant Secretary of Agriculture, a member of the committee, has given an outline of a course of study for the consolidated country school, the agricultural high school, and the agricultural college, articulated in a unified scheme. Professor Hays did this upon the request of the committee.

This is certainly a move in the right direction. It is time the gap between the country school and the college of

Fig. 128. Old Schoolhouse, No. 2, at Williamsburg, North Carolina

agriculture was filled. The agricultural high schools of Minnesota and Wisconsin do this in an ideal way; that is to say, the county agricultural high school stands in the same relation to the farm that the city high school does to the life in the city.

The consolidated country school with a two years' high-school course goes a long way towards filling up this gap.

I believe in the country high school with a course of study suited to the future life of the great majority of the boys and girls who attend such a school.

Space does not allow me to give the course for the first eight grades as outlined by Professor Hays, nor that of the agricultural high school or college. Only the suggested course for two years of work in the high-school department of the consolidated country school is here given. In time this corresponds to the first two years of a first-class city high school doing four years' work.

FIRST-YEAR HIGH-SCHOOL COURSE IN CONSOLIDATED COUNTRY SCHOOL

First Half Year

Agricultural botany	4
Elementary algebra	5
English	4
Drawing (farms and buildings)	2
Rhetoricals	1
Country engineering (boys)	3
Sewing (girls)	2
Agriculture (girls)	1

Second Half Year

Agricultural botany	4
Elementary algebra	5
English	4
Farm accounts	4
Rhetoricals	1
Fences and farm conveniences (boys)	2
Cooking (girls)	2

SECOND-YEAR HIGH-SCHOOL COURSE IN CONSOLIDATED COUNTRY SCHOOL

First Half Year

Plane geometry	5
Physiology (foods and feeds)	4
Civics	4
General history	5
Rhetoricals	1
Judging stocks and seeds (boys)	1
Carpentry	$2\frac{1}{2}$
Sewing (girls)	2

Second Half Year

Plane geometry	5
English	4
Agricultural mathematics	4
General history	5
Rhetoricals	1
Judging stocks and seeds (boys)	1
Carpentry	$2\frac{1}{2}$
Sewing (girls)	2

It is the country child's right to have just as good an educational opportunity as that enjoyed by the most favored city child attending the public school. If the average country school affords this opportunity both for elementary instruction and high-school privileges, then the consolidated country school has not much claim. But if the average

FIG. 129. Old Schoolhouse, No. 3, at Williamsburg, North Carolina

country school does not afford this opportunity, then the consolidated country school is worthy of earnest consideration.

Let us enrich and enlarge life for the country child.

Reference elsewhere has been made to a bulletin on the "Centralized Schools in Ohio," by Mr. A. B. Graham, Superintendent of Agricultural College Extension Work, State University, Columbus. Some of the illustrations in this chapter are from that bulletin, namely, map of Ohio showing extent of centralization, map of Wayne Township, the

$17,500 building in Wayne Township, two of the abandoned buildings in Wayne Township, and the centralized building in Gustavus Township. These speak for themselves with reference to this forward movement for the country child.

The following, from Mr. Graham's bulletin, will convey to the reader a correct idea of the types of centralized schools in Ohio :

1. In a few townships the subdistrict schools have been abandoned and the pupils conveyed to a village school centrally located. Such schools are found at Kingsville, Ashtabula County, and at Windham, Portage County. In Windham Township the Board of Education contracts with the village board of Windham for tuition. To Woodstock, Champaign County, sixty pupils from four schools in Rush

FIG. 130. The New Building for Nos. 2 and 3 Consolidated, Williamsburg, North Carolina

Township are transported in three comfortable wagons at a cost of one hundred dollars per month. The pupils from seven out of eight subdistricts from Fulton Township, Fulton County, are transported to the village school at Swanton.

2. In most completely centralized townships the central building, grounds, wagons, etc., belong to the township. In some places the wagons belong to the drivers or contractors. Such schools are to be found in Wayne Township, Clinton County; Mad River Township,

FIG. 131. The Interior of Schoolhouse, District 99, Winnebago County, Illinois

Champaign County; Copley Township, Summit County, and in about twenty others in northeastern Ohio (see map, Fig. 117).

3. At Selma, Clark County, and at Bidwell, Gallia County, are special districts created to include territory sufficiently extensive to require the transportation of pupils to school. They are known as the Selma Special and the Porter-Bidwell Special, and are the only school districts in our state organized to comply with section 3934.

4. The fourth type may hardly be considered centralized, but rather consolidated schools. Such are found in Madison Township, Lake County; Salem Township, Champaign County; Valley Township, Scioto County; Liberty Township, Ross County, and in about thirty others.

There are now 92 centralized and consolidated schools, divided as follows. One or two schools suspended and children transported to another school, 35; about one half or more of the township schools suspended, 25; nearly or completely centralized, 32.

Mr. Graham sent letters of inquiry to patrons asking several questions with reference to the working of the centralized schools. The following are some of the questions with replies :

" Does your child stand and wait for the wagon ? " Every reply so far is, " No."

" Is it necessary to clothe your child as heavily for the winter trips as under the old plan ? " Seventy-five per cent answer, " No "; fifteen per cent, " No difference "; and ten per cent, " Yes."

" Does your child attend school more regularly than under the old plan ? " Eighty per cent answer, " Yes "; twenty per cent, " See no difference."

" Does your child show increased interest above what it was under the old plan ? " Ninety per cent answer, " Yes "; ten per cent answer, " No."

" Do your teachers show an increased interest ? " Ninety-five per cent answer, " Yes "; five per cent answer, " No " and " Notice no difference."

" If it takes more time under the new way than the old plan, is it compensated for by better work ? " Eighty-five per cent answer, " Yes," and fifteen per cent, " Can't say " and " No."

" What effect has the centralized or consolidated school on the social and educational interests of the township ? " Most who have answered said, " There has been a great improvement." One replied, " In the beginning it stirred up a great deal of trouble, but everything is going along nicely now." A few replied, " No improvement; has not been established long enough to tell what it will do."

The entire bulletin needs to be read to be appreciated. More than that, it is an inspiration to visit these schools and note their working at first hand. Mr. Graham points out two main difficulties in Ohio:

1. Prejudice against a new thing and the sentiment that prompts us to quote " forty years ago," and to relate some of our childhood

experiences that are so vivid and so closely associated with the little weather-beaten schoolhouse, — which, when all sentiment is thrown by, did little more than house us, — sometimes prevent children from having modern advantages.

2. Bad roads and negligent drivers. The use that is being made of roads by the rural mail carrier, by milk haulers, and others who travel them daily is arousing an interest in road building that will make them of greater service to all. A negligent driver should meet the same fate that some have already met, — immediate dismissal. Negligence on the part of the driver is no more excusable than for a teacher.

CHAPTER XIII

THE TRAINING OF TEACHERS FOR COUNTRY SCHOOLS

The writer is well aware that it is a very easy matter to find fault. It is not so easy to point out a sane remedy. There is no disposition in this chapter to belittle the work that is done to-day by the country school-teacher. Most of the country school-teachers with whom I am acquainted are earnest, enthusiastic, loyal, and progressive, and they are getting things done. Many of them, even with the low wages paid them, are attending summer sessions at normal schools and earnestly striving to attain greater skill and efficiency as teachers. There are some poor workmen in the country schools, but that is true everywhere. Perhaps the critical observer will claim that there is more poor teaching done in the country schools of the United States than in the graded schools. If this is true, we ask our critics to be charitable enough to temper their criticisms with some knowledge of the hindrances to the best work in the country schools. I will not attempt to enumerate them all, or to name them in the order of importance. These are a few:

1. Insufficient supervision.
2. Low wages and insecurity of position.
3. Small schools with irregular attendance.
4. Low educational ideals in many districts.
5. Failure of normal schools to train teachers for the specific work of the country schools.

It is the last item that I wish to consider here.

In the *Prairie Farmer* editorial on "fads," quoted in Chapter X, the editor says, " We hope that the educator will be wise enough to fit the school for either of these innovations (study of agriculture and domestic science in the country school) rather than attempt to fit them to the school."

Now I suppose the term " educators " may be justly applied to the various members comprising the faculty of the normal school. They consider it their business to fit the school to do its work by fitting the teacher to conduct the school properly in all its relations ; and the term "school" has always meant the city graded system, — that is, it has meant that until within the last two or three years or so. It is safe to say that the narrow limitation of the words " city graded school " will be denied by the average normal school. But all normal — state normal — schools that I am acquainted with, so far as their training schools are concerned, are affiliated with city systems, and all the instruction of student teachers — that is, *practical work* — is directed toward solving the problems of the city schools.

It may be that the educators connected with normal schools do not consider the study of agriculture and domestic science as necessary for the country schools. If so, it must be confessed that they have plenty of company among the country people themselves, who do not yet see the possibilities of the new country school. But the leaders of agricultural thought do believe in these things, and it would seem that the leaders in pedagogical thought believe in them also, if one may judge from the recent expressions of some of them.

Superintendent Newell D. Gilbert, head of the training school connected with the Northern Illinois State Normal School at Dekalb, in discussing "The Sociological Basis of the Course of Study" at the Northern Illinois Teachers' Association at Kankakee, April 27–29, 1905, said:

From all that has been said, it is evident that social efficiency demands that the course of study in all its detailed outworking should be made a "local issue"; that it should utilize the local community life, — its occupations, resources, organization, traditions, customs. The school should be consciously in touch with all. To-day the serious charge against it is its isolation as a realm of child life and its failure to articulate closely and smoothly with the home, the neighborhood, and the community at large. Only so can the realities of the larger life come to the child; only so can the instruction of the school take on the reality needed to make it vigorously and practically effective.

Now it seems to me that a state institution supported by public taxation should have a department that will fit teachers to "utilize the local community life" for the country school, and that some practical training should be given to country school-teachers and graduates from city high schools who expect to teach in the country school as to how to "articulate" the country school "closely and smoothly" with the country home, because only in this way can "the realities of the larger life" come to the country child. Only in this way can the "instruction" of the country school "take on the reality needed to make it vigorously and practically effective."

But the normal schools may say: "Send on your country school-teachers. They do not come to our halls." The country school-teacher who does go — not in large numbers as yet, it is true — replies: "I do not get any help for the specific problems of the country school. If I am allowed to teach in the practice school, it is in a graded school with forty-minute recitation periods and the content of the course of instruction along city interests. I need help on how to organize a country school of fourteen pupils with twenty-six daily recitations, and how to get the most out of a seven-minute recitation in geography," etc.

Thus the difficulties of the situation are apparent.

It is reported that, during the last General Assembly of Illinois, the country members of the legislature objected to

Fig. 132. The Wisconsin Training School at Menomonie

voting for appropriations, to any great extent, for the state normal schools on the plea that the country, as distinguished from the city, did not derive any direct appreciable benefit from them. Yet the farms paid a large per cent of the public tax for the maintenance of schools that are supposed to help the entire school system. All of the above, or words to that effect, led to the passage of an act to quiet the complaint of the country lawmaker and taxpayer.

Just how much good it will do remains to be seen. The legislators recognize that something is wrong, for the first section says, "that in order to equalize the advantages of the state normal schools there," etc. But the entire act is here given, followed by a brief comment. This act took effect July 1, 1905. No definite plans have yet been formulated to make the law fulfill the mission for which it was passed.

NORMAL SCHOLARSHIP

An act to provide for scholarships for graduates of the eighth grade

SECTION 1. Be it enacted by the People of the State of Illinois represented in the General Assembly: That in order to equalize the advantages of the state normal schools, there shall be awarded annually, to each school township or fractional township, a scholarship which shall entitle the holder thereof to gratuitous instruction in any state normal school for a period of four years : Provided that any township having a population exceeding one hundred thousand inhabitants shall be entitled to five scholarships.

SECTION 2. The county superintendent shall receive and register the names of all applicants for such scholarships, and shall hold an examination, or cause an examination to be held, in each township for the benefit of graduates of the eighth grade : Provided that where a township is divided by county lines the county superintendent in whose county the sixteenth section is situate shall have charge of the examination in such township.

SECTION 3. All examinations shall be held on the second Saturday of May in each year, according to rules and regulations prescribed by the Superintendent of Public Instruction, and the pupil found to possess the highest qualifications shall be entitled to such scholarship : Provided, however, that such pupil shall be a resident of the township in which such examination is held : and provided, further, that where no application is received from any township the county superintendent shall assign the pupil found to possess the next highest qualifications to that township.

SECTION 4. The county superintendent shall certify the names and addresses of all successful applicants, with the number (and range) of the township to which each pupil is accredited, to the Superintendent of Public Instruction, who shall issue to each pupil a certificate of scholarship which shall be accepted by the authorities of any state normal school in lieu of any entrance examination, and shall exempt the holder thereof from the payment of tuition or any term, matriculation, or incidental fee whatsoever.

SECTION 5. Section 7 of an act for the establishment and maintenance of a normal university, as amended; Section 13 of an act to establish and maintain the Southern Illinois Normal University; Section 13 of an act to establish and maintain the Northern Illinois State Normal School; Section 13 of an act to establish and maintain the Eastern Illinois State Normal School; and Section 13 of an act to establish and maintain the Western Illinois State Normal School, are hereby repealed.

[Approved May 12, 1905.]

It is the plan of State Superintendent Bayliss to have a conference of the normal-school people and the county superintendents to settle on some plan for awarding scholarships. If this act results in many eighth-grade pupils attending the state normal schools, and if the normal schools give these eighth-grade pupils the proper training, then future country legislators can have no just ground for complaint.

In my humble judgment the possibilities of this law will not be attained if it merely results in a number of eighth-grade pupils getting free high-school privileges at a state normal school. It may fairly be questioned whether a state normal school should have a high school at all, in view of a greater work needed in the way of training student teachers to become efficient teachers. It remains to be seen, of course, whether the offer of a high school will induce many parents to send children away from home to get this high-school work. It may be claimed, to use a local illustration, that the country children of Winnebago County can get as good high-school training at the city high school of Rockford as at any state normal school of Illinois. To be sure, the pupils must pay tuition to the local school, but doubtless many of them prefer to do this, since with the facilities in the way of electric roads and the like they are able to board at home. What is needed on the part of the normal school to make this law most effective is a course of training and study that will enable these eighth-grade pupils to do fairly good work at the end of one year, — something similar to what the country training schools of Wisconsin are doing for the country schools. If these eighth-grade pupils can be induced to remain two years, all the better. There is no doubt that some high-school extension is needed badly in Illinois, but it does not seem proper to have it come *via* the state normal school, if by coming that way it is a substitute for normal training for the student teachers who will teach in the one-room district schools of the state.

But I have no doubt that the coming conference will agree on some plan to get out of the law all that was intended.

The reader is doubtless aware of most of the principal problems the inexperienced teacher meets with in carrying out the organization and administration of the average country school. I need not enlarge upon them here. A small school may be one of the best of schools, if the teacher has been trained to make the most of the material and the time. I give here a daily programme of an average country school of Winnebago County. The school has an enrollment of twelve pupils, with a daily attendance of nine. The teacher is a graduate of a local village high school with a four years' course of study.

DAILY PROGRAMME

SUBJECT	LENGTH OF RECITATION	PUPILS IN EACH CLASS	SUBJECT	LENGTH OF RECITATION	PUPILS IN EACH CLASS
Forenoon			*Afternoon*		
Opening Exercises .	10 min.	all	Opening Exercises	5 min.	all
Primer	10 "	1	Primer	10 "	1
Second Reader (*a*) .	10 "	3	Second Reader (*a*)	10 "	3
" " (*b*) .	10 "	1	" " (*b*)	10 "	1
Fourth Reader (*a*) .	10 "	3	First Physiology .	10 "	2
" " (*b*) .	10 "	2	Second "	10 "	3
Literature	15 "	1	U.S. History . .	10 "	1
Language	15 "	2	First Geography .	10 "	2
			Second "	10 "	3
			Third "	10 "	1
Recess	10 "	1	*Recess*		
Numbers	15 "	4	Primer	10 "	1
Arithmetic Reader .	10 "	3	Arithmetic Reader	15 "	4
First Arithmetic .	10 "	1	First Grammar . .	10 "	3
Third "	10 "	3	Second " . .	10 "	1
Second "	15 "	all	" Spelling .	10 "	2
Writing			Third " .	10 "	1

The reader at once suggests a reduction in the number of classes, so that there would be only one second-reader class, one fourth-reader class, and one physiology class. That depends upon the local circumstances, as every one acquainted with a country school knows full well.

One more programme is given. This is from a school that last year had three different teachers during the school year of eight months. One pupil in the school desired first-year high-school work, so a graduate of the Rockford High School taught the following programme for two months. The school had an enrollment of ten pupils, with a daily attendance of eight.

DAILY PROGRAMME

SUBJECT	LENGTH OF RECITATION	PUPILS IN EACH CLASS	SUBJECT	LENGTH OF RECITATION	PUPILS IN EACH CLASS
Forenoon			*Afternoon*		
Opening Exercises .	10 min.	all	*A.* Algebra . . .	10 min.	I
B. Reading . . .	10 "	I	*C.* Geography . .	7 "	I
G. " . . .	10 "	2	*D.* " . .	8 "	I
D. " . . .	10 "	I	*E.* Physiology . .	10 "	2
C. " . . .	10 "	I	*B, C.* " . .	10 "	2
F. " . . .	10 "	2	*E.* Language . .	10 "	2
E. " . . .	10 "	2	*G.* Spelling . . .	5 "	I
B. Arithmetic . .	10 "	I	*A.* Physical Geog-		
A. Latin	10 "	I	raphy . .	10 "	I
			E. Geography . .	10 "	2
Recess	15 "		*Recess*	15 "	
D. Arithmetic . .	10 "	I	*B.* History . . .	10 "	I
C. " . .	10 "	I	*C.* " . . .	10 "	I
B. Language . .	5 "	I	*F.* Spelling . . .	10 "	2
G. Arithmetic . .	10 "	2	*B, C, D.* Spelling .	15 "	3
F. " . .	10 "	2	*D.* History . . .	10 "	I
E. " . .	10 "	I	*E.* Spelling . . .	10 "	2
D. Language . .	10 "	I	*A.* Commercial		
B. Geography . .	10 "	I	Arithmetic	10 "	I

Here are thirty-two daily recitations, nineteen of them having one pupil each and twelve having two pupils each.

To the state of Indiana, so far as I know, belongs the honor of having a model country training school in connection with the State Normal School at Terre Haute. This school has been in successful operation for two years. It is a typical country school, presenting the usual peculiarities and difficulties of such a school. It is located six miles east of Terre Haute on the interurban electric road between Terre Haute and Brazil. Part of the expense of running this school is borne by the State Normal School and part by the township in which the school is situated. This school is used by the students of the Indiana State Normal School as an observation and practice school, the students going there on the interurban cars. One provision of the agreement between the trustees of the normal school and the trustees of the township in which this

FIG. 133. A Model Country School connected with the Indiana State Normal School

model country school is situated is "that the teacher during the seven months of the school year (the period during which the schools of the township continue) shall be paid the maximum salary by the trustees and a certain fixed amount in addition by the Board of the Indiana State Normal School, and that during the continuance of the school beyond the seven months, so as to complete the period of ten months, the teacher shall be paid by the Board of the

Indiana State Normal School." This school is equipped as it should be, and is designed to show what a country school should be and what can be done there in the way of effective work. The following very interesting and valuable letter is self-explanatory.

INDIANA STATE NORMAL SCHOOL,
TERRE HAUTE, INDIANA, July 26, 1905

Superintendent O. J. Kern, Rockford, Illinois

Dear Mr. Kern : It affords me pleasure to furnish you the information you request concerning the country training school which is connected with our school.

Answers to questions:

1. Number of children enrolled? *Ans.* Fifty-two.

Note. This enrollment was too large, but could not be avoided last year. We have an understanding that the enrollment is not to exceed about thirty, on account of accommodations.

2. Average attendance? *Ans.* Forty.

Note. This is for ten months, and six graduated at the middle of the year.

3. Qualifications of training teacher in charge? *Ans.* She is a high-school graduate and a graduate of the Normal College at Ypsilanti, Michigan.

4. Salary of training teacher? *Ans.* She is paid by township trustee fifty-five dollars per month, and by the normal school board fifty dollars per month. Total, one hundred and five dollars per month.

5. How do student teachers get to this school? *Ans.* The students get to school by means of the interurban car. It costs them twenty cents per round trip.

6. How many student teachers at a time do observation work at this country training school? *Ans.* Every student who reaches the practice work in the normal school spends from one to three weeks in observation and teaching in the training school. They are sent there in groups of from eight to fifteen, as the circumstances determine. Then observation classes are taken there for observation in a body, depending upon the size of the class, but they are only taken there

a few times in a term (three months). Other students, by their request, are allowed to observe as often as they wish. This is all under the direction of the Department of Methods, Observation, and Practice in the normal school.

7. Something in general of the character of the work done in this school? *Ans*. The effort is to make this a first-class country school. They follow the course made by the state superintendent for such schools and try to do the work in accordance with the principles of education. We endeavor to do as good work there as we do in the city training school. The teacher is just as careful about her assignments and her presentation as if she had only one grade to teach.

8. The course of study for this school? *Ans*. The regularly adopted state course.

Note. This is so from choice. We have the right to modify it if we wish, but, as I said, our aim is to conduct a first-class country school according to the science of education under the conditions they have given them.

9. Daily programme:

8.30 Opening Exercises.
8.45 Penmanship (all grades).
8.55 Music (grades 1–4 and 5–7).
9.05 Reading (second grade).
9.15 Reading (first grade).
9.30 Arithmetic (seventh grade).
9.45 Arithmetic (fourth grade).
10.00 Arithmetic (third grade).
10.15 Arithmetic (first grade).
10.30 *Recess*.
10.45 { Geography (seventh grade), or History (second and third grades).
11.00 Arithmetic (second grade).
11.10 Spelling or Reading (seventh grade).
11.25 Reading (fourth grade).
11.40 Spelling (third grade).
11.50 Spelling (first grade).
11.55 Spelling (second grade).
12.00 *Noon Intermission*.

12.40 Reading (first grade).
12.50 Grammar (seventh grade).
1.05 Spelling (fourth grade).
1.15 Language (second and third grades).
1.30 Geography or History (fourth grade).
1.45 Physiology or Reading (seventh grade).
2.00 Reading (third grade).
2.15 Arithmetic (second grade).
2.25 Reading (first grade).
2.35 Physical Culture (all grades).
2.40 Language (fourth grade).
2.55 History or Geography (seventh grade).
3.10 Nature Study (second and third grades).
3.20 History or Geography (third grade).
3.30 Discussion with student teachers.

Note. The above programme is frequently varied to accommodate the work of the normal students.

10. What expense to students who attend, in the way of tuition, etc.? *Ans.* None except their car fare to and from school.

11. What do you regard as the most important features of this school? *Ans.* First, that it affords an opportunity for student teachers to study the country-school problem in a first-class school; second, it furnishes a good standard country-school work for teachers and school officers to visit, and thus gradually elevates the standard of country-school work; third, it meets in a practical way the question we are asked so often in our normal classes, — " This theory may be all right for city schools, but will it work in the country schools?"

Note. That the school is accomplishing something under the second point may be seen from the following facts: first, during the last school year (ten months) there were three hundred and twenty-three visitors to this school; second, they were from eleven different counties of Indiana (some of the near counties have sent all their teachers for a day's visit in the school); third, several were from Illinois and one from Buenos Ayres, South America.

Note. It is fair to say that the one from South America did not come to Terre Haute for the purpose of visiting the country training school.

Now if I have provoked any other questions, I should be glad to answer them if I can. I will mail photos as soon as finished.

Very truly yours,

A. R. CHARMAN,
Head of Department of Methods,
Observation, and Practice

Perhaps Illinois is to have the second model country school in connection with a state normal school; for State Superintendent Alfred Bayliss, President of the Board of Trustees of the Western Illinois Normal School, in a letter to me dated July 22, 1905, says:

You can say that the training school at Macomb is a very complete one and has as part of its organization a typical country school, located in the country, and in which one of the most competent critic teachers is employed. This school is available for observation purposes to all students of the normal school, and some practice in it is required of every graduate. There is also a school for individual instruction, to which pupils of the grades, up to a certain number, who may have become irregular and unclassifiable by reason of sickness, other necessary absence from school, indolence, or slow development are admitted, and whatever is necessary to help them over temporary rough places is done.

The reader will note that in the cases of model country schools in Indiana and Illinois the location is in the *country*, in country environment. One may say, Why not

FIG. 134. An Interior View of the Model Country School connected with the Indiana State Normal School

build a model country-school building on the campus of the normal school and take the children there from some district school in the country? Such a school is not a country school. It is not in country environment. The same objections hold here that obtain in the proposal to consolidate surrounding country districts with a large city and send the country child to the city school by wagon or trolley line. We must not give up the country school.

If it is a consolidated school, let it be a consolidated *country* school. A small village of one hundred and fifty or two hundred people is essentially country.

Wisconsin has gone one step farther by establishing county training schools for county schools. These training schools exist for a specific purpose, namely, to train teachers for the work of teaching in the one-room district school.

State Superintendent Cary, of Wisconsin, says of these county training schools :

It may be said without exaggeration that counties which maintain these county training schools have, as a general thing, a corps of country teachers above the average in efficiency. In the immediate future, without doubt, more of them will be established. In addition to the training of teachers to do actual teaching in the country schools, these county training schools have become feeders for the state normal schools, and have furnished a very desirable product. The course of study consists of branches that are required to be taught in the common schools.

The counties of Buffalo, Dunn, Marathon, Manitowoc, Richland, Waupaca, and Wood, in 1904 maintained county training schools.

COURSE OF STUDY FOR DUNN COUNTY TRAINING SCHOOL

First Quarter

Reading, Orthoëpy.
Arithmetic, Manual.
Grammar, English Composition, Manual.
Psychology.

Second Quarter

Reading, Manual.
Arithmetic.
Grammar, English Composition, Manual.
Theory and Art Teaching.

Third Quarter

History, Manual.
Civics.
Geography, Physical.
Physiology.

Fourth Quarter

History.
Geography, Manual.
Observation and Practice.
Agriculture.

Library readings and rhetoricals given throughout the course.

Spelling and penmanship given as needed.

Algebra will be allowed to those who apply for it and whose regular work will permit.

The normal is to prepare teachers for the rural schools of Dunn County, and tuition is free to students of the county. Nonresidents are charged forty dollars a year tuition. Nonresidents are admitted on the same basis as other students when there is room.

It was my pleasure to attend the graduating exercises of the Dunn County Training School in June, 1905. The practical benefit of these schools can be best understood from those at work in them. Here follows the report of the principal of the Dunn County Teachers' Training School at Menomonie for the year ending June 30, 1904:

To the County Superintendent, H. E. Layne, Dunn County, Wisconsin :

Permit me to render to you the fifth annual report of the Dunn County Teachers' Training School.

The total enrollment for the year has been seventy-four. Had there been no limitations placed upon applicants by an entrance examination, there would have been an enrollment of about ninety.

The school has graduated thirty-seven students this year, twenty-four of whom taught during the spring term. These twenty-four completed the course in April, but did not take their diplomas until the close of the year, June 24. We hear their work well spoken of by the patrons of the several districts where they have taught.

The number of graduates produced by the training school since it started is one hundred and forty-eight. Of this number ten have worked for a season in the schools ; two have gone to the Superior State Normal, three to Stevens Point, and five to River Falls.

The presidents of these schools have each made a satisfactory report upon the attainments of these students upon entering these state schools. Each of the ten has entered the normal without being required to take an entrance examination, and four have completed the elementary course.

We have undertaken a measure this year which seems to have given a great stimulus to the teaching power of our students in the country schools. Through the wisdom of the local board, it was made possible for the training-school faculty to spend some time in visiting our student body while at actual work in their several schools. Thirty-six of these visits were made where they seemed to be most needed. It is the judgment of the principal that no better service has ever been rendered to the schools of Dunn County.

We believe the school has done a strong year's work, and it is sufficiently popular in the state and county to warrant its continuance.

There are about thirty-five this year's students who are held over into next year, besides thirty applicants to date, who have notified the principal of their intention to take the entrance examination next fall. Many more will write next fall than have applied this time.

Respectfully yours,

W. L. MORRISON

The expense of these county training schools is borne jointly by the state and the county in which the school is located. Michigan is following the lead of Wisconsin in establishing county training schools.

At Menomonie, Wisconsin, during the summer of 1905, the Dunn County School of Agriculture, a different institution from the County Training School or the Menomonie City School, conducted a teachers' institute and summer school for teachers of common schools. The following outline indicates the character of the work done :

SUMMER-SCHOOL TOPICS IN DOMESTIC ECONOMY

I. *Home economy :* General care of the home ; drainage around house ; arrangement of house ; care of rooms (sweeping, dusting, etc.); floors and their treatment ; walls and wall coverings ; ventilation of house ; household pests.

II. *Sewing:* Hand needlework; all stitches used in plain sewing; mending, patching, and darning; sewing on buttons; button-holes.

III. *Cooking:* Kitchen range; fire; draughts; oven tests; foods. Principles of cooking; experiments to show effect of heat on eggs, meats, etc.; composition of foods.

Proteids, or tissue-building foods, as casein of milk, albumen of egg, albumen of meat, gluten of wheat.

FIG. 135. A Teachers' Training School at Menomonie, Wisconsin

Carbohydrates, or energy-producing foods, as starches of potato, wheat and other grains. Iodine test for starch.

Fats, or heat-producing foods.

Water, — its value in the diet.

IV. *Food sets:* Their preparation. Food sets are to show the relative amounts of the various nutriments in our common foods.

V. *Laundry work:* Removal of stains; fixation of colors; washing powders and bluings; treatment of silks, flannels, laces, embroideries, etc.

VI. *Emergencies:* Hemorrhages; dressing of wounds; bandaging; treatment of burns; fire; drowning; poisons and antidotes.

VII. *School hygiene:* Ventilation of schoolroom; lighting of school-room; position of pupils.

Topics in Agriculture for School-Teachers

I. *Practice and principles of pruning.*

II. *Practice and principles of grafting; starting home fruit gardens.*

III. *Methods of seed testing.*

IV. *Treatment of grains for prevention of smut.*

V. *Treatment of potatoes for prevention of scab.*

VI. *Simple spraying mixtures.*

VII. *Treatment of clover and other legumes with nitrogen-fixing bacteria.*

VIII. *Plans for school gardens:* How to lay out and prepare ground; what plants and seeds to use, and how; where to secure plants and seeds free; the question of tools; care of growing garden plants.

IX. *Planning school grounds for improvement and beauty:* What to plant and how to get plants; where to plant vines, trees, shrubs, etc.; how to plant and care for plants.

Ten to two hundred or less of the best experiments concerning soils, crops, weeds, insects, diseases, etc., outlined in *Rural School Agriculture.* (This manual is available free for all rural districts in Dunn County.)

Topics in Manual Training for all School-Teachers

I. *Woodwork:* Simple preliminary exercises introducing the knife, ruler, square, saw, hammer, plane, chisel, brace bit, etc. (Dunn County rural schools have the free use of a number of suitable and excellent tool sets, through the beneficent interest of Senator Stout.)

The woodwork to conform to the environment of the country boy or girl, and to be of such practical nature as to commend the work to the country patron.

II. *Models in woodwork:* Plant label, fish-line winder, pencil sharpener, book rack, sled, pen rack, mail box, desk letter box, bushel box, applied models of schoolroom ventilation.

III. *Rope tying and splicing:* The long splice, valuable on the farm for mending hay ropes.

Tying knots : Knots for end of rope, the square knot, the bowline, half hitch, and timber hitch.

IV. *Paper and card work:* Perceptional cutting: massive objects; smaller objects grouped to show social ideas; free cutting of familiar objects.

Conceptional cutting: Poses; animals; animals in action; figures illustrating familiar songs, stories, trades, and games.

Symmetrical cutting: Half fold (geometrical forms of familiar objects); fourth fold and eighth fold (ditto); geometrical forms repeated to make simple border and center designs; weather signals.

The Normal School at New Paltz, New York, has begun a series of important educational conferences for the purpose of helping the country school to become the power that it should be in the new country life now upon us. The country school-teachers, school officers, and influential patrons are invited to confer with the normal-school faculty regarding the best means of promoting the welfare of the country districts, — of enabling the country school to vitalize the lives of the young people living on the farms, — and how a normal school can help in this work.

Some of the subjects being considered are the preparation of normal-school students in manual training, home science, and in important branches of agriculture and handicraft; the institution of traveling libraries from school to school; the improvement of school buildings and the beautifying of school grounds; the school garden, etc.

A course of lectures in contemporary educational problems was given recently at Teachers College, Columbia University, New York City. The following bibliography was prepared by Principal Myron Scudder, of the New Paltz Normal School, for use in his lecture on Country Schools and the Teaching of Agriculture:

BIBLIOGRAPHY

List of articles on consolidation, centralization, transportation, etc. (very comprehensive and carefully compiled by State Superintendent Fowler, of Nebraska), National Educational Association report, 1903, pages 924–929.

"Bibliography of School Gardens," Carter, State Normal School, Greeley, Colorado, March, 1904.

Reports of the National Educational Association

"The Rural-School Problem." Circular of Information No. 5 (Sabin *et al.*), July, 1895.

Report of the Committee of Twelve, pages 383–385, 1897.

Report of the Committee on Industrial Education in Schools for Rural Communities (published in separate pamphlet), 1905.

(See also the index in reports for 1894, 1895, 1897, 1901, 1903, and 1904.)

Reports of the Commissioner of Education

YEAR	VOLUME	PAGE	SUBJECT
1893–1894	I	288–289	"School Gardens in Berlin Common Schools."
1894–1895	I	380–403	"Rural Schools in Germany."
	II	1457–1467	"The School District."
	II	1469–1482	"Conveyance of Children to School."
1895–1896	II	1199–1206	"How Agriculture is Taught in Prussia and France."
		1353	"Transportation of Children to School."
1896–1897	I	79	"Rural Schools in Denmark."
	I	811–873	Report of the Committee of Twelve.
	II	1535	"Conveyance of Children to School."
1897–1898	I	224	"School Gardens in Europe."
	II	1614	"Instruction in Agriculture in the Normal Schools of France."
	II	1623	"Gardener's Schools in Russia."
	II	1623	"School Gardens in Russia."
	II	1701	"Conveyance of Children to School."

YEAR	VOLUME	PAGE	SUBJECT
1898–1899	I	1067–1082	" School Gardens."
1899–1900	II	1447	" School Gardens in Sweden."
	II	2581	" Transportation of Pupils to School."
1901		161–212	" Consolidation of Schools and Transportation of Pupils."
1902		650	" Agriculture in Rural Schools."
		752–754	" Agricultural Schools in Italy."

Foreign Reports

1902 New South Wales : Department of Public Instruction, conference of inspectors, etc., pages 122, 143, 158.

1903 New South Wales : Interim report of the commissioners on certain parts of primary education, pages 66, 78, 95, 100, 116, 117, 119.

1904 New South Wales: Report of the Minister of Public Instruction for the year 1903, pages 87, 92, 98, 108, 113, 133, 134.
Rapports du jury internationale : Groupe I, Éducation et enseignement. Première Partie — Classe I. See references to Austria, Belgium, Bosnia, Herzegovina, Bulgaria, Finland, and Hungary.

The Rural-School Problem

" Rural Schools : Progress in the Past ; Means of Improvement in the Future." Circular of Information No. 6, Bureau of Education, 1884.

" Some Problems of the Rural Common School." A. C. True. Reprint from the yearbook of the Department of Agriculture, 1901.

" Study of the Rural Schools of Maine." Superintendent Stetson, 1895.

" The Rural-School Problem in Massachusetts." Fletcher, agent of Massachusetts Board of Education.

" Evolution of the Rural-School System : Present Status in Michigan." Burnham, in Proceedings of fifty-second annual meeting Michigan State Teachers' Association, 1905.

" Rural Schools and how to Improve Them," and other articles. Institute Bulletin No. 11, State Board of Agriculture, Michigan, 1905.

"Conditions and Needs of Iowa Rural Schools." State Superintendent Riggs, Des Moines, Iowa.

Rural Sociology

"Social Problems of the Farmer." Publications of the Michigan Political Science Association, Ann Arbor, Vol. IV, No. 6, July, 1902. $1.00.

"Federation of Rural Social Forces" (reprint). Butterfield, American League for Civic Improvement, Chicago.

"Social Phases of Agricultural Education." Butterfield, *American Journal of Sociology*, Vol. X, No. 5, March, 1905.

"Social Phases of Agricultural Education." Butterfield, *Popular Science Monthly*, August, 1905.

Consolidation and Transportation

"Consolidation, etc., and the Conveyance of Children." Fletcher, Massachusetts Board of Education.

"Consolidation," etc. State Superintendent Cary. See eleventh biennial report of the Department of Public Instruction, Wisconsin, 1902–1904.

"Consolidation of Country Schools." University of Illinois Bulletin, Vol. II, No. 3, December, 1904.

"Report of a Visit to the Centralized Schools of Ohio." Superintendent O. J. Kern, Rockford, Illinois. See also his annual reports for 1901, 1902, 1903, 1904, and 1905 (especially 1905), profusely illustrated.

School Gardens

Nature Leaflets, Nos. 29, 30, 31, and 32. Massachusetts State Board of Agriculture.

"Philadelphia School Gardens." Civic Club, Philadelphia.

"Municipal School Gardens." Board of Public Education, Philadelphia.

"School Gardens." B. T. Galloway, United States Department of Agriculture, Bulletin No. 160, 1905.

"How to Make School Gardens." Hemenway. Doubleday, Page & Co. $1.00.

"Hints and Helps for Young Gardeners." Hemenway. 35 cents.

"School-Garden Movement." Spillman, Reports of American Civic Association, Philadelphia, Vol. VI, Part III; and Vol. VII, Part III. 25 cents each.

Teaching Agriculture in Country Schools

Report of Commissioner on Teaching Agriculture, etc. Circular No. 32, United States Department of Agriculture.

"Elementary Agriculture in our Public Schools." Dumas, *The Normal Seminar*, State Normal School, Cheney, Washington. 50 cents.

"Agricultural Instruction in District Schools." Report of State Superintendent Harvey, Wisconsin, 1902.

Bulletin of Information No. 8. Issued by Superintendent Harvey, 1902.

"Rural School Agriculture." Bulletin No. 1, Department of Agriculture, University of Minnesota, St. Anthony Park, Minnesota.

FIG. 136. Teacher and Pupils in a Rural School
in Dunn County, Wisconsin

Courses of Study and Methods of Instruction, including Agriculture and Nature Study

"Course of Study for the Common Schools of Illinois" (third general revision), August, 1903. Published by C. M. Parker, Taylorville, Illinois. 25 cents.

"Course of Study for Elementary Schools." New York State Educational Department, Albany, 1905.

"Manual for the Use of Members of County Teachers' Institutes." State of Maine, Educational Department.

Helps for Teachers — Bulletins, etc.

" The Nature Guard " (monthly). Rhode Island College of Agriculture, Kingston, Rhode Island.

" Reading Course for Farmers." Cornell University Agricultural Experiment Station.

" Reading Course for Farmers' Wives." Cornell University Agricultural Experiment Station.

" Teachers' Leaflets on Nature Study." Cornell University Agricultural Experiment Station.

" The Study of Farm Crops " (monthly). University of Illinois. Published by C. M. Parker, Taylorville, Ill. 25 cents per year.

Also free bulletins from Illinois Experiment Station, Urbana, Illinois; Agricultural Experiment Station, Madison, Wisconsin; Iowa Agricultural Experiment Station, Ames, Iowa; and other similar stations.

Text-Books in Agriculture

" Development of the Text-Book of Agriculture in North America." L. H. Bailey, United States Department of Agriculture (reprint from annual report, 1903).

" Principles of Agriculture " ($1.25); " Garden Making " ($1.00); " Practical Garden Book " ($1.00). L. H. Bailey. The Macmillan Company, New York.

"Agriculture for Beginners." Burkett, Stevens, and Hill. Ginn & Company. 75 cents.

" New Elementary Agriculture " (for rural schools). C. E. Bessey *et al.* University Publishing Company, Lincoln, Nebraska. 60 cents.

" First Principles of Agriculture." Edw. B. Voorhees. Silver, Burdett & Co. 75 cents.

" Principles of Agriculture for Common Schools." I. O. Winslow. American Book Company. 60 cents.

In the Magazines

(See also Carter's " Bibliography of School Gardens ")

Arena: " Value of School Farms " (Gordon), XXIII, pages 544–553, May, 1900.

Charities: " Children's Farm School in New York City " (F. G. Parsons), XI, pages 220–223, September 5, 1903.

Charities: " Junior School of Horticulture in St. Louis " (Stevens), XI, pages 223–224.

Current Literature: "Agricultural Education on the Continent" (De Reimer), XXVII, pages 57–68, January, 1900.

Education: " How the Common Schools can Help the Farmer " (Warren), XVI, pages 417–425, March, 1897 ; " Courses of Study in Agriculture " (Bogen), XXVII, pages 89–94, October, 1901; " The Enrichment of Rural School Life " (Jones), XXII, pages 373–377.

Educational Review: " School Garden in Thuringia " (Lukens), XVII, pages 237–241; " Newer Ideas " (Bailey), XX, pages 377–382 ; "Significant Factor in Agricultural Education " (Butterfield), XXI, pages 301–306 ; " Rural Schools in France" (Anna T. Smith), XXIV, pages 471–483.

Fortnightly Review: " Present-Day Need in Agricultural Education " (Tremayne), LXXIX, pages 1068–1092, June, 1903.

Forum: "University Extension in Agriculture" (True), XXVIII, pages 701–707, February, 1900 ; " Bussey Institution " (Hersey), V, pages 558–560.

Independent: "Agriculture in the Public Schools," LV, pages 1641–1642, July 9, 1903.

Journal of Education: "Agriculture in Schools" (Whittaker), XLV, page 320, May 20, 1897.

Nation: " Rural Education in France," LXXI, page 231, September 20, 1900.

New England Magazine: "Government of Boys for Boys by Boys " (Thrasher), New Series, XXII, pages 193–208, April, 1900.

Popular Science Monthly: "Agricultural Education on the Continent," LVI, pages 218–233, December, 1899 ; "American Agricultural Education " (Butterfield), LXIII, pages 257–261, July, 1903.

Public Opinion: "Opening of a National School Farm (for Jews) at Doylestown, Pennsylvania," XXIII, page 44, July 8, 1897.

Review of Reviews: "State as a Farmer" (Ellis), XIX, pages 706–709, June, 1899; "Our Farmer Youth and the Public Schools" (Ellis), XXVIII, pages 449–455, October, 1903; "Learning by Doing for the Farmer Boy" (Kern), XXVIII, pages 456–461.

Scientific American: "Children's School Farm in the Heart of a Great City" (describes Mrs. Parsons's great work), LXXXIX, page 279, October 17, 1903.

The World's Work: "Teaching Farmers' Children on the Ground" (Iles), VI, pages 3415–3420, May, 1903 ; "Farmer Children Need Farmer Education" (Poe), VI, pages 3760–3762.

Yale Review: "City Farm Training Schools," pages 95–97, May, 1898.

Michigan, like Wisconsin, is moving along the line of improving the country schools by improving the teachers for country schools in special training classes in the county normal schools, and in 1903 eight such normal schools were in operation. In June, 1904, eighty-six young people graduated from the one-year course and went into the country schools to teach. The average age of the graduates was twenty years. The minimum age at which certificates to teach may be granted is eighteen years. By September, 1904, twenty normal schools for country teachers were in operation, an increase of twelve over 1903. State Superintendent Fall, in his report for 1904, advocates trained teachers and consolidation as two very efficient means of improving the country schools.

CHAPTER XIV

MANUAL TRAINING IN THE COUNTRY SCHOOL

The following quotation from a recent article by Calvin Milton Woodward on "Manual Training: Theory and Method" (see the *Outlook*, December 16, 1905) will serve as a good introduction for this chapter. This quotation expresses the experience, no doubt, of thousands of boys raised on the farm, and the purpose of the chapter is to secure, if possible, a different system of training in the country school and in the country home that will give a richer experience to the country boys and girls of the future.

Says Mr. Woodward:

We are frequently told that the boy from the farm has had manual training; and it is true that he has had some manual training, but he has had a great deal of manual labor with it. I know, because I was a farm boy and learned everything that could be learned on a farm previous to my college course. I learned to use correctly the hoe, the shovel, the plow, the scythe, the cradle, and the ax; but I never learned the proper use of bench tools, nor had we a machine tool of any kind till the mowing machine and the reaper came. I knew nothing of drawing, nothing of the mechanic arts, properly so called. Nineteen twentieths of my time was spent simply in hard labor, which had no education beyond an incidental and imperfect knowledge of crops and soils and the market. Manual training would have been of great value and a few lessons would have saved me much time and money.

Because the average farmer has not yet distinguished the difference between manual training and manual labor, the former will be slow in coming into the country school.

But it will surely come; indeed, it is already here in many places. Manual training is a phase of industrial training for the country school. It is a little unfortunate that we do not have a better term to express this thought; for a great many excellent people to-day, moving along the educational avenue that leads up to the public school, shy and stop still at the sight of the word "industrial" as applied

FIG. 137. The Beginning of Manual Training in a Country School of Winnebago County, Illinois

to the work of the public school. Any attempt to lead them closer for a more careful inspection of the word proves unavailing. To their thinking, industrial training means the elimination of "culture," whatever that may mean, and the substitution of the reform school or the trade school. For them the thought has not yet come that education should be for service as well as for sweetness and light; that the children in our schools should be able to do things as well as to know about things; and that in the right doing of things by the country child there is as great opportunity for culture as there is in studying the printed page to learn what men have said and thought in the past.

The distinction between higher education and industrial education has no real foundation upon which to rest. It is a survival of the aristocratic ideas of the Middle Ages. The thought that farming and blacksmithing are just as "high" as law and theology is not original with the writer. Whether it is better to be a blacksmith than a minister

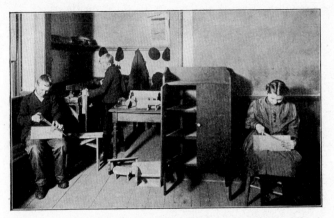

FIG. 138. Manual Training in a Winnebago County District School

depends. As has been well said recently, "It is better to pound an anvil and make a good horseshoe than to pound a pulpit and make a poor sermon."

This same writer adds:

There is a real distinction between education for self-support and education for self-development, between culture and what the Germans call the bread-and-butter sciences. In order, if not in importance, the bread-and-butter sciences come first. The first duty every man owes to society is to support himself; therefore the first office of education is to enable the pupil to support himself.

As President Roosevelt said in an address to the young men of an eastern college, "Every young man ought to be able to carry his own weight," the thought being that a young man should be self-supporting and not be a dead weight on society or depend upon inherited wealth.

I am indebted to Director W. C. Smith of the Winona Technical Institute, Indianapolis, Indiana, for the following interesting tabulation of children in the public schools of the United States. The data are taken from the report for 1903 of William T. Harris, United States Commissioner of Education. It is worthy of careful notice.

PUBLIC-SCHOOL EDUCATION

GRADE	AGE	NUMBER OF PUPILS IN EACH GRADE	
1	6	5,149,296 children enter first grade	
2	7	2,912,462	By second year nearly one half drop out
3	8	2,426,263	Still leaving school
4	9	2,168,956	
5	10	1,288,814	Breadwinning by children begins
6	11	705,885	The call of the " Dollar "
7	12	405,693	
8	13	323,697	Compare this line with the first. About 17 per cent of pupils in school finish eighth grade
9	14	243,433	enter high school
10	15	147,192	
11	16	101,903	
12	17	73,596	leave high school. A very small dot. 30 per cent finish high school

So over 10,000,000 children leave school to go into trades without complete schooling. Among these millions is found the field of the trade school.

627 universities, colleges, and technical schools in the United States have 114,130 students.

43 of these are technical schools, with 13,216 students.

32,000,000 breadwinners, — 2,000,000 by brain work, and 30,000,000 by manual labor trades.

The reader will note the comparatively few who enter the high school. The number is relatively smaller for the country schools. This should emphasize the establishment of country high schools, so that more of the country children may have opportunity for manual training.

Mr. William T. Bawden, Director of Manual Training in the normal school at Normal, Illinois, gives the following as compiled from the United States census for 1900. The total number of persons engaged in gainful occupations is placed at 29,286,000, classified as follows:

Agricultural pursuits, 10,438,000, or 35.7 per cent.
Professional service, 1,264,000, or 4.3 per cent.
Domestic and personal service, 5,691,000, or 19.4 per cent.
Trade and transportation, 4,778,000, or 16.3 per cent.
Manufacturing and mechanical pursuits, 7,113,000, or 24.3 per cent.

Commenting on these statistics, Mr. Bawden says :

During the last fifty years there has been a marked decrease in the proportion of the number of individuals engaged in agricultural pursuits, and there has been a large increase in the percentage of those employed in trade and transportation and in manufacturing and mechanical pursuits. These figures show what a large part manual work, and especially the constructive industries, play in our national life. It is instructive to note what a large proportion of these methods of gaining a livelihood employ the hand more or less directly. We are preëminently an industrial nation, and if we are to maintain our supremacy among the nations of the world, we must be, even more than we have been, a manufacturing nation. This can only be accomplished by raising up generations of children who can do something with their hands. This does not imply, as has been already indicated, the teaching of trades in the common schools; but it does mean that children should be brought up to know something at first hand about " things,"— the realities of life and the elements of such typical industries as it may be possible to introduce into the work of the school (see bulletin, " Manual Training in the Schools," by W. T. Bawden, Illinois Normal University, April, 1904).

With the country high schools — that is, the village high schools — and the consolidated school as centers, manual training for the country child should begin. From these schools this particular phase of educational activity will soon spread into a large number of one-room country schools. The progress will be slow for two reasons : first, the teachers are not yet trained for this work ; second, as was said above, the farmer, the patron of the country school, does not yet distinguish the difference between

FIG. 139. Manual Training Products in Cottage Hill
School, near Springfield, Illinois

manual training and manual labor. Enough of the latter, certainly, the country child gets, and he is sent to school to study a book. We must not neglect book study, to be sure; but a careful observer of the average country school must be impressed with the great waste of time in much of this alleged study of books. A reasonable amount of manual training could be given in the country school without doing violence to the study programme, and the study of books would be better for the manual activity. This is no theory;

it has been and is being demonstrated beyond the shadow of a doubt ; and if we wait till every teacher is properly trained and every farmer is converted, nothing will be done. A demand must be created where none now exists. It is the duty of educational leaders — teachers and superintendents and school officers — to create this demand. Manual training did not come into the city schools because of a great spontaneous demand on the part of the city people. The history of the movement shows that it was regarded

FIG. 140. The Workshop of Cottage Hill School. Workbenches used for Lunch Counters

as a "fad" by the great mass of the people and also by no inconsiderable part of the elect, — the educational leaders, — who were supposed to know. But time changes some things ; and in view of educational progress in the past one should hesitate before he determines for time and eternity that manual training has no place in a sane, rational system of education for the country child.

Here is a great opportunity for the school to coöperate with the country home, for through the inspiration and help of a live teacher a workbench can be installed in the home workshop, if it seems impracticable to install one in the country schoolhouse. The boy and girl at home, along the lines of farm activity and domestic economy, can make a collection of simple tools and receive instruction from the teacher as to processes of work. The country school and the country home must come more closely together. Many of the old-time activities on the farm and in the country home have gone since the introduction of improved machinery. With this change have gone some of the elements in the training of the country child, which the new country-school training must supply.

Superintendent Brown of Edgar County, in an address before the Eastern Illinois Teachers' Association at Tuscola, February, 1906, emphasizes this point as follows :

Our schools must take up the neglected work of the home. Much credit was given the schools of the olden time for the power of character formation in the youths of fifty years ago. We may be in error, but our candid opinion is that the great men and women of fifty years ago were produced by the home in spite of the school. The character of our grandparents was the result of a home training such as no child in this day and generation is the fortunate possessor of.

It has been well said that when a boy is learning the mechanics of home-keeping and a girl the chemistry of home-keeping, they are gaining as much self-culture as when they are learning what kinds of homes the ancient Greeks and Romans possessed. Our present self-development is too narrow. We need to broaden it. Manual training is necessary to make the "all-round" man.

It will be impossible to note every country school and every county, normal, and training school where some manual training for the country school is carried on. The data are not yet at hand, and if they were, there would be material enough on this subject for a large book, to say nothing of a single chapter. So the writer cannot give credit for all the good work that is being done, and certainly he makes no pretension of saying in one brief chapter the last word about manual training in the country school. It is hoped that what is given here, together with the account of what is being done, will quicken public interest in this particular phase of the education of the country child.

As an illustration of what may be done by a country teacher in a one-room school, the account of the Cottage Hill School, near Springfield, Illinois, as given by State Superintendent Bayliss at the Department of Superintendence at Cincinnati, Ohio, February, 1903, is worthy of careful study. Mr. Bayliss made a study of that school and has kindly loaned some of the photographs for this chapter. The illustrations show that the workbench is in the basement. When the new schoolhouse was built only enough of excavation was done to provide room for the furnace and for fuel. The teacher and boys dug out enough more to place a workbench, and upon Superintendent Bayliss's suggestion to the school officers the entire basement was made available for manual training purposes, as shown in the illustration. In the erection of country schoolhouses in the future the possibility of a good, dry, well-lighted basement should not be overlooked.

The teacher stayed in this school for six years, with a steady increase of salary. He had no special training for this particular work, but had a willingness to learn and to do. In speaking with Superintendent Bayliss he said:

When I came into this district six years ago the schoolhouse had nothing in it and was falling to pieces. After the new house was built the school grew, and I just couldn't keep those little fellows studying books all day, and so had to do something to keep them busy. The older children just naturally "got busy" because they wanted to.

We quote further from Superintendent Bayliss's paper, read at Cincinnati:

Results count. This man's pedagogical method may be vulnerable, but, beyond a peradventure, he has achieved the prime result in any school district, — a genuine and public interest in the school.

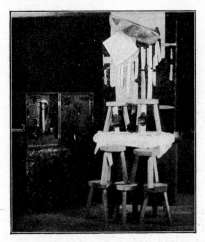

FIG. 141. Articles made in a Rural School in Dunn County, Wisconsin

The bane of the detached school, in the small independent district, is the withering apathy, — the utter indifference to anything but petty grievances that, in the last analysis, can be usually traced to the intolerable dullness of the conventional school routine. Children are confined to a single mode of expression, and that upon matter derived from books, which, as far as they can see, has no sort of relation to anything whatever of interest to them; and they naturally go to sleep. Why shouldn't they? Whatever wakes them up is justifiable. If the waking is followed by a new attitude of mind, extending beyond the school to the community, uniting directors, people, children, and teacher, the result is a distinct gain, apparent pedagogical crudeness to the contrary notwithstanding. Saul, the son of Kish, is not the only man who ever found a greater thing than he sought.

The following will illustrate what can be done in a county as a unit. County Superintendent Duggan of Hancock County, Georgia, has issued a bulletin entitled

" Manual Training in Hancock County Schools." The first
paragraph reads :

Hancock County is the only county in Georgia, or elsewhere so far
as we are informed, where any serious effort has been made towards
the systematic introduction of manual training into the courses of
study of an entire county system of rural schools.

The work has been going on for two years, — not time
enough, it is true, to establish it firmly or to demonstrate

FIG. 142. The Manual Training Class at Work in a Rural
School in Edgar County, Illinois

its worth to other counties. But the interest and value
are certainly great enough to justify the fondest hopes of
those who believe in it. The conditions under which the
work was inaugurated are similar to those of thousands of
communities. Superintendent Duggan says :

The large majority of the teachers had no ideas, or incorrect ideas,
as to the methods or purposes of manual training in school work.

Citizens and patrons generally knew or thought but little about educational methods, and regarded any innovation as unorthodox and therefore unwise ; while a few leaders of educational thought and progress, from whom wise counsel and coöperation was confidently expected, looked upon the movement with skepticism or jealousy, thereby well-nigh discouraging the most ardent promoters and interposing serious hindrance to a full, fair, and impartial trial.

But there were some decided advantages. There are only twenty-six public rural schools in the county and one city high school at Sparta, the county seat. Thus the territory is more compact, with fewer schools than in the average county in Illinois and the Middle West. Then again there was a liberal donation from the General Education Board of New York towards the establishment of a system of manual training in connection with the county's public schools. Thus most of the funds were realized without the necessity of relying on local sources not friendly to the scheme ; and last, but not least by any means, the county superintendent was able to have an expert supervisor in charge of the work, — a person " who received her preparation at Teachers College, Columbia University, and who was also familiar with southern institutions, native materials, and Georgia rural-school conditions, and who was well educated, thoroughly trained, and had had successful experience in this particular line of educational work."

Now no county superintendent should be cast down under such conditions. Given twenty-six country schools and one high school, a liberal amount of money, and a trained supervisor to a thousand county superintendents scattered over this country, and you will see things done in spite of unprogressive patrons and educational leaders, by courtesy so termed.

Most of the pupils beyond the seventh grade in the twenty-six country schools go to the high school at Sparta. On the high-school ground a manual training building of three rooms was erected, and this is open on Saturdays for the country school-teachers. The supervisor and the superintendent outline the work from month to month, and a copy of the outline is sent to each teacher at least ten days before the first of the month. The teachers study this and receive help from the supervisor at the manual training shop on the first Saturday of each month. The instruction and direction for the country school-teachers is not limited to one Saturday, but the supervisor is ready every Saturday. At the first meeting practically every teacher in the county attends; the attendance at the other meetings depends upon the weather, etc. A two weeks' manual training institute is carried on during the summer vacation.

The following is given to illustrate the work:

HANCOCK COUNTY SCHOOLS

(*Manual Training Department*)

OUTLINES FOR NOVEMBER

(Furnished by Miss Emily P. Wilburn)

First Three Grades

1. Draw from large red apple.
2. Tear from paper an apple. Mount best picture of an apple of contrasting color.
3. Make drawing of a large pear.
4. Draw to illustrate something in connection with language or nature-study lessons.
5. Make drawing from spray of red leaves.
6. Draw simple landscape.
7. Illustrate story of three bears.
8. Draw to illustrate some personal experience.

Constructive Work

1. Make needlebooks. Decorate with sewing two pieces of cardboard. Make leaves of flannel and tie together with bright-colored ribbon.

2. Decorate card with pumpkins or turkey and sew with bright-colored thread. Use as Thanksgiving card.

Lessons for Grades above Third

1. Select spray of autumn leaves and draw, placing in a panel of good proportion.
2. Give lessons in landscape drawing.
3. Continue lessons in landscape drawing.
4. Make drawing of pumpkins placed in inclosure. Use table line to give the appearance of resting on something.
5. Draw to illustrate some portion of reading lesson.
6. Make drawing of pod of pepper. Let each child have a pod if possible.
7. Use the drawings of pepper for making a border design.

Constructive Work

1. Waste basket. Make bottom of wood. Weave sides of willow, native rattan, or braided buffalo grass.

2. Comb-and-brush tray. Make by sewing pine needles or native grass with coil stitches.

Teachers are requested to study these outlines and bring them to the class on Saturday, November 5, 1904, where any point not fully understood will be explained.

Teachers are also expected to confer freely with Miss Wilburn at any time in regard to any feature of the work or its introduction into their schools.

In the preceding chapter is an account of the great work being done in Dunn County, Wisconsin, in training teachers to give instruction in manual training in the country schools

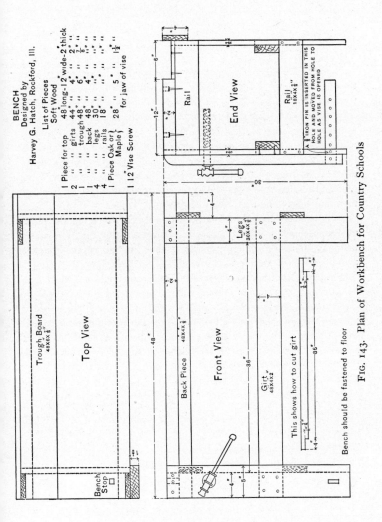

BENCH
Designed by
Harvey G. Hatch, Rockford, Ill.

List of Pieces
Soft Wood

1 Piece for top	48" long	12 wide	2" thick
2 " " girts	44" "	4" "	2" "
1 " " trough	48" "	6" "	7/8" "
1 " " back	48" "	4" "	1" "
4 " " legs	30" "	4" "	1" "
4 " " rails	18" "	2" "	1" "
1 Piece Oak or Maple }	28" "	5" "	1 1/2" "
1 12" Vise Screw		for jaw of vise	

Rail

End View

Rail 18 X 4 X 3/4"

A IRON PIN IS INSERTED IN THIS HOLE AND MOVED FROM HOLE TO HOLE AS VISE IS OPENED

Trough Board 48 X 6 X 7/8"

Top View

Bench Stop

Back Piece 48 X 4 X 1"

Front View

Legs 30 X 4 X 1"

Girt 48 X 2 X 2"

This shows how to cut girt

Bench should be fastened to floor

FIG. 143. Plan of Workbench for Country Schools

323

of that county. A reference to the account given will reveal the course of study. Principal K. C. Davis of the county School of Agriculture, writes :

Senator J. H. Stout has helped materially in the introduction of the woodwork in the rural schools by providing fifteen sets of wood-working tools in neat cases, to be used as loan sets. These travel from school to school, staying in one place only long enough to create a demand for such work in that district. The district itself is then expected to buy a set of tools to be used in the future. The agricultural school has provided workbenches and brackets for the same, made by its students. These go with the loan sets mentioned. Very practical results have already been obtained, and in many cases much more has been done than could be expected.

The teachers find the work useful in helping to keep the older pupils in school, in interesting pupils otherwise listless, and in making better equipment for their schools, to say nothing of the training actually gained from the work itself.

We should not fail to consider the important influence which has surrounded the teachers of this county because of the presence of the Stout training schools, located at the county seat. The spirit of manual training pervades all. This paves the way for the introduction of such work into all schools; and since it has helped the city schools of Menomonie, it is reasonable to suppose that such work will help the country schools also, as it does.

State normal schools are seriously studying the question of manual training for the country school. The oldest normal school in Illinois, the one at Normal, offers four courses in the training of teachers for the country schools: (1) bench work in wood; (2) construction work for primary grades; (3) hand work for intermediate grades; (4) mechanical drawing.

Special attention is given to elementary hand work during the first summer term of each year, when a great number of teachers from the country schools are in attendance.

This instruction is helpful, as Assistant County Superintendent Brigham of McLean County, the county in which the normal school is located, reports to Director Bawden that twenty per cent of the country schools of this county have some hand work going on, and that the number is increasing. This increase is to be expected in a county in which a great training school has been located for fifty years. But what about counties far removed from the direct influence of such a school?

A very important investigation has been going on, which must result in an awakening on the subject of manual training in the country schools, especially those of Illinois. During the past year a committee of the

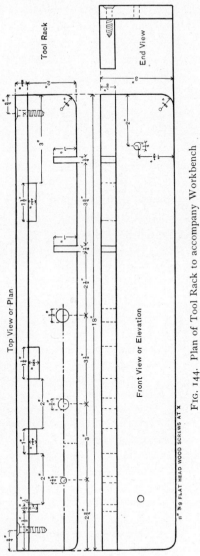

FIG. 144. Plan of Tool Rack to accompany Workbench

Illinois Manual Arts Association has been making a study of the country-school problem.

This committee made its report on manual training for rural schools to the Illinois Manual Arts Association at the third annual meeting at the University of Illinois, Saturday, February 17, 1906.

It has not yet been decided what will be done with the report, but through the kindness of the chairman, Mr. Bawden, I am permitted to use portions of it here, the committee reserving the right to publish it entire or in part in the future. No definite conclusions have yet been determined in this report concerning manual training in the country schools beyond the belief that something can and should be done.

So far the committee has used the following outline as a guide in making investigations :

I. Given certain conditions, some hand work is possible.
   1. Country school with one room and one teacher.
      a. A teacher having some natural interest in and some aptitude for hand work, and willingness to make some effort. Or
      b. A teacher having had enough training in hand work to be able to get at least a few things started and the pupils interested.
      c. Officials not absolutely opposed to the idea of manual training, but no funds available.
   2. Conditions similar to 1, but small sum available (five or ten dollars).
   3. Conditions similar to 2, except that the schoolhouse has an entry or vacant space in which a workbench or table might be placed.
   4. School with two rooms and two teachers, one of whom fills conditions of *a* or *b* in 1 ; permission to spend ten or fifteen dollars.

    a. What conditions are desirable?

    b. What conditions are essential if hand work is to be attempted?

    c. What may be undertaken in any of the cases cited?

    d. How may it be done?

    e. How arouse interest?

    f. How meet opposition?

    g. How secure material or equipment?

II. Discussion of source of initiative.

   1. The citizen.

   2. The teacher.

   3. The school directors or board.

   4. The county superintendent.

   5. Any teacher or supervisor of the manual arts within reach.

   6. The Illinois Manual Arts Association.

   7. Educational institutions.

    a. Who should make the first move?

    b. What may each do?

    c. How secure coöperation of two or more?

    d. How secure or disseminate information, advice, practical suggestions?

III. Description and discussion of results actually accomplished.

IV. How can we make use of the important work already accomplished along the lines of nature study and elementary agriculture?

   Can we get from the leaders of this movement a list of definite and concrete problems that we may systematize and put in shape from the standpoint of the hand work involved?

Thus far only two members of the committee have submitted the results of their investigations.

Mr. Kendall, Supervisor of Manual Training, Lasalle Township High School, offers suggestions on "How to begin Manual Training in the Rural Schools." He says at the outset of his suggestions:

This beginning has to do with the school that has no special equipment and no provision for any regular appropriation. At the outset it may be said that there is no beginning for the teacher who has no interest in the work; such a teacher has no business to attempt the work. A teacher with the proper incentive and adequate information will succeed as well in manual training as in any book subject.

Mr. Kendall approaches the subject from the educational point of view, which is the correct one in the end, and groups the work in three divisions. The first division comprises Grades I, II, and III; the second comprises Grades

FIG. 145. Manual Training in a Country School of
Winnebago County, Illinois

IV and V; while the third comprises Grades VI, VII, and VIII. With each division is given an outline of work suitable for each grade. Some may claim that the proper beginning is with Grades VII and VIII by making some things that will appeal to the average farmer from a usable point of view and still be educational in the processes of work. Mr. Kendall says on this point:

The need in all this work is a well-arranged, logical as well as natural, course through the first six years. The usual method of procedure in the installation of manual training is to begin in the eighth

FIG. 146. Manual Training in a Country School of
Winnebago County, Illinois

or ninth year, and then the work is slid up and down until all the grades are provided with their several lines of work. The proper place in which to begin manual training is in the kindergarten or first grade, and then develop the work year by year through the upper grades. The teacher will be able to make the course fit the special needs of the school when the scope of the work is understood from a study of the literature and materials that may be obtained from the resources at command.

The above is sound in theory, but manual training has had to start in almost any way in many city schools. The problem is more complicated for the country school, and it may be that the utilitarian aspect will have to be emphasized with the farmers at the outset rather than the educational aspect. The educators should, of course, keep both in view.

The report has an account of the literature available on the subject, and gives the experience of two country school-teachers in installing manual training in their schools. The chairman closes by asking the following general questions :

1. First, what can the supervisor of drawing or manual training in the town or city do to help the rural school-teacher? How many supervisors here present have Saturday morning meetings for teachers? Is it practicable for such supervisors to extend an invitation to such rural school-teachers as are within reach, and who can be interested, to come in and attempt to prepare themselves for this work?

2. My second question is, Are the conditions ripe for the publication of a small manual prepared especially for the rural school-teacher and dealing with the subjects of drawing, hand work, and nature study? A beginning could be made with a small pamphlet of say thirty or forty pages, profusely illustrated ; it should specifically suggest a *few* things that may be done in any rural school by any intelligent teacher. The processes should be simple, the materials cheap and easily obtained, the equipment reduced to a minimum, and all details worked out and fully explained. Suitable references to the literature of the manual arts would furnish the teacher with a clew as to what to do next.

A progressive county superintendent in Minnesota, Miss Fanny Gies of Mower County, states how manual training is carried on in a county where there is no special supervisor. Her account is a type of what, doubtless, is being done in many counties. Miss Gies says:

I believe the manual training courses as laid out for our city schools under the direction of a trained specialist are not suitable or practical for our country schools. We have neither the time nor the trained instructor, but we can do something to bring into our schools and develop the manual training spirit. We can do something to meet that innate desire of every child to make something that is of use, that desire which, when materialized, supplements and strengthens our work in other directions. Since manual training courses are planned to train the eye and the hand to work together under the direction of the mind, I believe we must put into our country schools something which will tend to accomplish this result.

In this county I have introduced drawing into the one-room schools partly for this reason. We need not fear that we shall destroy the beauty idea by making it a training; for the closer the union of mind, eye, and hand, the better the artistic result as well as the training. Drawing to measurement with rulers and the making of designs should be often introduced into the work of the older pupils. The practical and decorative is often combined in making articles for definite uses, such as notebook covers, portfolios for drawing and writing material, programmes and invitations, and objects for holiday purposes.

In the primary grades we find the little folks become very skillful in the use of the scissors in making free-hand cuttings to illustrate some mental picture derived from a story. Paper folding and weaving of paper, cloth, or yarn are forms of industrial work adapted to the lower grades in our country schools.

Some of our schools have done excellent work in cardboard construction. This demands great accuracy in measurement, drawing, and cutting. The pupils have taken great pleasure in making brackets, boxes, cardcases, match holders, furniture for dolls, etc. Because of its excellent training I hope to make this work general in the schools of this county. Some teachers have attempted raffia work in their schools, but say they find it more difficult to use in the one-room schools. This last form of work has not been urged upon the teachers.

The kinds of industrial work that have been emphasized in Mower County are drawing, paper cutting, folding, and weaving, and cardboard construction. For the teachers who have not had previous preparation for this work we have provided special instruction at the summer training schools, and also at the county teachers' meetings held during the school year.

Something may be done at the annual teachers' institute of only a week's duration to help country school-teachers to a better understanding of the importance of manual training. A few of the teachers will receive enough help and inspiration to really accomplish something in their regular school work. For two years manual training has had a place on the programme of the institute of Winnebago County. The work has been in charge of Mr. Harvey G. Hatch, Supervisor of Manual Training in the city schools of Rockford. This work may be taken as a type of what may be done in a week in the way of aiding teachers and helping to answer the question how a city supervisor of manual training may help the country school-teacher. This question was raised before by Mr. Bawden. The following is Mr. Hatch's thought on the subject :

At first sight it seems that manual training forms so natural a part of the farm boy's life that he does not need school influence to stimulate him to activity. We have heard over and over again from city men whose careers had their rise in farm life that they did not lack for manual training in those early years; in fact, it was manual training from early morning till late at night. But we do not hear from the old-time farmer boy that manual training ever meant anything more than long-drawn-out drudgery and unending toil. The city man sees his early life as a means, while the farmer sees his early life in the light of an end. It is for the farmer of to-day to see that in manual training he has a means that will help his children directly, and himself indirectly, to better understand and enjoy farm life.

No matter how involved the present situation may be, it takes no great prophet to see what the end will be. The country boy is capable of and has great necessity for the fine adjustments of muscular

control which the planing of a board means. Without doubt the
country boy needs to have more of a chance to use his hands under
school auspices, and when the time comes that the country boy may
be seen on his way home from school with a book under one arm
and under the other an evener, a towel rack, or some useful thing
which he himself has made in school, it will be safe to say that that
boy will look upon his school as a more useful place, and there will
be some natural connection between living on a farm and going to a
country school. I doubt not that the country boy likes to feel himself a part of the life which is all about him, but he gets only a slight

FIG. 147. Winnebago County Teachers doing Tool Work at the
March (1906) Annual Teachers' Institute

view of it through the present country school. Action is a part of
life, but ordinarily action is ruled out in school business.

Many machines are used on a farm, and machines break. Repairs
are necessary, and often the loss of a day's use of a machine means a
great deal. Suppose the country schoolboy could make an intelligent
working drawing of the necessary part and take it to town himself,
explaining to the mechanic just what repairs would be needed. Here
again the boy would feel himself a prime factor and not a drudge
factor in the development of the farm.

From my point of view, then, it is necessary to emphasize the
need of what the educator calls the purely utilitarian. I urge this as

the next step, for it is the logical thing to do. Without doubt the passing of time will reveal a broader application.

No doubt the county institutes may be made a great help in giving teachers some rudimentary ideas in the details of tool work. While this is an opportunity by no means to be neglected, it cannot be considered to meet the situation adequately; but if the city manual training schools could give the matter some consideration, they would be of great assistance. I doubt if it would be difficult to form Saturday classes in cities for country teachers, if enthusiasm and backing were forthcoming from county officials.

The manual training high school of the city must aid in the solution of the manual training problem of the country school. Township high schools and the regular city high schools are attracting many country boys, and almost without exception they find large satisfaction in the manual training courses. From these young people must come the supply of teachers for the country schools; they are the ones who can give the greatest help, since they are in sympathetic touch with the life of the country and can best see and realize country needs.

Ofttimes teachers in the country school find the need of a suggestive outline of work for the different grades, together with some good practical reference books, which the teacher may own or put into the local school library as the result of a school social. The following, taken from the *Manual Training Magazine*, is to the point, and is particularly valuable to the country school, as shop equipment is not necessary:

POSSIBLE KINDS OF HAND WORK

From the following outline one or two or possibly, in some cases, three kinds of work may be selected for each grade.

GRADES I AND II. Equipment: pencil, ruler, scissors, needle:
   a. Paper folding: geometric, square of paper given (see "Construction Work in the Primary Grades," by Julia C. Cremins in Yearbook of Council of Supervisors of the Manual Arts, 1904).

FIG. 148. A House constructed by Grammar-School Boys, to be furnished by the Children of the Primary Grades

Work done in the Hyannis (Massachusetts) Training School

335

b. Paper cutting: freehand (see "Freehand Cutting," by Olive Wills in *School Arts Book*, Vol. IV, pages 265–271).

Cutting natural forms and illustrating stories.

c. Paper weaving: strips of paper given (see *Educational Handwork Manuals*, Part I, by Arthur H. Chamberlain; also *Suggestions in Handwork*, by Wilhelmina Seegmiller).

d. Paper construction work (see *Paper Sloyd or Primary Grades*, by Ednah A. Rich).

e. Work with raffia or shoe strings: braiding, winding, knotting (see *Educational Handwork Manuals*, Part I, by Arthur H. Chamberlain).

f. Weaving: rugs and other simple objects of yarn or strips of cloth or raffia.

GRADE III. Equipment: pencil, ruler, scissors, needle, two or three ticket punches for the class.

a. Cardboard work: very heavy manila paper, one square corner given (see *Paper Sloyd for Primary Grades*, by Ednah A Rich; or *First Years in Handicraft*, by Walter J. Kenyon).

FIG. 149. Learning to Cook: Manual Training for Girls

b. Card work: macramé cord, shoe strings, or wrapping cord (see Chapter XXIII in *Practical and Artistic Basketry*, by Laura R. Tinsley).

c. Basketry (see *Practical and Artistic Basketry*, by Laura R. Tinsley).

GRADE IV. Equipment: the same as provided for Grade III, with compasses added.

a. Cardboard construction: heavy manila paper or bristol board; find square corners (see *Cardboard Construction*, by J. H. Trybom; or *Paper and Cardboard Work*, by Arthur H. Chamberlain).

b. Basketry (see reference in Grade III).

FIG. 150. Macdonald Consolidated School, Guelph, Ontario, Canada. Manual Training Room

c. Clay working (see "Clay Working in the School," by Cheshire L. Boone in Yearbook of Council of Supervisors of the Manual Arts, 1905; also " Pottery in the Public Schools," by Forrest E. Mann in *Manual Training Magazine*, January, 1906).

GRADE V.

a. Knife work. Equipment: knife, try-square, compasses, ruler, and pencil for each pupil, and small hammer, two hand screws, oilstone, oil can, and brad awl. Material: basswood, $\frac{1}{8}$ by $\frac{3}{16}$ inches thick; pad of drawing paper 6 by 9 inches; liquid glue, small brads, sandpaper, stains and wax for finishing (see *Elementary Knife Work*, by W. C. A. Hammel; and *Art Crafts for Beginners*, by Frank G. Sanford).

b. Bent-iron work. Equipment: flat-nose pliers, round-nose pliers, rule, and pencil for each pupil; snips for every four pupils, small hand vise, small hammer, Morrill punch, and paint brush for general use. Material: $\frac{1}{4}$-inch ribbon iron, $\frac{1}{4}$-inch binders, rivets, black paint (see " Bent Iron," by Henry T. Bailey in *School Arts Book* for February, 1905).

c. Basketry (see reference in Grade III).

d. Clay working (see reference in Grade IV).

GRADE VI.

a. Knife work. Continuation of work in Grade V.

b. Bent-iron work (see references in Grade V).

c. Basketry (see references in Grade III).

d. Sewing.

e. Clay working (see references in Grade IV).

GRADE VII.

a. Knife work. The same as Grade V, adding the use of thicker wood (pine) in the middle of the year. To the equipment should be added one backsaw (10 inches), one bench hook, one bit brace, three drill bits, in sizes to suit work to be done (see *Advanced Knife Work*, by W. C. A. Hammel).

b. Tooled leather work. Equipment: modeling tools, small board of hard wood, knife, ruler, sponge (see *Manual Training Magazine*, July, 1904, and October, 1905; also *Art Crafts for Beginners*, by Frank G. Sanford, and "Simple Metal-Working in the Public Schools," by Forrest E. Mann in *Manual Training Magazine*, Vol. IV).

c. Sewing and garment making.

Note. The girls may take sewing while the boys take knife work. Then for a part of the time both boys and girls may unite in either tooled work or in sheet-metal work.

GRADE VIII.

a. Mechanical drawing. Equipment: "Springfield Kit," compasses, ruler, pencil, eraser (see *Mechanical Drawing*, by Anson K. Cross).

b. Paper-box making and the elements of book binding; use of strawboard and lining paper. Equipment : straightedge, knife, scissors, ruler, pencil, folder. Material: strawboard, lining paper, cover papers, linen, paste, glue (see "Some Phases of Constructive Work in the Grammar Grades," by Julia C. Cremins in Yearbook of Council of Supervisors of the Manual Arts, 1905).

c. Tooled leather work (see reference in Grade VII).
d. Sheet-metal work (see reference in Grade VII).
e. Sewing and garment making.
f. Cooking.

Following is a carefully prepared list of the most useful works on the various phases of manual training :

REFERENCE LIST

THEORY

Baldwin, W. A., Industrial School Education.
Dewey, John, The School and Society.
Dopp, Katherine E., The Place of Industries in Elementary Education.
Goetze, W., Hand and Eye Training. (From the German standpoint.)
Ham, C. H., Mind and Hand.
National Educational Association, Report of the Committee on Industrial Education in Schools for Rural Communities, 1905.
Salomon, Otto, The Theory of Educational Sloyd. (From the Swedish standpoint.)
Washington, B. T., Working with the Hands.
Woodward, C. M., The Manual Training School.
Woodward, C. M., Manual Training in Education.

PRACTICE

Schoolroom Handicrafts

Chamberlain, Arthur H., Basketry, Clay, and Paper Weaving for the Elementary Grades.
Chamberlain, Arthur H., Paper and Cardboard Construction.
Hammel, W. C. A., Elementary Knife Work.
Hammel, W. C. A., Advanced Knife Work.
Hapgood, Olive C., School Needlework. Teacher's Edition.
Kenyon, W. J., First Years in Handicraft.
Rich, Ednah A., Paper Sloyd for Primary Grades.
Sage, Elizabeth, and Cooley, Anna M., Occupations for Little Fingers. Work in textiles.

Sanford, F. G., Art Crafts for Beginners. Sheet-metal work, tooled leather, pottery, bookbinding, pyrography.

Seegmiller, Wilhelmina, Suggestions in Handwork. Paper weaving, work with tilo matting.

Todd, M. P., Hand-Loom Weaving.

Trybom, J. H., Cardboard Construction.

Trybom, J. H., Correlated Handwork, Book I.

Walkeman, A. V., and Heller, L. M., Scientific Sewing and Garment Cutting.

Williams, Mary E., and Fisher, Katharine R., Elements of the Theory and Practice of Cookery.

Worst, E. F., Construction Work.

Woodworking

Foster, E. W., Elementary Woodworking. A text-book for schools. It is intended to supplement class instruction concerning tools, fundamental tool processes, wood, and trees.

Goss, W. F. M., Bench Work in Wood. Contains an excellent chapter on tools and their use.

Hoffman, B. B., The Sloyd System of Woodworking.

Murray, M. W., Problems of Woodworking. Forty selected working drawings ready for class use.

Pinchot, Gifford, A Primer of Forestry. Part I, The Forest ; Part II, Practical Forestry. Bulletin No. 24, United States Department of Agriculture.

Wheeler, C. G., Woodworking for Beginners. Tells the amateur how to make furniture, implements for sport, small boats, house boats, summer cottages, and the like.

Drawing and Design

Batchelder, E. A., Principles of Design.

Cross, A. K., Freehand Drawing.

Cross, A. K., Light and Shade.

Cross, A. K., Mechanical Drawing.

Equipments, Cost, etc.

Rouillion, Louis, The Economy of Manual Training.

Gardening

Hemenway, H. D., Hints and Helps for Young Gardeners.

PERIODICALS

Amateur Work.
Craftsman.
Manual Training Magazine.
School Arts Book.
Yearbooks of Council of Supervisors of the Manual Arts.

CHAPTER XV

A LAST WORD

In this concluding chapter I do not expect to say the final word with reference to increasing the usefulness of the country school. This will be a last word so far as this work is concerned. There needs to be an awakening among country people and educators generally with respect to the possibilities of the country school. How this awakening is to be brought about is another matter.

It is a hopeful sign for the country schools of any state when the state university begins to "sit up and take notice" of the district schools. This is what is happening in the great state of Illinois. So far as I know, for the first time in the history of the state the University of Illinois held a special summer session in the interest of country schools, June 12–30, 1905; also a special state conference in the interests of the country schools of Illinois was held by the University, June 26–30, 1905.

During the summer session of three weeks such subjects as agriculture, household science, manual training, teaching, economic zoölogy, commercial geography, school architecture, and school consolidation — all for country schools — were considered by men of mark in the educational world.

The reader's attention is called to the following resolutions, adopted at the close of this conference:

Resolutions

University of Illinois, Urbana,
June 30, 1905

.   .   .   .

Whereas: We sincerely appreciate the importance of the movement whereby the great University of Illinois, the apex of the educational pyramid of our state, extends a helping hand to the ten thousand six hundred and seventy-seven country schools of Illinois at the base of our educational pyramid, where were enrolled three hundred and eighteen thousand two hundred and eighteen boys and girls of the Prairie State; and

Whereas: Fully ninety per cent of these boys and girls will get their only training for life's duties, so far as books are concerned, in these ten thousand six hundred and seventy-seven one-room country schools under more or less favorable conditions ; therefore

Be it resolved: That we, as school officers, teachers, and patrons assembled in this first conference in the interests of the country schools, recommend that a united effort be made all over Illinois, by individual school districts or larger communities, to increase the usefulness of the country school along one or more of the following general lines.

First. Increase the usefulness of the country school as a spiritualizing force in country life by planting trees, flowers, shrubbery on the school grounds so that the one thousand seven hundred and sixty-six country-school grounds now without a single tree, and the three thousand three hundred and thirty-two country-school grounds with insufficient trees, may exert as wholesome an influence as do the three thousand nine hundred and fifty-four well-kept, beautiful country-school grounds now scattered over our state. It is also true that beautiful buildings, equipped with necessary apparatus, a library, choice works of art on the walls, etc., do exert quite as much influence for right thinking and doing as does a study of what men have said or done in past ages.

Second. Increase the usefulness of the country school by an enrichment of the course of study for the country child, so that the country child may be put into sympathetic and intelligent relation to his environment. That there shall come into the country school something in an elementary form, with reference to agriculture, manual training, and domestic arts. That in the things surrounding the child on the farm is a body of material that possesses a high cultural value as well as practical utility.

Third. Increase the usefulness of the country school by consolidating weak country schools and transporting children when conditions are favorable. This will give a country graded school and make

FIG. 151. A Schoolhouse built in the Early Fifties

possible the distinctly country high school with a course of study flavored with country life and interests. We fully recognize that consolidation is not feasible in many localities *now*, nor perhaps desirable; but it is practicable in many localities, and we are heartily in favor of an educational campaign whereby the people may be thoroughly informed on this question. Then it is theirs to do or not to do.

Resolved: Our thanks are hereby extended to the authorities and faculty of the University of Illinois for their efforts to make this first conference the success it has been.

.   .   .   .

Under the leadership of State Superintendent Cary, Wisconsin has already made most significant advances. It was my pleasure to attend a recent convention of school directors in Rock County, Wisconsin. These conventions can be made a great force in an educational campaign for an educational uplift for the country child. The Wisconsin law with reference to school directors' meetings reads as follows:

SECTION I. A paragraph is hereby added to Section 461 of the statutes of 1898, to be numbered and to read as follows: 9. The county or district superintendent of schools shall annually call and hold at least one school board convention for his superintendent district, at the county seat or some other convenient place, for the purpose of consultation, advice, and instruction upon matters pertaining to the management of our schools. Each district clerk shall, and the director and treasurer may, attend such convention. Each member present shall be allowed two dollars and mileage at the rate of three cents per mile each way, going and returning to and from said meeting, and said sum to be paid from any moneys in the school district treasury not otherwise appropriated. The county superintendent shall issue to each member in attendance a certificate which shall be filed with the school district clerk and serve as a basis or evidence for drawing the necessary warrant upon the district treasury.

The last legislature of Wisconsin made provision for a State Inspector of Country Schools. The new inspector, Mr. L. W. Wood, has a great field before him. From my conversation with him at the Rock County school board convention I judge him to be a man in full sympathy with the country school. It is safe to say that the school directors, county superintendents, and country school-teachers will find in the new inspector a safe and sympathetic colaborer. The *Journal of Education* (Boston), in a recent editorial, has the following with reference to this forward step for the country schools of Wisconsin. Speaking of Inspector Wood's duties, the editor says :

In July and August he is to familiarize himself by careful reading with all the recent literature on rural schools and their improvement. He is expected to be master of the best things so far written on all phases of the subject. In September and October he will visit, in and out of the state, those places in which the new work is done in and for the country schools. From November to March there will be seventy county conventions of the boards of education in rural districts. At least one man from each district is required to attend, and his expenses are paid, and he further draws a per diem honorarium for attendance.

The county superintendent arranges the meeting, though Inspector Wood will largely dominate the programme. In this way he will enlighten and inspire some school official in every local rural district in the state.

From March to June he will be visiting schools, selecting typical regions, visiting rural schools faithfully and actively for five days each week, and on Saturday will hold a teachers' meeting at which every teacher visited shall be present. From time to time bulletins will be issued for the advantage of the teachers, superintendents, and the public.

The state department has set about improving school buildings and grounds, notably in heating and ventilating; securing better teachers, and better salaries for the better teachers; reducing the number of small schools through consolidating schools and transporting the pupils. Mr. Wood was born in an agricultural community, went to a country school, has taught in ungraded schools, and has the purpose and the vigor to do a great work for the rural schools of Wisconsin.

Why not something of this kind for every state? Why should the country school be the last part of our educational system to receive attention? State Superintendent Miller of West Virginia is conducting an educational campaign in his state. The *West Virginia School Journal* for June, 1905, contains the following editorial:

State Superintendent Miller believes that the educational progress of the state is not keeping up with its industrial progress, and that in our wild scramble for wealth we are losing sight of the more important things of life. In order to get the people to think upon these things he organized an educational campaign in three sections which he called "The Ohio River Tour," "The North Central Tour," and "The Tour on the Main Line of the Baltimore and Ohio," respectively. County Superintendent O. J. Kern of Winnebago County, Illinois, was the chief speaker on the first of these tours; Dr. A. E. Winship, editor of the *Journal of Education* (Boston), on the second; and State Superintendent W. W. Stetson of Maine on the third. Superintendent Miller had personal charge of the meetings for the first two weeks, after which he was obliged, by the serious illness of Mrs. Miller, to remain at home. Professor Thomas E. Hodges of the University was a member of the party for the first week and a part of the third, and Dr. Waitman Barbe of the University was with the various tours the whole three weeks. The campaign began April 24 and closed May 13. At least fifteen thousand people heard the addresses. The meetings were attended by the most influential people, and in most cases the interest and enthusiasm were quite marked. In some instances receptions and banquets were held, and orchestras, as well as the best vocal music, were brought into use, and the occasions were emphasized in a most encouraging way.

State Superintendent W. W. Stetson of Maine organized, in 1898, the School Improvement League of Maine, for the improvement of the country schools of that state. The objects of the league are to improve school grounds and buildings, to provide suitable reading matter for pupils and parents, and to provide works of art for the schoolroom. How successful the league has been may be judged from a report of the state president and state secretary issued from the office of Superintendent Stetson. The material results are summed up as follows:

1. Planted over five thousand trees.
2. Purchased a hundred thousand books.
3. Purchased over five hundred casts.
4. Purchased about seven thousand pictures.

Other important results are given as follows:

1. The league has created a higher standard of equipment for schools.
2. Harmony has been strengthened between the school and home.
3. Self-help has been emphasized.
4. The usefulness of the country school has been increased.
5. School life has been made more attractive to the children, civic pride has been cultivated, and the taste for good literature has been encouraged.

Superintendent Stetson reports that the country schools of Maine constitute sixty-one per cent of the whole number in the state, with forty-four per cent of the children attending them. Since these same country schools are, in some respects, the most important in the state, Superintendent Stetson has instituted what he is pleased to call "standard schools." He does not quite believe in either "ideal" or "model" schools. To quote from his booklet on standard schools :

The "ideal school" is not attainable. It is doubtful if it is desirable. If we had it, we would not be able to use it in such a way as to derive benefit from it. We have to grow up to the higher planes before we can be helped by ideal conditions.

The "model school" has filled such large spaces in so many reports that it is in bad odor. The "model school," like the "ideal school," is both illusive and delusive. Each is one thing to-day and something quite different to-morrow. Before either can be built it will have outgrown the conception upon which it was constructed.

The "standard school" is achievable. It has metes and bounds and may have a local habitation.

It may be said in passing that no "ideal" is absolutely attainable, for the moment it is attained it is no longer an "ideal" ; and it may be fairly questioned whether a "model school" need necessarily be "both illusive and delusive."

However, among the excellent "ideals" which Mr. Stetson sets forth for his "standard school," which may serve as a "model" for the improvement of the country schools of Maine, are the following :

1. The grounds shall comprise at least three acres with plots for forest trees, fruit trees, school garden, and playground, and with neat, tasteful walks, etc. This is an excellent "ideal," and in several states is being attained, thus serving as a "standard" for other country communities.

2. The building should be constructed of wood and of such a size as to afford plenty of cloak room, etc. The architecture should be simple and attractive, the floors and wainscoting to be of yellow birch with walls and ceiling of steel, the former painted a light buff and the latter a light cream.

3. The windows should be at the left and rear of the pupils when seated.

4. The furniture should consist of a slate blackboard, single adjustable desks, recitation settees, chairs for teacher and possible visitors.

5. A library case and suitable books.

6. Pictures and statuary of real artistic merit.

7. Necessary maps, globe, etc.

8. Stove with jacket, and ventilating shaft in chimney.

9. Water supply ample and pure.

10. Outbuildings in the rear of lot surrounded by evergreen trees.

11. A good fence around school ground.

12. A workshop for the boys and one also for the girls.

And to educate the people up to his ideal of a standard school Superintendent Stetson has issued a pamphlet entitled "Sketches, Designs, and Plans for School Buildings, School Grounds, and Outhouses"; also one on "Improvement of School Buildings and Grounds."

Mr. Stetson claims that the "standard school" will help the people of his state to see that :

The homes of Maine should be domestic universities.

The common school should be the social, literary, and art center of the community.

The safety of the nation is not in the hands of its rulers, but in the lives of its common people.

West Virginia, under the excellent leadership of State Superintendent Miller and Dr. Waitman Barbe of the University of West Virginia, has an active league for the same purposes. The membership fee of the West Virginia league consists of a pledge to devote at least one day during the year towards improving the school grounds and buildings, and to maintain libraries in the schools. Much good work is being done.

From the Pine Tree State to the Palmetto State is shown a quickening of the public interest with reference to the country school. The pamphlets issued by State Superintendent O. B. Martin of South Carolina, in 1905, reveal the new educational spirit in the South land. Special attention

Fig. 152. Bare and Uninviting

is here called to Mr. Martin's pamphlet, "School Improvement, Law, Designs, and Suggestions for Schoolhouses," which cannot help creating a new "ideal" as to the character of the school plant. Design No. 16 in the above pamphlet is "an ideal eight-room school building built in Illinois."

Superintendent Martin well says :

People will not patronize merchants who have uncomfortable, dingy, ill-furnished storehouses, nor do they accept accommodations in box cars when they ride on railroads ; and yet, when it comes to the training of children, they often risk the health, lives, and character of their children in buildings which have but little more comfort or architectural beauty than a cheap barn or a box car. If we judge a man's business by his place of business, it is no wonder that our people are becoming dissatisfied with the average school building, its equipment and its environment. It is impossible to keep the best teacher in an uncomfortable, ill-fitted schoolhouse.

All of which is true of many other states as well as of South Carolina.

A most valuable pamphlet entitled "Better Schools in South Carolina" contains the papers read at a conference of South Carolina educators held at Charleston, April 11, 1903. The papers discuss the following subjects :

1. The Value of Education.
2. Local Taxation.
3. School Consolidation.
4. The Improved Teacher and the Improved Trustee.
5. School Supervision.
6. The School Building and its Equipment.
7. Beautifying School Grounds.
8. The School Library.
9. Country High Schools.
10. The Industrial Side of the Public School.

One quotation from the last will bear reading :

Teach the great mass of the people how to produce something, as well as how to speak and write something, and we have filled an aching void which has long existed in our educational system. We shall then look forward with new hope and inspiration to better things generally, remembering that no civic, religious, or educational system can long exist and succeed without support, backed by the ability of its people to produce.

South Carolina is moving in the matter of consolidation of country schools. State Superintendent Martin says : " The strongest argument that I have heard in favor of consolidation is that wherever it is tried the people like it and usually become its best friends and supporters when it is put into operation."

Following the above conference a campaign for education was carried on in many counties in the state, and great results are following. The report of the state superintendent gives the following interesting fact :

Not long since, in a mountain community known as the " Dark Corner," I was very much gratified to know that the school had secured a library, and I was even more pleased to hear one of its patrons say that he preferred to send his children five miles to a well-equipped school rather than send them to a poorly taught and unfurnished school near his own door.

December 15, 1905, was Library Day for South Carolina, and the expectation was to put twenty-five thousand new books into the school libraries.

Georgia is making strides in the improvement of the country school and is undergoing a general educational awakening, as shown by the 1904 report of State School Commissioner William B. Merritt. In that report is a joint address to the southern people by the state superintendents of all the southern states. The following extract shows the importance of the country school in the South :

The rural schools. Between eight ninths and nine tenths of the population of the South is rural and agricultural. The great mass of the people of the South, therefore, are dependent upon the rural schools for education. The rural schools, then, are the strategic point in the educational system of the southern states. Farming is still the greatest institution in the South. The preservation and improvement of its greatest industry and its greatest institution depend upon the improvement of these rural schools. Because of the sparse population, the large territory, the bad roads, the geographical barriers, the small amount of taxation, and the small school fund, these rural schools are the most poorly equipped and the most inefficient public schools in the South. Unless they can be made equal in merit to the

best public schools of the towns and cities, and adapted to educating
farmers' children for farm life rather than away from farm life, many
of the best people in the country will continue to leave the farms;
and the disastrous drain upon the best blood of the country will be
kept up until there may be left there only the poorest peasant population, too ignorant to know the value and blessing of education, and
too indifferent to care to secure it for their offspring.

The women's clubs of Georgia are doing most excellent
practical work to secure better conditions for the schools.
A representative of the Women's Club of Macon writes

FIG. 153. Pleasant to Look Upon

most interestingly of the work done there, — how the
coöperation of the superintendent and the board of education was secured, also that of the teachers and school
children ; and when they would reach the parents of the
children, the ladies of the club wondered in the spirit of
the story of a tenement district in New York. This is
the story :

"Mrs. Malone, and did the settlement visitor see you this morning?"
"Sure she did that; came telling me about sanation and high
genny, and telling me to give my baby civilized milk, and I said, ses
I : 'Have you any children?' and she says, 'No.' I ses : 'Then what
do you come telling me how to bring up children? I guess I knows;
I buried eight already.'"

This antagonistic spirit did not prevail with the parents at Macon. They heard and received gladly. Improvement for the schools meant to them books, magazines, pictures, fence, and seed.

Georgia has many school-improvement clubs scattered over the state and doing a noble work.

In Missouri the cities and towns are spending annually nearly five times as much for school buildings and school equipment as do the country districts, notwithstanding the fact that there is a much larger percentage of pupils enrolled in the country districts. The poor attendance in the country is attributed to lack of organization and lack of high-school opportunities. State Superintendent Carrington is working for more efficient supervision for the country school and advocating making the county the unit for school-revenue purposes. Mr. Carrington is making some progress with consolidation. He says :

Too long have we striven to locate a school on every hill and in every valley. Instead of ten thousand school districts in Missouri it would be better if there were only a thousand. We would then have a thousand high schools instead of the three hundred at present. If properly distributed, there would be a high school within six miles of every home, — a thing to be desired. Until this is accomplished Missouri cannot claim to have a school for every child.

He has also issued a course of study in the elements of agriculture for the country schools of his state. The subjects are grouped under the following general heads:

      1. Studies on soil.
      2. Roads, — importance and improvement.
      3. Studies on seeds and related subjects.
      4. Studies on plants.
      5. Orcharding and gardening.
      6. Studies of insects.
      7. Stock raising and feeding.

A list of reference books on elementary agriculture, together with a list of Farmers' Bulletins as issued by the Department of Agriculture at Washington, are given for study and reference by both pupils and teachers.

In Minnesota, for the year ending July 31, 1904, a total of eight hundred and thirty country schools received state aid to the extent of one hundred and twenty dollars each. The country schools receiving such aid must satisfy the State Department of Public Instruction that the heating and the ventilation are adequate to the purpose for which they are intended. State Superintendent Olsen has issued a bulletin giving directions for installing a practical system of heating and ventilation for a one-room country school. Because of this stimulus in the way of state aid not only have eight hundred and thirty country schools made a much-needed improvement, but also two hundred and seventy semigraded schools have been helped along similar lines. The force of the example of these districts will influence neighboring ones.

The state of Virginia has recently conducted a notable educational campaign in which special emphasis was placed upon country-school conditions.

The state of North Carolina is making wonderful progress in the improvement of country schools. Since June 30, 1902, a total of 1133 country schoolhouses has been built at an aggregate cost of $490,272.44. The value of the entire public-school property of the state has been increased from $2,632,659 to $4,666,770. By act of the General Assembly, in 1903, a loan fund was established, which now amounts to $254,065. This sum is increasing every year by the four per cent interest on the amount loaned and by the proceeds of the sale of swamp lands belonging to the State Board of Education. Of this loan fund one tenth, together with the interest on the entire fund and the annual proceeds of the sale of swamp lands, is available annually as a loan for the building and improvement of schoolhouses.

FIG. 154. Such a Tree as this Ought to be in Every School Yard

The state school law has been amended so that every new schoolhouse erected must be in accordance with plans approved by the State Superintendent of Public Instruction and the County Board of Education. The number of school districts without houses of any description has been reduced from eight hundred and forty to five hundred and fifty-three, and the number of log schoolhouses has been decreased from eight hundred and twenty-nine to five hundred and forty-nine. In the same length of time, also, much valuable work has been done in furnishing and beautifying schoolhouses, improving school grounds, etc.

A recent pamphlet issued from the office of the State Superintendent of Public Instruction for North Carolina gives a clear and definite account of the valuable assistance the earnest women of the state are rendering in the improvement of school conditions. It shows how women, properly organized with a plan for work and working the plan, may create a public sentiment for better things for the country child.

The Woman's Association for the Betterment of Public Schoolhouses in North Carolina was organized at the State Normal and Industrial College at Greensboro, in March, 1902. The organization comprises a state association, county associations, and local associations. Article II of the state constitution reads as follows :

The object of this association shall be to unite the women citizens of North Carolina for the purpose of awakening their interest in the improvement of public schoolhouses in our state. It will undertake to have local associations in every county. Through these it will endeavor to interest a volunteer association in the neighborhood of every public schoolhouse, which will help to beautify the premises by planting trees and flowers, placing pictures on the walls, or otherwise improving the school environment of our future citizens; to furnish entertaining and instructive amusements, and to encourage the establishment of local public libraries.

Article II of the county constitution reads :

The purpose of this association shall be :

1. To arouse interest in the educational conditions, problems, and work in —— County.

2. To interest the people of the county in the improvement of their schools.

3. To establish a local association in every school district in the county.

Article II of the local constitution reads :

The purpose of this organization shall be :

1. To arouse interest in education and to insist upon the importance of every child being in school every day of the school term.

2. To unite all the people of this community for the improvement of our public school (1) by placing in the school facilities for health, comfort, and education, together with objects of beauty; (2) by planting trees, shrubs, and flowers in the school grounds; (3) by encouraging the establishment of a public library in connection with the school; (4) by making the school the center of the community by furnishing wholesome and instructive amusements; in a word, to improve the physical and intellectual environments of our future citizens.

During the first three years of the existence of the Woman's Association fifty-four county organizations have been formed, with nearly two hundred local branches. The state organization employs five field workers, who have visited forty-five counties, visiting schools and addressing meetings of teachers and patrons of the schools.

The report from one or two counties will show the extent and importance of the work of the association.

Cleveland County reports:

During the year 1903 the county association raised one hundred and fifty dollars for improvements. There were twelve libraries established and twelve houses improved through the influence of the association, the value of which was increased from eighteen hundred dollars to five thousand dollars.

Rockingham County:

There was a large association organized, affecting seventy-two schools. They raised fifty dollars for pictures, one hundred and sixty-five dollars for libraries, and twenty-five dollars for other improvements. During the year five hundred pictures were hung on the walls of the public schoolhouses and twelve libraries were established. Two houses, valued at twenty-three hundred dollars, were built through the influence of the association.

Surry County:

An association was organized, with seventy-five members. Every school in the county was reached. Through the influence of the association twenty-three new houses were built, increasing the valuation from $1200 to $5750.

Wayne County:

An association was organized, with two hundred and thirty active members and fifteen associate members. During the year forty-three schools were reached. The association raised seventy-five dollars for pictures, four hundred and sixty-four dollars for libraries, one hundred and twenty dollars for other improvements, hung two hundred and six framed pictures, and helped to establish forty-one libraries.

The influence of a similar organization for the improvement of conditions for the country school ought to be felt in every state. It is not North Carolina alone that needs this awakening. The following picture of the average country schoolhouse in North Carolina may not be the "average" in many other states, but such a picture can be seen in too many places in too many states. This picture is given in the pamphlet issued by State Superintendent Joyner (1905) which describes the work of the Woman's Association, and shows the urgent and patriotic duty of the noble women of North Carolina.

The average house is accurately and faithfully described by Mr. Charles L. Coon as follows:

The schoolhouse is a shabby-built board structure one story high. The overhead ceiling is not more than nine feet from the floor. There is one door in the end of the house; there are six small windows, three on either side. There are no blinds and no curtains. The desks are homemade, with perpendicular backs and seats, all the same size. There is a dilapidated wood stove, but no wood box, the wood for the fire being piled on the floor about the stove. The stove is red with rust and dirt, never having been polished and cleaned since it was placed in position for use. The floor of the house is covered with red dirt and litter from the wood. There are several broom-sedge brooms lying in one corner of the room. The occupied blackboard space in this house is just eighteen square feet. The blackboard is, however, too high for the children to use well, and it is too small for anything but a bulletin board. There is no teacher's desk or table. There is one chair. The children's hats and cloaks are hung on nails around the room. The walls and windows are covered with dust and seem never to have been washed. All the children's books are soiled and look very much like their surroundings. There are no steps to the schoolhouse; an inclined plane of dirt answers that purpose. The yard is very muddy during the winter, and the general appearance of the place anything but attractive.

The reader, perhaps a country school-teacher, perhaps a teacher in a fine city-school building, no doubt wonders, What in the world should I do if placed in a schoolhouse like this? In truth, there are tens of thousands of country teachers teaching school under conditions very much like those in the "average school" described above. Many of them are making heroic and effectual efforts to improve conditions, although the world does not hear enough of their great work. Now for the teacher who has done nothing so far, but wants to know what to do, the following true picture is given in contrast with the one hung above. This country school-teacher, Mr. John S. Teague, won a scholarship to the Agricultural and Mechanical College summer school, offered by the Wayne County Association of North Carolina to the teacher of the county who should make the greatest improvement in his or her schoolhouse and grounds during the year. This is what he tells of things done:

When I first came to Watery Branch, Wayne County, two years ago, I found a house with not room enough for the children, situated in the woods, with a path in front leading to the door. The building was surrounded with shrubbery of every description, from the tall oak to the tiniest fern, intermingled with dead brush and decaying leaves that could count their age by decades. Dead stumps of all sizes peeped up here and there, with their snaggled teeth offering defiance to the passer-by. A wash in front, on the side of the road, was slowly but surely eating its way to the house. Many of the limbs of the trees were kissing old mother earth. All the trees needed an

introduction to the pruner's knife, and not a few were anxiously waiting in old-maid fashion for a husband by the name of Mr. Ax, who
would lift them from their sad state and dress them in costumes to
be an ornament to the people.

If an artist had by chance gone into the building, he would not
have found anything to tickle his fancy or please his eye save the
children, and perhaps the teacher. Here were children hungering and
thirsting for books to read, but sadly waiting to be filled. Nothing
there to woo them to come to this sacred place save the whistle of
the wind and the song of the mocking bird. With very few books to
read, no yard to play in, no flowers in the yard or house to send forth
their fragrance for them, no pictures on the walls for them to look at,
no shades on the windows, not comfortable room enough in the
house, is it any wonder that so many of the boys and girls never
came to school?

To-day, by the coöperative work of parents, pupils, and teacher,
we have turned these dry bones into a living personage. Fifty stumps
have been taken up, thirty trees uprooted, logs cut and put into the
wash and dirt thrown over them and made level. There are flowers
of several kinds in the house on shelves made for the purpose, and
flowers in the yard. The limbs from the trees have ceased to kiss the
earth, but with the aid of the pruner's knife those left are pointing
heavenward, inviting all to let their lives do likewise.

Twenty pictures are in the house, seven of them nicely framed.
Shades are over all the windows. We have a library of books neatly
cased. Our seating capacity has been enlarged one third by taking
out an old rostrum.

We gave two nice entertainments and collected forty-two dollars
with which to pay for our library, pictures, shades, etc. We still have
on hand fourteen dollars and twenty-five cents with which to have
planted two rows of shrubbery from the front of the house to
the road.

It is with pride that I point to the fact that the children were the
most anxious to help in this beautiful work. Instead of disliking the
old place, they are proud of their school. Their books are kept neater,
their faces and hands cleaner, and their hair is usually combed.
Somehow the boys do not mind building fires, sweeping the yard, or
cleaning off their feet at the door. The girls are delighted to sweep

the floor and dust the desks. No spider has a chance of life on those premises, and last, but not least, our worthy county superintendent enjoys visiting us.

Comment is unnecessary. Go thou and do likewise.

The corresponding secretary of the state organization, Miss Mary Moore, furnishes the following paragraph with reference to coöperative work :

Since the organization of the association many hundred letters have been written to the county superintendents, officers of local associations, and teachers. Literature has been distributed over most of the counties of the state. Through Mr. J. B. Upham, who has charge of that department of the paper, the *Youth's Companion* has very kindly given us a large number of pamphlets on " Ideal Public Schools," " How to Set out Shrubbery," etc. ; also three thousand copies of *Free Public Education*, a little pamphlet setting forth the need for free public education and having the name of the Woman's Association printed on the back. The *Youth's Companion* also gave pictures, which many of our schools have been fortunate enough to secure. Mr. O. J. Kern, Superintendent of Public Instruction, Winnebago County, Illinois, sent many valuable suggestions on the improvement of houses and grounds. The Perry Pictures Company furnished a large number of mounted pictures suitable for schoolroom decoration, and many sample pictures to be distributed among teachers. Mr. L. H. Bailey of Cornell University sent one hundred and fifty copies of Agriculture Bulletin No. 160, which have been distributed. Mr. Clarence H. Poe, editor of the *Progressive Farmer*, offered to publish any article on our work that we would send. Letters have been received from many county superintendents which show that they are in hearty sympathy with our work. On all sides the association receives expressions of hearty sympathy and coöperation.

In the report of Mr. John T. Prince, Agent for the Massachusetts State Board of Education, as given December 31, 1904, that gentleman has the following with reference to the country-school problem of the Old Bay State. Writing about the future of rural schools, he says :

> In this statement of the conditions underlying the work of the rural schools a rather hopeful view has been presented, partly because they show a great improvement over conditions which formerly existed, and partly because they indicate a spirit of activity and progress. It must be admitted, however, that in actual work done they are, as a rule, inferior to the schools of the cities and large towns; but the success attained in some rural schools warrants the belief that with the improved conditions these schools have yet a great work to do.
>
> Besides carrying on the so-called "regular studies" in a practical and effective way, they may, through lessons in nature study, help the children to a genuine love of nature and country life. They may be the means of introducing into the home artistic and useful occupations ; and they may, as some have done already, do much in manual and industrial work to prepare the pupils to choose and follow efficiently some vocation in life. Indeed, it is not too much to hope that some time in the future the farms themselves will be made more productive than they are, through the agency of proper instruction in the school. By some such means as these life in the country may be made more attractive, and the present rush of young people to the cities may be stayed.

For the present, besides consolidation, the country schools of Massachusetts are being helped by increasing the efficiency of the teaching force, — a very important improvement. This is being done, as Mr. Prince says, by (1) better salaries because of increased state aid; (2) by increasing the number of normal schools so that more persons may receive a training for teaching ; (3) by the changed character of the supervision.

North Dakota may well lay claim to being a very progressive state educationally. For five years a law has been in force whereby the county superintendent may call a directors' meeting in each county for the purpose of discussing educational topics and policy. Thus it seems that North Dakota is the first in this regard.

It is also claimed for this state that better wages in general are paid county superintendents. Counties with more than fifty schools must provide a deputy to assist the county superintendent in the discharge of his duties. Mileage is paid each county superintendent at the rate of ten cents per mile for every mile he travels in the discharge of duty.

Again North Dakota strikes twelve. The minimum-wage law for teachers is forty-five dollars per month for the second grade. Teachers of a higher grade must receive more. All third-grade certificates are to be eliminated after 1908. Other states having a minimum-wage law are Indiana, West Virginia, Pennsylvania, Maryland, and Ohio.

The following is the law recently enacted in Ohio:

MINIMUM-SALARY AND STATE-AID LAW

SECTION 1. That no person shall be employed to teach in any public school in Ohio for less than forty dollars a month; and that, when any school district in Ohio has not sufficient money to pay its teachers forty dollars per month for eight months of the year, after the board of education of said district has made the maximum school levy authorized by law, three fourths of which shall be for the tuition fund, then said school district is hereby authorized to receive from the state treasury sufficient money to make up this deficiency. Any board of education having such a deficit shall make affidavits to the county auditor, who shall send certified statement of the facts to the state auditor. The state auditor shall issue a voucher on the state treasurer in favor of the treasurer of said school district for the full amount of the deficit in the tuition fund.

SECTION 2. Any school district shall have the state aid provided for in Section one, provided it has in it not less than twenty times as many persons of school age as it has teachers.

SECTION 3. All acts and parts of acts inconsistent herewith are hereby repealed.

A STATISTICAL TABLE SHOWING THE IMPROVEMENT IN THE RURAL SCHOOLS OF TENNESSEE FROM 1900 TO 1905

Scholastic Population

1900 658,238
1905 645,237

Pupils Enrolled

1900 433,759
1905 507,423

Average Attendance

1900 302,111
1905 348,688

Average Length of School Term

1900 . . . . 96 days
1905 . . . . 113 days

Entire Amount Expended

1900 . . . . . . $1,809,246.34
1905 . . . . . . 3,101,847.33

Amount per Capita of Scholastic Population

1900 . . . . $2.35
1905 . . . . 4.54

Amount appropriated by State

1900 . . . . . . $129,413.16
1905 . . . . . . 635,494.78

Amount appropriated by Counties

1900 . . . . . . $1,679,833.18
1905 . . . . . . 2,466,352.55

Number of Schoolhouses

1900 7043
1905 6855

Value of School Property

1900 . . . . . . $1,459,958.18
1905 . . . . . . 2,701,162.00

Average Monthly Compensation of Teachers

1900 . . . . $31.16
1905 . . . . 34.87

Per Cent of Graduates from Public-School Course

1900 . . . . 67%
1905 . . . . 171%

And now for the last word. *The country child is entitled to every whit as good an educational opportunity as that now enjoyed by the most favored city child attending the American public school.*

In order to have this equality of educational opportunity for the country child, the country people must spend more money on the country school and spend it in a better way.

THOU SHALT ENRICH AND ENLARGE THE LIFE OF THE COUNTRY CHILD.